HARRY'S GAMES

Also by John Crace

Vertigo: One Football Fan's Fear of Success

Brideshead Abbreviated: The Digested Read of the 20th Century

Baby Alarm: Thoughts from a Neurotic Father

HARRY'S GAMES

John Crace

Constable • London

Constable & Robinson Ltd
55–56 Russell Square
London WC1B 4HP
www.constablerobinson.com

First published in the UK by Constable,
an imprint of Constable & Robinson, 2013

A copy of the British Library Cataloguing in Publication
Data is available from the British Library.

ISBN 978-1-78033-911-5 (hardback)
ISBN 978-1-78033-912-2 (ebook)

Typeset by TW Typesetting, Plymouth, Devon

Printed and bound by CPI Group (UK) Ltd, Croydon, CR0 4YY

1 3 5 7 9 10 8 6 4 2

For Jill

Contents

Ring the bells that still can ring
Forget your perfect offering.
There is a crack in everything
That's how the light gets in.
From 'Anthem' by Leonard Cohen

Acknowledgements

It seems to have taken a fuller than usual complement of family, friends, psychiatrists, doctors, therapists, surgeons and physiotherapists to help me write this book. So my apologies in advance to anyone whom I have accidentally omitted . . . and to anyone whom I have included who would rather not have been.

Thanks must first go to all those who agreed to be interviewed either on or off the record, including Steve Claridge, Trevor Morley, Erik Thorstvedt, John Sissons, John Williams, Sam Delaney, David Conn, Julian Guyer, Mike Leigh, Arild Stavrum, Pete Crawford, Rick Mayston, Mat Snow, Martin Cloake, Trevor Jones and Pete Haines.

Thanks also to Andreas Campomar, Matthew Hamilton, Charlotte Macdonald, Angela Martin and Jon Davies for guiding my hand and not objecting too strongly to the inclusion of a Leonard Cohen quote; to the brilliant Julie Welch for reading the manuscript and giving it her seal of approval; to John Sutherland for his forensic eye and unwavering support; and to Richard Nelsson and Jason Rodriguez for their painstaking trawls through the archives.

To Jill, Anna, Robbie, Alex Benady, Theo Delaney, Patrick Barkham, Steve Chamberlain, Neil Pearson, Matthew Norman,

Malik Meer, Suzie Worroll, John Rullestad, Terry Blake, Hunter Davies, Angie Stanger-Leathes, John Kaare Hoversholm, Tim Parks, Simon Hattenstone, Bob Granleese, Tom Butler and Rob White goes my gratitude for sharing their lives, having a laugh and not shouting at me too loudly.

Thanks to Clive Hebard, Craig Hepburn, Phyl Fenton, Mervyn Sloman, Frankie Murrey, Trevor Jones, Pete Haine and Pete Crawford.

And to Herbert Hound, my profound apologies for not having provided you with your own Monaco bank account.

Introduction

8 February 2012

Shortly after 11.30 a.m. on Wednesday, 8 February 2012, the tannoy crackled inside Southwark Crown Court: 'All parties in Mandaric and Redknapp to go to Court One.' The journalists, TV reporters and football fans – who had been kicking their heels and drinking too much coffee ever since the jury had been sent out just before lunch the previous day – formed a scrum outside the door to Court One. The media ticketing system that had been introduced on the first day of the trial to guarantee everyone a place throughout had ceased to be operational on the second day. Ever since, it had been every man and woman for themselves in a land grab for the key seats in court. Or any seat, for that matter.

'Good old Harry,' said one radio reporter. 'His timing always has been impeccable. He's just made sure the verdict is the lead item on every lunchtime news bulletin. What a pro!'

With the also-rans of the press and fans in situ, the seating reserved for family, friends and FA and Tottenham Hotspur officials began to fill up. As so often on the pitch, Redknapp was the top attraction in town. Finally, the two defendants – Milan Mandaric, the Serbian billionaire and former owner of Portsmouth FC, and Redknapp – entered the court. They both gave nervous smiles but their faces were drawn and they looked understandably edgy.

You could smell the excitement and fear in court. We were just minutes away from two versions of history. In one, the defendants would be found guilty and almost certainly sent to prison with Redknapp's reputation and career in tatters. In the other, Redknapp would walk free, the allegations of tax evasion and financial chicanery that had dogged him for years wiped clean, leaving him a clear run at the top job in football. His Spurs team had been playing the best football in the Premiership and were in contention for the title and, ever since Fabio Capello had announced he would stand down as England manager after Euro 2012, he had been everyone's favourite successor.

Finally, something was going to have to give. These two differing histories could no longer run in parallel as they had done for the best part of two years, ever since the authorities had decided there was a case for Redknapp to answer over this latest investigation into his tax affairs. There had even been rumours the FA had asked sports editors not to make a big deal of the impending court proceedings in the run-up to the trial as they didn't want to queer the pitch for their chosen one. Normally, the idea of any sports editor obliging the FA would have been laughable, just another oddity in the long line of myths and legends that seem to surround Redknapp wherever he goes. It was impossible, however, to ignore the fact that the case had received remarkably little attention alongside consideration of Redknapp's football credentials in the sports pages.

It was odd that these two versions of Redknapp's future had managed to co-exist at all, let alone survive for so long. With any other man, the two charges of tax evasion would have thrown serious doubt on his suitability for the England job. But Redknapp wasn't any ordinary man: he was everyone's exception. Other British football managers may have had more success, but few have been more universally loved, and, over the years, he has acquired the status of a national treasure. Football writers like him because he always gives 'good quote' and the fans like him because his teams generally play entertaining football. His weaknesses are part of his charm.

Redknapp is a man whom other men – myself included, at times – are not ashamed to love. There is something about him that makes you feel as if you know him when you don't; he has genuine charisma. Unlike other public figures who often appear to regard dealing with the press or meeting the riff-raff as an unavoidable hazard of the job, Redknapp gives the impression he enjoys it. He'll stop the car and wind down the window for a chat and he has the knack of making eye contact with you. He makes it feel natural, relaxed.

At one point in the trial, a mobile phone had rung in the public gallery. The ring-tone of 'Glory, Glory Tottenham Hotspur' had been greeted with a smile by everyone other than the judge and the prosecution, and during the first break in proceedings afterwards Redknapp had made a point of sharing the joke with the fan whose phone had rung. When he talks, it's as if he knows you, as if you're an old mate with whom he's sharing a confidence. Above all, he makes you feel as if you aren't imposing; that his time is your time.

As with most with other national treasures, people tend to read into Redknapp whatever it is they want to see. For some, he is the what-you-see-is-what-you-get, always-ready-to-have-a-laugh character out of an Ealing comedy; for others, including the police and the Crown Prosecution Service (CPS), he is the East End working-class wide boy. The archetypal dodgy geezer.

Both versions of Redknapp are hopelessly simplistic. You don't get to manage one of the top clubs in England just by cracking jokes and being charming. Many modern footballers have egos as big as their weekly earnings and require a manager with a will of iron. While faced with a possible prison sentence, Redknapp had got his Spurs side playing better than they or the fans ever dreamed possible. Hardly a soft touch, then. He even appeared to take heart surgery in his stride just before Christmas the previous year.

Neither did the dodgy geezer caricature entirely stack up. There had been rumours swirling around about Redknapp's financial dealings for more than a decade, the most vociferous of which had been Tom Bower's allegations about Rio Ferdinand's transfer from West Ham to Leeds in his 2003 book, *Broken Dreams*. Redknapp had always denied them but had never sued Bower for libel. Rather, he had been cleared of taking bungs by the Stevens inquiry into corruption in football in 2007. He'd then been released without charge in November of the same year after being arrested on suspicion of conspiracy to defraud and false accounting in connection with the Amdy Faye transfer.

You'd have thought that having been cleared twice might have put an end to the whispers about Redknapp, but the rumours continued to persist and the City of London Police and the CPS seemed to be determined to have one last crack at making them stick. It was their judgement, as well as Redknapp's career, that was in the balance and would be determined in the next few minutes. Yet just who Redknapp really was – what really made him tick – would still be up for grabs either way.

'The thing is this, John,' a former top manager said when I told him I was planning to write a book about Redknapp, 'no one's going to talk to you right now. I mean, his friends will, but they will just tell you what a wonderful bloke he is, which is really dull and not much help. You might get a few of his old enemies to say something, but everyone has heard what they've got to say many times over already. And the people who are more neutral and could give you a more balanced view are going to keep their mouths shut now Redknapp is a bit of a national hero. So you're a bit stuck.'

'Would you be willing to give me any insights?' It seemed worth a try; I had nothing to lose.

'You've got to be joking. I work in this world. I've got to live with these people.'

This wasn't particularly worrying, as the manager hadn't told me anything I hadn't suspected myself. I didn't see any future in approaching Redknapp himself for an interview, even though the Spurs media bods I'd chatted to at the trial hadn't ruled out the possibility of him agreeing to talk to me. Redknapp had already written one autobiography in the late nineties, had given dozens of interviews since and I couldn't imagine that he would have anything much to add until such time as his agent negotiated a seven-figure advance for the second instalment of his autobiography on his retirement.

Neither could I run the risk of falling even more under his spell. During the course of the trial, we had had a number of brief conversations – we'd never met before – and each time he had held me spellbound. This was partly because I could never rid myself of the childish football fan within – 'I can't believe the Spurs manager is actually talking to me' – but mostly because of his seemingly innate ability to generate a sense of intimacy where none exists. If I felt like this after a few brief encounters, what would I be like after some lengthy conversations? I had the feeling that Redknapp had the power to make me believe anything he wanted me to believe, so a little distance might be useful.

Even more to the point, these were delicate times for Redknapp. With the trial over and his future up for grabs, Redknapp's advisers would be giving him a crash course in being as bland as possible, so even if he did give me an interview he would be bound to say next to nothing and still require copy approval of anything I wrote. So, much as I personally couldn't think of anything better than hanging around the Spurs training camp and shooting the breeze with Redknapp, I had to accept it would be a waste of time for both of us. Another time, another book, maybe.

In any case, I didn't want to write a standard biography. Most of the important events of Redknapp's life were already public knowledge and trawling through his career, season by season, looked unlikely to turn up anything new. One of the most interesting men in football deserved better than that. I didn't want to indulge in either empty praise or bitchy back-stabbing – I wanted to understand Redknapp, to think about what he had achieved, to see how many different Redknapps there actually were and whether they could be unified into a consistent, if complex, whole. And given that the first six months of his sixty-sixth year were shaping up to be as dramatic as the previous sixty-five years put together, it would be especially fascinating to watch the present unfold and piece together just how much it was informed by the past.

But how to do it? Like many football fans, I've wasted rather too much time thinking about the managers of the club I support; in my case, Spurs. The manager is the club's heartbeat, the man who gets the credit when things go well and gets a kicking when they don't; he is the club's most visible symbol. So over the years, I've thought a great deal about Bill Nicholson, Keith Burkinshaw and Martin Jol and spent as much time trying to forget others, such as George Graham, Christian Gross and Jacques Santini. But of all the Spurs managers whose teams I've watched, I've spent more time thinking about Harry Redknapp than anyone else, principally because he's infuriating – yes; intoxicating – yes; heartbreaking – yes; embarrassing – yes. But dull? Definitely not. He's rarely out of the newspapers and his teams switch from the divine to the incompetent in the blink of an eye. Redknapp is nothing if not watchable.

Football specializes in narratives that are either dramatic or sentimental. Last-minute equalizers, heroic underdogs and come-back kids are its lifeblood. It has no time for the narratives that are more mundane, the everyday unremarkable ups and downs of unremarkable games in unremarkable seasons. Yet these are precisely the narratives that committed football fans live and breathe. Newspapers don't care what a manager said a month ago, or even a week ago; all that matters is the next fixture, the next press conference, the next deadline. The only time a manager is held to account for the past is when he's sacked, and even then the slate is wiped clean within seconds, with everyone's attention focused on his replacement.

But fans remember the little things. They remember if a manager says he was going to buy a new striker and doesn't; they remember the bad substitutions; and, along with the triumphs, they keep a running tally of the chinks, the inconsistencies and the contradictions in the narrative. They make the connections others miss. And right from the start of his time at Spurs, it became clear that Redknapp would be worth watching as much for the way the team played under him as for his subtle manipulations of history.

Spurs were bottom of the Premier League with just two points from eight games when Redknapp took over as manager in October 2008; by Christmas, the team was comfortably positioned in mid-table and the football world had come to accept as gospel Redknapp's frequent assertions that he had turned a rubbish side into a good one. Everyone except the hardcore Spurs fans, that is. The way Redknapp had been talking, you could easily have believed he had taken over Northampton Town rather than the club that, in the three previous seasons before his arrival, had finished fifth in the Premier League twice and won the Carling Cup with near enough the same squad. Spurs weren't a bad team made good; Spurs were a decent team who had been playing badly.

That may sound like semantics, but it's not. It's an important, if subtle, difference that was largely overshadowed by Redknapp's more dramatic and self-serving account. It wasn't that Redknapp's version was an outright lie; it was just that it was only about eighty per cent of the truth; and it was the other twenty per cent that was the most interesting and was the true connection between the past under Jol and Ramos and the present under Redknapp. After that, Harry-watching became an essential weekly pastime. The man was so charming, and his teams sometimes so good, that you'd find yourself believing anything given half a chance . . . and enjoy doing it.

There were practical drawbacks to relying on Harry-watching for the connections. Most obviously, I'd only become a proper Harry-watcher when he came to Spurs. Before that, he had just been another – if somewhat livelier than most – football manager. What I knew about him had all come from newspapers and I'd probably forgotten most of it. So I decided to track down the other Harry-watchers: the old-school, hardcore Bournemouth, West Ham, Portsmouth and Southampton faithful who had been paying good money to watch their teams long before Redknapp came on the scene and had continued to do so long after he had left. Like me, they would have observed Redknapp with an affectionate, yet objective, eye and remembered the connections others had missed.

And why stop there? It was time to track down the old local sports reporters who had turned up at deserted press conferences when no one from the national media would give Redknapp air time. Or talk to a sports psychologist who had worked closely with footballers from all divisions. And perhaps talk to the minor characters in the Redknapp story, people who had seen a lot but had previously said little. Put together all these people along with some of those who had had first-hand experience of Redknapp and I might just make sense of the man himself.

I talked to a football club chairman about my plan. I was

expecting him to knock it, to wheel out the usual canards that only those who have played the game or been on the inside of it are qualified to talk about it. But he didn't. 'The supporters who watch the team week in, week out, home and away, aren't stupid,' he said. 'They know their club and can see quite clearly what's working well and what's not. You can't pull the wool over their eyes. People sometimes try to make out football is a tremendously complicated game. It's not. If it was that complicated, most of the players wouldn't be able to make a living out of it.'

Traditional methods of biography hadn't really come close to pinning Redknapp down. He had remained everyman and no man, an elusive character in whom everyone saw the reflection that suited them. So maybe a less orthodox approach might just work. It might not reach the whole truth of Redknapp, but it would hopefully capture a truth – a recognizable, if different, truth. And if it didn't, then I'd be no worse off than anyone else who'd looked for the meaning of Harry Redknapp. At the very least, the journey couldn't fail to be fun and interesting. Just like Redknapp.

Some of the material I obtained in this way was eye-opening. Another chairman of a football club Redknapp had managed – he, too, would only speak anonymously – said, 'Harry is a nice enough guy. You can have a lot of fun with him and he's certainly no worse or better than any other manager. What you've got to remember, though, is this: football isn't as bad as people say it is. It's ten times worse. The manager and the players are all in it just for themselves. The game should be called "selfish" not "football". The only way to survive is to trust no one. That was my mistake. I did trust and it just about bankrupted me.'

Other stories and observations were just too potentially libellous to use. They may or may not have been true. But no one would put their name to them and, as Redknapp generates at least as many fictional stories as factual, I couldn't take a chance.

One remark did stand out, though, because it just about summed up everyone's feelings about Redknapp. It came from a former player who had been managed by Redknapp: 'He's the best manager I ever played for and I can't help loving him. If I had a chance to sign for him again tomorrow, I would. But he can also be a complete arsehole.'

1

Harry Kicks Off

'A true Cockney' . . . 'Times were hard but we never went without' . . . 'Always had a smile on his face' . . . 'There was always a lot of love around' . . . These are just some of the standard, catchall phrases that everyone – Redknapp included – tends to trot out to describe his childhood, an easy shorthand for the typical working-class East End, post-Second World War upbringing that has become lodged in the national consciousness of those who didn't have to live it. Remember those feel-good Pathé newsreels of cheeky ten-year-old boys in shorts playing on old bomb sites without a care in the world? One of them could have been our Harry.

That isn't to say that Redknapp didn't have a reasonably happy childhood, or that his was any better or worse than many others growing up in the East End at the same time. Rather, that to sugar-coat it in a familiar sentimental gloss is to miss an important part of the picture. Redknapp was born on 2 March 1947, the only child of Harry (senior) and Violet. His father was a docker and decent amateur footballer and his mother worked for the Co-op. His grandmother, Violet, who made Harry his dinner when he came home from school, was a bookie's runner and often in trouble with the law. 'Quite often my nan would be getting carted away in a police car,' Redknapp once said. '"Your dinner's in the oven," she'd shout to me. "These bastards won't keep me for long. I'll be home in an hour, boy." The police would have her down the station for a couple of hours, warn her off, and then she'd be back and do exactly the same again. They never put her off. She loved it.'

You couldn't have come up with a more stereotypical East End version of Redknapp's childhood: the ducking, the diving, the smooth-talking patter to dodge trouble . . . here it all was, handed down from one generation to the next. Redknapp makes it sound attractive – fun even – to have been a working-class boy in post-war London. So it probably was at times, but the more so in memory because it must also have been tough growing up in a family where rationing was severe and money was short. It must also have been frightening for him to see his grandmother being carted off by the cops on a regular basis. What ten-year-old child wouldn't be a bit scared? What most kids want most is to feel secure, for life to be predictable. Redknapp's was anything but.

And what of his parents? Harry's father had been a Prisoner of War and must have returned home scarred in some way. He must have seen and experienced things that would have had a profound impact on his subsequent relationships. The same would have been true of his mother, to a lesser extent, having experienced the uncertainty, terror and personal loss that the war meant on the home front. No one could go through something as extreme as that and expect to emerge easily able to form normal, healthy relationships; indeed, a whole generation was similarly traumatized.

Something had to give and the breaking point varied from person to person. But it's worth observing that those who work hardest to create an image of happiness about themselves are often those in whom the need to do so is greatest, as they are those for whom the idea of unhappiness is least bearable.

Taking Redknapp at face value is almost always a mistake; he's a far more complex man than he would want the world to think. Listen to Redknapp talking to the media with a big smile and his easy one-liners and you might be lulled into thinking he's a man with boundless self-confidence, a man who can handle himself in any situation. And so he can, but what if the way he handles himself isn't through self-confidence so much as learned bravado? Perhaps a big smile and a smooth patter were the principal tools of his trade out on the streets, the way he dealt with awkward situations. And perhaps he learned to keep his more vulnerable feelings hidden and chose instead to present to the outside world the versions of himself he thought people wanted to see. It would certainly make Redknapp a more interesting and attractive character; someone for whom it is easier to feel empathy. And it would also make a great deal more sense of the apparent contradictions his critics are often only too quick to expose.

Many Spurs fans gave a hollow laugh when Redknapp went out of his way to stress his connections to the club after his appointment as manager in 2008 by saying, 'I am a big follower of the history of the game and Tottenham have been a great club over the years. I followed Tottenham, I trained there as an eleven- and twelve-year-old so I know the history of the club . . .' Those Spurs fans remembered that in earlier versions of his life he had claimed he and his father were 'avid fans' of the North London club's main rival, Arsenal, and suspected it was this attachment that was the more real.

Redknapp's bullshit was soon smelt out. Most fans have little time for false protestations of loyalty; they understand that everyone in football is in the game to make a living and much prefer a manager who talks straight – 'I've come to the club because it's a good move for me and I'll do my best to get the results everyone wants' – than one who trades in pathos and sentiment. Those two qualities are the preserve of the fans alone. So Redknapp's arrival at Spurs immediately caused suspicions that he was a man not necessarily to be trusted, a man whom the fans should handle with caution.

Was it bullshit? His long-term affection for Spurs was unquestionably, at best, a very partial truth, but bullshit requires some intentionality. Was Redknapp deliberately trying to hoodwink the fans or was he just saying something he thought would go down well? There is a distinction to be made. Redknapp wouldn't thank anyone for suggesting he had anything less than an idyllic childhood – he has an image to protect – but, given everything that was going on, he can't have felt as secure as all that. And insecure children tend to grow into people-pleasing adults. They have learned the necessary mechanisms to hide their vulnerability, and the automatic response to any new and unfamiliar situation is to avoid any possible conflict by saying whatever they feel is required: a joke, a half-truth, whatever. It's worth bearing in mind, given the question marks raised over his loyalty and integrity at various points throughout his career.

What is for certain about Redknapp's childhood was that school didn't feature highly on his list of priorities, other than as a place to showcase his football talent. That he would go on to play professionally seemed self-evident to most people who watched him as a slightly built, but devastatingly quick, teenager. But then these same judges often have a tendency to forget the many other youngsters for whom they predicted great things and whose football careers never got further than schoolboy trials.

So just how good a player was Redknapp? These days, it's much easier to reach an objective assessment of a player's ability. Every game in every division is televised and, for those with the time and inclination, you can make a detailed analysis of every minute of a player's entire career. Not just the goals scored and the assists made, but the yards run, the tackles missed, the passes uncompleted and the team-mates blamed. It may not give you the player's whole story, but it will give you more than enough to make an informed judgement.

You can't do that with Redknapp. When he began his professional playing career, very few matches were televised; fewer still were shown in their entirety. The BBC's Saturday-night *Match of the Day* programme featured the highlights of just one, sometimes two, of the afternoon's First Division fixtures. ITV's Sunday-afternoon show, *The Big Match*, had just one game. A bit of bad luck with an injury or loss of form and even one of the best footballers could go through a whole season without appearing on television once. Search all the available archives, and you'd be lucky to come up with even ninety minutes of Redknapp's career on film.

What you're left with then are memories of those who played both with and against him, of those who paid a few shillings at the turnstiles to stand on the terraces of Upton Park and Dean Court. And memories fade over time, so that the distinctions between what's real and what's imagined become more blurred. This is especially true for a player like Redknapp, whose contributions, even at the time, were frequently overshadowed by those of his more famous team-mates, in particular Bobby Moore, Geoff Hurst and Martin Peters, the triumvirate of World Cup winners. Some memories will be rose-tinted, some unduly negative, and a great deal more almost certainly blank. There are few clear ways to differentiate between questionable contemporary evidence and hard fact. So whose word is to be believed – that of Redknapp's friends and admirers, which is likely to be spun in the most favourable light, or that of his detractors, which will most definitely not be? And where does this leave Lord Macdonald, Milan Mandaric's defence QC – a man who one would hope would favour evidence over opinion – who described Redknapp in court as a not very good footballer?

The bare bones of Redknapp's career are 149 first-team appearances for West Ham between 1965 and 1972, 101 for Bournemouth between 1972 and 1976 and just 26 for Brentford, Seattle Sounders and Bournemouth (again) in the final six years up until his retirement in 1982, with a total of just 12 goals for all clubs. It does indeed appear to confirm the 'below-average journeyman' of Lord Macdonald's description. But what the statistics don't provide is an answer to the more interesting question: Was Redknapp a talented player who underperformed, or an unskilled makeweight who did well to play professional football at all? Here, as is so often the case with Redknapp, the waters quickly become very muddied.

One long-time West Ham fan remembered that Redknapp arrived at the club as a youngster with a big reputation. 'Harry was a local Cockney boy so everyone knew he had been a good sprinter and a very promising right-winger at school,' Dave Newton told me. 'We all had high hopes for him.' As did others, as Spurs and Chelsea had also been in the mix to sign Redknapp as an apprentice teenager in 1963.

Initially, his career at West Ham flourished; he was an integral member of the team that won the FA Youth Cup in his first season, was picked for the England Youth team the same year and had a promising first couple of seasons in the first team. But, somehow, the sparkle vanished and he struggled to hold down a regular first-team place.

John Sissons, the left-winger who joined West Ham at much the same time as Redknapp in the early 1960s, is still not entirely sure why Redknapp's career didn't flourish more. 'When I played alongside Harry in the youth team, he was always the quickest player on the pitch,' he says, 'and we all had him marked down as someone who would go far. He was outstanding in our FA Youth Cup run, a real live wire who was more than a handful for anyone. But then he didn't quite develop in the way we imagined.

'I think he may have been a bit unlucky. Harry was a winger, pure and simple; he'd push the ball past defenders and outrun them. And he was a good crosser of the ball. But wingers began to go out of fashion in the game . . . Ron Greenwood started to play 4-3-3 and Harry couldn't adapt his style of play so he gradually became marginalized.'

Sissons isn't alone in reckoning Redknapp was a bit unlucky. Several other ex-footballers have voiced a similar opinion that Redknapp just didn't get the right breaks every player needs at certain points of his career. Luck only gets you so far as an explanation, though. To dismiss the random completely is to misread the universe, to fail to understand what it is to be human; it is equally so to throw up your hands and, like the hero of Luke Rhinehart's satire *The Dice Man*, leave every decision to a metaphorical roll of the dice and relinquish all personal responsibility. The timing of the winger's decline in English football may have been beyond Redknapp's control, but his ability to adapt his game to the new reality wasn't.

Redknapp's loss of form wasn't a particularly unusual phenomenon. Kids develop at different rates, both physically and emotionally, and many child prodigies fade into obscurity; very few England schoolboys go on to play for the full international side. In his autobiography, Redknapp offered his own explanation: 'Looking back,' he wrote, 'I know I should have done better, but the game was changing a lot then. Full-backs suddenly weren't slow any more. Now they were as quick as wingers, not giving you a yard to control the ball. Suddenly, whenever you got the ball you were clattered within a split second. It was getting harder to play in that position, unless you played in a dominant team which enjoyed a lot of possession and could feed the winger regularly. We stayed out wide, never came in, and were expected to do something with the ball on the few occasions we got it. Suddenly, wingers died out, as Sir Alf Ramsey underlined with his England side. As my form dipped, so did my popularity at Upton Park. My confidence was draining and, for a long spell, the punters hated me.'

All of which makes sense, yet doesn't quite tell the full story. It's the comments Redknapp almost throws away as asides that are the most fascinating. Consider his phrase 'unless you played in a dominant team which enjoyed a lot of possession'. West Ham was unquestionably not a dominant team at that time. In the years that Redknapp played for the club, it only had one top-ten finish – eighth in 1968–9; in the other seasons, it finished twelfth, fourteenth (twice), sixteenth, eighteenth and twentieth. That's a horrible series of results for a club that was generally lauded for the style of its football and, in Ron Greenwood, had one of the league's most respected managers. It's even worse when you take into account the team had Bobby Moore (one of the best centre-backs in the world), Geoff Hurst (one of the two best strikers in the country), and Martin Peters (one of the country's best mid-fielders). With these players at its spine, West Ham was a team that ought to have been contesting the league title, not propping up the division. If Redknapp was underperforming, he wasn't alone; underperformance was endemic in the club culture.

'It's the million-dollar question every one of us is always asked about that team,' says Sissons. 'With the players we had, we should have achieved far more than we did. You could argue that in some cases Ron Greenwood just wasn't ruthless enough and failed to accept some players were past their best until a couple of seasons too late. You could also say Ron didn't control the team as firmly as he should have done . . . he was too nice and he let the bigger personalities dominate him. But the bottom line is that it was our fault. We knew we were a talented team but we just weren't professional enough.'

You have to be careful making judgements across generations. Back in the 1960s, diet and fitness weren't taken nearly as seriously as they are now. A pre-match steak and chips followed by a couple of cigarettes to get the lungs working properly was considered fairly standard, almost self-denying. And a post-match drinking binge was often obligatory for some players. But even by these standards, West Ham acquired the reputation of being a party club. And wherever there was a party, Redknapp seems to have been at its centre. 'It was a good time,' Rodney Marsh, another footballer noted as much for his fondness for the high life as his on-field brilliance, said in Les Roopanarine's biography of Redknapp. 'We drunk a lot and ate a lot and we laughed a lot, and Harry was at the forefront of all that.'

Bobby Howe, a West Ham team-mate of Redknapp's, also agreed that Harry was the life and soul of the dressing room. 'Harry was a real product of the East End,' he said. 'His wit and story-telling were fantastic. He was also a prankster and incredibly street smart.' In his autobiography, Redknapp tried to play it both ways; he couldn't resist telling great stories about how he and the lads – Bobby Moore in particular – would go out on the lash but still turn up for training on time and play out of their skins. As far as Harry was concerned, he was doing nothing wrong; he wasn't 'giving it large' in the West End like some of the glamour boys, he was just going out and having a few bevvies down the local with the lads. He didn't help his cause, though, by calling that particular chapter 'Win or Lose – on the Booze'.

It's hard to avoid the image, then, of Redknapp as a gifted player who rather took his talent for granted and let it slip slowly, like grains of sand, through his fingertips. There was no spectacular George Best-style self-destruction – he wasn't an alcoholic. Rather, he was an ordinary young bloke who never thought too much about the future at the time. He'd shown talent as a kid, and those who knew him had always said he'd play professional football and he'd gone on to do just that. The achievement had almost been preordained. Redknapp had never had to think about a career; the career had come to him. And like many young men in that situation he had thought himself immortal – that life would somehow stand still and the good times would roll for ever. But eventually the lifestyle found him out; the bottom line was that he didn't quite have the innate talent – or possibly the desire – of a Bobby Moore who could perform flawlessly week after week, no matter how hard he had been partying. Redknapp was good, but not that good. His sharpness was blunted and the cracks began to show.

The other phrase that stands out in Redknapp's self-assessment is 'Suddenly, whenever you got the ball you were clattered within a split second.' The key word here is 'clattered'. In the 1960s and 1970s, by the time the season had reached the winter months many pitches were mud-baths and the balls were heavy and waterlogged; as a result, skinny, nippy wingers like Redknapp did not have the advantage their counterparts do today. Both the ball and the winger got stuck in the pitch, making it easier for opposing full-backs to neutralize their threat – as often as not, by crunching them as hard as possible in the tackle. If the winger didn't bounce back up immediately, so much the better. A limp made him even less of a problem for the rest of the game.

And Redknapp was regularly injured; the knee injury that forced him out of English professional football in 1976 was just the last in a long catalogue that had gradually destroyed his pace and effectiveness. Perhaps if he had been playing these days with better pitches, better physiotherapy and higher levels of fitness his career might have fulfilled its early promise, but that's another story.

John Sissons has a lot of sympathy for Redknapp. As a fellow winger, he was often on the wrong end of the treatment himself. 'It was a tough, tough game for a winger,' he says, 'especially as you didn't get much protection from referees. If you went past some players, such as Norman Hunter, early in a game they'd make a point of catching up with you a little while later and saying, 'If you do that again, I'll break your legs.' You tried to ignore them and just get on with the game, but it did make you think twice, because you knew they were being serious.'

The impact of the 'clattering' wasn't just physical. Intimidation is just as much in the mind; a full-back who knows that a forward is going to pull out of any 50-50 ball has a significant advantage. And a few early, heavy tackles – with possibly a yellow card as collateral – can shift the balance even more, with opponents not going for the balls that are 60-40 in their favour. Then the game really is up for the forward, and this is the reason that one old-time West Ham fan gave for the Upton Park crowd turning against Redknapp. 'We never doubted his ability,' he said, 'and no one had a problem with him being a bit of a joker. What annoyed us was the sense we began to get that he just didn't really fancy it that much. When the chips were down and the studs were flying, he would go AWOL.'

Football fans can be an unforgiving bunch; they expect things of their players that they wouldn't dream of doing themselves and offer little thanks for it in return. They demand their players make that potentially career-ending tackle, and when the bone does break or the ligaments do snap, they say, 'That's a shocker', before wondering whom the manager is going to bring on as a substitute and whether the formation will have to be switched. Even before the mega salaries of the Premiership, footballers were just a commodity in an ongoing entertainment, and a relatively cheap commodity at that. But supporters can read the game, and if they can sense the fear from the terraces, then it must be obvious to the players and the manager.

Fear isn't something often admitted in football. In a tough game, with big egos, any sign of vulnerability is almost always vilified. 'Call me a bad footballer if you like, just don't call me a pussy' is the mantra of just about every professional. But it's equally hard to imagine that some players weren't – and still aren't – physically intimidated. When you've been badly injured once, why would you necessarily be fully committed in every subsequent tackle? Look at it from a forward's perspective. It's not as if pulling out of a tackle is likely to cost your side that much, unless you are clean through; so the worst that can happen is that your side loses possession. And as you can probably make it look as if you were really going for it, there's no harm done. Balance that against the possibility of being crocked for several months, and it's a no brainer.

It's no great surprise that neither Redknapp nor any of his teammates have ever so much as hinted he may have lost his nerve a touch – that topic is strictly off limits – so only he can know for sure whether he did or not. But it does make rather more sense of Redknapp's transfer from West Ham to Bournemouth in the summer of 1972. In his autobiography, Redknapp explained the deal like this: 'Bondy [John Bond, the Bournemouth manager] had made an early attempt to lure me from West Ham but at that stage I didn't fancy going from the top flight down into the lower divisions . . . But as it became clearer I was out of the picture at West Ham, I decided a move would be in my best interest . . . Bournemouth were going places at the time. The chairman was a man called Harold Walker, who was pumping a fortune into the club and Bondy was spending it. He had top players like Ted MacDougall and Phil Boyer at the club, and signed me and ex-Everton star Jimmy Gabriel on the same day.'

Or to put it another way, moving to Bournemouth was a deliberate act of career advancement. Somehow, that doesn't ring quite true. Redknapp says he resisted an earlier offer to go to Bournemouth because he didn't fancy moving down two divisions. Who could blame him? What player would? When he did agree to the transfer, he was still only twenty-five; at that age, he should have had at least three or four years left in him in the First Division. More, maybe, given Redknapp's natural talent. Bobby Howe had described Redknapp as one of the best crossers of the ball in the game while at West Ham, and Jimmy Gabriel said much the same about him at Bournemouth. So if he was that good, why were no other clubs interested in signing him?

Injury-prone or not, you might have thought that another first- – or even second- – division team might have been willing to take a punt on Redknapp. Just give him enough time to recover from his niggles, get him strong, fit and motivated, then let him loose against the full-backs. Except there were no other offers from anyone else. So either Redknapp was a great deal more physically knackered than West Ham chose to let on – in which case Bond took a £31,000 gamble signing him to Bournemouth at all – or there was a general feeling that he no longer had what it took mentally to succeed at the highest level.

Redknapp went on to dismiss his four-year playing career at Bournemouth in less than a paragraph. And most of that paragraph was about how Bond had gone on to manage the first-division club, Norwich, and how a proposed transfer – then loan deal – for Redknapp to join him had collapsed along with his knee. If Bournemouth left little impression on Redknapp as a player, the fans reciprocated by feeling he had left little impression on them. 'I think the basic problem was that every full-back in the Third Division targeted Harry,' says a Bournemouth old-timer. 'They wanted to make it clear right from the start they weren't going to be shown up by some fancy Dan who had just moved down a couple of divisions, so they all got their retaliation in early.' Perhaps, even, some of them had been tipped off about the best way of dealing with Redknapp by friends playing in the higher divisions. Either way, it was the same old, same old.

*　　*　　*

With his knee and playing career in England grinding to a halt, Redknapp was granted an unexpected three-year lifeline with the offer to play for the Seattle Sounders in the newly formed North American Soccer League. The football in the US at this time was as undemanding as the lifestyle was good, so the state of Redknapp's knees didn't automatically rule him out of contention. And for some great footballers coming towards the end of their careers – Pelé, Carlos Alberto and Franz Beckenbauer among them – it was a handsome and stress-free last payday. Redknapp secured an invitation through his old Bournemouth mate, Jimmy Gabriel, and quickly renewed his West Ham connections, moving into the same apartment complex as Geoff Hurst and Bobby Moore who were also playing out time Stateside.

'We all trained quite hard and there some were very enthusiastic American youngsters as well as us ex-pros coming to the end of our careers,' says John Sissons, who joined the Tampa Bay Rowdies the year before Redknapp joined Seattle. 'But it was a completely different game. The North American Soccer League didn't play offside at the start, so all the tactics we had learned over the years counted for nothing. When you had an opposition forward who seldom left your penalty area, it was impossible for your backs to push up. So we'd play these weird games where very little was happening in the middle of the park! Still, it was good fun and we all enjoyed our stay in the US.'

Redknapp's time in the US was undoubtedly more rewarding for him than it was for his employers. Redknapp managed just twenty-four games for Seattle – a lot fewer than the number of barbecues, beach parties and horse-race meetings he managed to fit in – yet even so it wasn't the final collapse of his knees that forced him back home. It was the collapse of Phoenix Fire, a US club that had offered Redknapp and Gabriel megabucks to player-manage the team. Within weeks, Redknapp realized the money he was being offered wasn't silly so much as non-existent.

This particular American dream really was just a dream after all; Redknapp was left with a wife and two young kids to support and with no obvious source of income.

Life always looks much simpler when it's replayed in reverse; motives and intentions that are sometimes weak, non-existent even, while going forward, take on an air of concrete inevitability. So by 2010, when Les Roopanarine published his biography of Redknapp, there were several of his ex-colleagues who were queuing up to say how Redknapp had always been a brilliant coach.

'We did a tremendous amount of technical stuff in training [at West Ham under Ron Greenwood],' said Bobby Howe, 'and I think that anybody who played in that era and went on to coach believed in that philosophy as well . . . Harry was one of the players that we took on the preliminary badge . . . I would have to say that Harry was one of the better coaches, even then – and it was a very long time ago.'

Frank Lampard Senior, Harry's brother-in-law and father of Chelsea's Frank Lampard, also described how he and Redknapp 'nurtured young talent, encouraged it and then gave players a platform on which to develop'. 'Like all good managers,' said Jimmy Gabriel, who had asked Redknapp to be his assistant coach in the US, 'Harry can get the most from his players – and he did that right from the start, right from when he was coaching young kids in Seattle.'

It's a heart-warming and compelling image: the young pro anxious to learn his trade and to pass on his knowledge and skills to the next generation. But just how accurate is it? In his own autobiography, written some twelve years earlier in 1998 while he was in charge at West Ham and there was much less of a cottage industry in the Redknapp legacy, Redknapp didn't make a single mention of having enjoyed coaching kids or wanting to build a career in the management side of the game during his years as a player. Not one.

And when Roopanarine interviewed him over a decade later, he didn't sound a great deal more enthusiastic. 'When we had finished training,' he said, 'me and Frank Lampard used to go to a place in Canning Town called Pretoria School and they had a lovely sports master called Dave Jones. We used to teach the kids and play a game of football in the gym. We loved it and as we were only on £6 a week, £2.50 for the afternoon didn't half come in handy.'

The kids probably learned a great deal, and even if they didn't they would definitely have had a great afternoon laughing, joking and running around. An hour or so with Redknapp could hardly fail to be anything else. You'd guess that Redknapp had had an equally good time himself. But would he have done it without the inducement of an extra £2.50? That's a much tougher call. Since he's become a comparatively wealthy man, Redknapp has done more than his fair share for charity, so to write him off as a man who wouldn't get out of bed unless there was money involved is plain wrong. But was he the type of twenty-year-old who would have willingly given up a few hours of his spare time because he had a burning desire to help kids improve their football skills? Probably not. It's not the image of him that Geoff Hurst remembered in a radio interview some forty-five years later, when he said that of all the footballers he had played with, Redknapp was about the last one he would have predicted to become a manager. But then there's no reason why Redknapp at that age should have been any different from most other twenty-year-olds of his generation. They would have been the exception, not the rule.

Redknapp was a professional. Football may have been a game he started out playing for fun but it soon became something he did for money. He had skills for which people were prepared to pay cash; not as much cash as they do now, but enough to make a living. Football was his job and if he could earn a bit extra on the side then he was happy to do it. He'd got married and had two kids while still in his twenties so there was no room for manoeuvre. With his career in America coming to a sudden end, he needed an income to keep the family afloat.

'Was he really interested in being a football coach?' says Pete Johnson, a veteran local news reporter who was close to Redknapp throughout his many years on the south coast. 'Yes and no. He loved the game but I couldn't have seen him going off to do a bit of coaching in his spare time at a local amateur club. Coaching was initially just a passport for him to earn a living doing something he enjoyed while hanging around with his mates.'

And it was his mates who came to the rescue – no surprise there. Friendships in football weren't then the short-term marriages of convenience they so often are now. Players tended to stay with the same club for more than a few seasons so they got to know each other, they also earned pretty much the same salaries and socialized in the same pubs. They had relationships that were forged not in idle visits to the Ferrari showroom – the occasional dodgy TV being sold on the cheap outside the training ground was about as good as it got – but out of a genuine sense they were in it together. And the friendships frequently lasted. Football may have looked like a closed shop to outsiders but, for those in the game, it was good mates looking out for one another; not so much an old boy's network as an act of charity.

Bobby Moore was the first to offer Redknapp a helping hand by taking him on as his assistant at non-league Oxford City where the former England captain had been appointed manager. It was in the main a fairly miserable year for Redknapp, commuting between Oxford and Bournemouth for just £120 per week to help coach a team he didn't really know or care that much about. But it was a job, it was football and he was working with an old mate.

Redknapp has never made any secret of how much he admired Moore. 'Mooro was a God, there are no two ways about it,' said Redknapp. 'When I first broke into the team in the early sixties after a golden youth career, Bobby was top man at Upton Park. Everybody looked up to him. You'd have thought given his stature that he would be aloof with kids coming into the side, but from day one he looked after me. He took me under his wing and really made sure I was OK. We got on great but he treated everyone the same way.' Moore was everything Redknapp aspired to be: better looking, better mannered, better leader, better player, better drinker. And a better better as well, probably.

The two remained close right up until Moore's death from bowel cancer in 1993. 'He spent a few days in Bournemouth with me towards the end of his life,' Redknapp said, 'and we went to watch the horses working at racehorse trainer David Elsworth's yard. Not once did Bobby complain that things were getting too much for him. He'd go for his treatment to a clinic in Scotland and not say a word to anyone. I remember I went to see him after he'd had his operation. I could have cried. Bobby was always a big lad, a powerful build, but suddenly his trousers were hanging off him at the back because he had lost so much weight. It slaughtered me to see him like that. He'd say to me he was going OK but he knew all along he wasn't. He knew what was coming but faced it with incredible bravery. That was how he was – unflappable. You couldn't help but love him.'

As a role model both on and off the pitch, Moore was one of the most – if not the most – influential figures in Redknapp's life. He was the man who taught the young Harry how a footballer should live, the man who gave him his first chance when his playing days were over, the man who showed him how to die. Significant as all these things are, though, Pete Johnson believes that if you want to understand Redknapp's managerial career, Moore's greatest legacy to Redknapp is probably to be found elsewhere in a gift he almost certainly had no idea he was giving.

'Harry had Bobby on a pedestal,' he says. 'And though he was thrilled to be offered the job at Oxford, he told me he was shocked at how far Bobby had fallen. It had never occurred to him that a World Cup-winning captain and football legend could end up managing a non-league side, playing against opponents who openly disrespected his reputation in front of just a few hundred spectators.

'It was a real wake-up call for Harry. If it could happen to Bobby, it could happen to anyone. And from that point on, I think Harry was determined that he wasn't going to end up as one of the vast number of bitter, ex-footballers who had been spat out and left broke and broken by the game. He was going to keep his wits about him and not let anyone take advantage of him. From then on, whatever career he could make in football was going to be on his own terms as far as possible. And he certainly wasn't going to end up penniless.'

2

In the Dock and the Dugout

23 January 2012

Southwark Crown Court is a vast, red-brick sprawl on the south bank of the Thames between Tower Bridge and London Bridge. It is the last word in Ronseal functionality, a building designed to process the law with as little fuss as possible. If anything, the interior is even more featureless: windowless, often airless, with slightly grubby, off-white walls with pale wood panels. Court Six, where Harry Redknapp's trial was due to start, had the feel of justice at its most municipal. It all felt wrong somehow. The setting for Redknapp's trial should have had the pomp of a Wembley cup final; instead, it felt like an away game at Millwall.

There was no drama, no fanfare, as Redknapp, Mandaric and their separate entourages entered the courtroom. Harry just gave his son, Jamie, a reassuring pat on the back – you'd have thought it might have been the other way round, but paternal habits die hard – and took his seat next to Mandaric in the dock, a self-contained room within a room with shatter-proof glass for walls. Moments later, the usher entered the court and Judge Anthony Leonard made his first appearance. It took a while to understand what he was saying – not just because he was softly spoken, but because he was extremely posh and pronounced 'about' as 'abite'.

The gulf between his world and Redknapp's couldn't have been plainer.

Courts operate in their own space-time continuum, one that is instinctively understood by every member of the legal profession, yet remains a mystery to the uninitiated. 'The case will last for two weeks,' said Judge Leonard at the start of the trial, apparently able to predict in advance exactly how long everyone was going to speak. He certainly knew how long he needed himself. After hearing a morning of legal argument in the absence of the jury, he announced, 'I will deliver my judgment in fifteen minutes, at 12.55.' If you didn't know better, you might have thought he'd already decided on the outcome in advance and fancied getting everything conveniently wrapped up in time for lunch.

The first adjournment was the setting for the first of many bravura Redknapp performances. Having just spent the morning listening to various barristers and police officers argue over matters that might affect whether he was going to prison or not, a normal defendant would want to get the hell out of the courtroom as fast as possible to relax with his family and take stock with his legal team. Not Redknapp. He was all smiles, sharing a joke with several football reporters he had known for years and announcing to the galleries, 'There's absolutely nothing to worry about, I can promise you.'

It was as disconcerting as it was impressive, because whatever he was really feeling he wasn't giving anything away. Many people who have known Redknapp for years joke about what a bad gambler he is, but he could have held his own playing poker with anyone in that court. Sure, he had arrived knowing – as did the press, though it couldn't be reported at the time – that Mandaric and Peter Storrie, the former chief executive of Portsmouth FC, had already been acquitted of similar charges, but, as all barristers warn their clients, juries can be very unpredictable and Redknapp wouldn't have been taking anything for granted.

There was a tactical change at the start of the afternoon's proceedings, with Jamie Redknapp swapping seats in the public gallery with Richard Bevan, chief executive of the League Managers Association, to make sure Jamie was directly in the line of sight of the jurors. Bevan may have many qualities, but celebrity eye-candy isn't one of them. Jamie was to remain in pole position in the gallery throughout the trial. Someone, somewhere, was paying attention to detail.

If anything, time seemed to pass even more slowly over the next day and a half, as barrister John Black QC outlined the case for the prosecution; ninety minutes in the hands of this lawyer was merely the time required to ask one question. In TV courtroom dramas, these opening remarks are invariably a short, snappy, damning resumé of the charges. This was more of a tortuous, soporific, detailed plod, characterized as much by Black saying, 'If the jury could now turn to page 467 behind divider 8 . . .' as by any startling allegations. It was all so long and convoluted, it was hard to keep track, although Redknapp tried manfully to pick his way through several ring binders full of evidence.

Mandaric preferred just to listen. The guard who sat next to the accused in the dock concentrated on his book of word puzzles while, for many of those in the public gallery, checking their emails on their Blackberries every five minutes or so suddenly became a priority. During one of the breaks, Redknapp joked, 'This man could put a glass eye to sleep.' I certainly knew how he felt. Even the judge gave the impression proceedings were drifting, from time to time enquiring how much longer Mr Black thought he was likely to be. It was a curious performance from the prosecution. Black is an experienced QC and must have given a lot of thought to how best to play his hand but he can't have failed to realize he had lost his audience's attention for long periods of time.

The essence of the case was this: in March 2002, Portsmouth

had sold Peter Crouch to Aston Villa for £4.5 million, generating a profit of more than £3 million on the £1.25 million the club had paid Queens Park Rangers for the striker the year before. As director of football, Redknapp's contract had specified he was due ten per cent of the net profits of the sale, but, the week before the sale was agreed, Redknapp was appointed manager of the club and the terms of his contract were changed. He now received a much higher basic salary but his share of any profits on the sale of players was reduced to five per cent. And that five per cent of the Crouch transfer was paid to Redknapp, net of PAYE and National Insurance, in April 2002.

It was what happened next that was of most interest to the authorities. Four days after receiving his five per cent of the Crouch bonus, Redknapp flew to Monaco to open a bank account under the name of 'Rosie47' – Rosie being Redknapp's much-loved pet bulldog and 1947 being the year he was born. Just over a month later, Mandaric paid $145,000 into the Rosie47 account. Thereafter, the Monaco account lay dormant for six months until early January 2003, when Redknapp faxed the bank a request to transfer $100,000 to First Star International Ltd, one of Mandaric's investment companies in America.

Just over a year later, in April 2004, a further $150,000 was paid into Rosie47 by Mandaric and thereafter the account lay dormant for more than two years until November 2006 when Redknapp volunteered the information that he had an offshore bank account in Monaco to the Quest inquiry into illegal payments in football. In January 2008, Redknapp closed Rosie47, transferring the remaining $207,498 to his HSBC account in England, with his accountant sending a cheque to HM Revenue & Customs (HMRC) for £4,415 in respect of untaxed interest on the Monaco money.

Eight months later, Redknapp's accountant again contacted HMRC, this time indicating the possibility that PAYE and NI had not been accounted for in respect of Mandaric's two payments to Rosie47 and offering to put this right if necessary. This, the City of London Police concluded, was clear evidence that the monies Mandaric had paid Redknapp via the Rosie47 account were the other five per cent of the bonus Redknapp had been due as part of his original contract with Portsmouth as the club's director of football and that the pair had deliberately set out to avoid paying any tax on it. In June 2009, the City of London Police formally interviewed Redknapp in connection with this matter for the first time and, early the following year, both he and Mandaric were formally charged with two counts of tax evasion.

It was to everyone's relief when the prosecution barrister finally concluded his opening statement and the judge adjourned proceedings. I went outside to get a coffee and wake myself up and fell into conversation with Redknapp's counsel, John Kelsey-Fry QC.

Kelsey-Fry was a man with almost as stellar a reputation as his client. Over a meteoric career, he has acted for, among others, Roman Polanski, Sharon Osborne and Steven Gerrard and is considered one of the stars of the bar. It wasn't hard to see why. In cross-examination he is sharp, succinct, witty and charming; juries love him. Even his wig oozes class. 'It used to belong to Christmas Humphreys,' he told me. 'He was the barrister who prosecuted Ruth Ellis [the last woman to be hanged in this country]. He was also a Buddhist and refused to sit on any capital cases. So he was a curious man . . . someone who was prepared to prosecute a woman to the gallows but not pass sentence.'

I asked Kelsey-Fry how he thought the case was going so far. Like most lawyers, he responded with a question of his own. 'How do you think it is going?' he said.

'Um . . .' I hesitated, unsure of the exact protocol for these exchanges. 'I'm not sure the prosecution is exactly dazzling the jury.'

Kelsey-Fry smiled and said nothing.

'But some of the evidence does seem quite compelling,' I added.

'Every defendant always looks as guilty as sin after the pros-ecution's opening speech. It will all look very different by the end of next week. Just you wait and see.'

'So you're confident then?'

I can't be a hundred per cent certain, but I have no memory of him replying to that question.

It's often been said of Redknapp that he's a lucky man, a man with the knack of being in the right place at the right time – although I doubt he would have considered himself that lucky to be standing trial. But it was undoubtedly fortunate that it had taken more than two-and-a-half years for the case to come before a jury as the prosecution's main witness was a *News of the World* journalist, Rob Beasley. He had interviewed both Mandaric and Redknapp over the phone in February 2009 and had recorded both conversations, the most damning part of which appeared to be Redknapp referring to the monies in his Monaco bank account as his 'Crouchie bonus'. At the time, this must have felt like gold dust to the CPS as the *News of the World* still had a reputation for investigative reporting alongside its standard celebrity gossip. Indeed, even if the case had been heard just a year earlier, then the newspaper's evidence might still have looked very strong, especially as it had exposed match-fixing during the Lord's Test match between England and Pakistan.

But all that had changed over the course of the previous summer when illegal phone-hacking was shown to have been conducted on an industrial scale by the *News of the World* and the newspa-per had been closed in a damage limitation exercise by its propri-etor, Rupert Murdoch.

Much to the disappointment of the CPS, it was Beasley's reli-ability and reputation that were under scrutiny in court every bit as much as that of the accused. It's always the duty of the defence lawyers to try to muddy the waters, but as the first week – and the case for the prosecution – came to a close, it rather felt as if the prosecution had been contributing to the murkiness itself. There had been a few headline-grabbing detours, such as 'Rosie47' and 'Crouchie bonus', but there had been no conclusive paper trail of who had done what, when and, most importantly, why. Or if there had, Mr Black hadn't been able to keep everyone in court awake for long enough at the same time to establish it.

It wasn't just Redknapp who was happy for the court to adjourn early on the Friday afternoon as Spurs had an away fourth-round FA Cup tie at Watford for him to go to; the rest of us also needed time off for good behaviour.

'You coming for more of this punishment next week?' Redknapp joked with me as I bumped into him in the lobby on the way out.

'Sure am,' I said.

'You must be a glutton for it. I don't have any choice.'

'Good luck tonight, Harry.'

'Thank you very much.'

It wasn't until the second week that things became marginally clearer. No one was disputing the basic facts that Redknapp had opened a bank account in Monaco in 2002, that Mandaric had made two payments, totalling $295,000, into the account and that $100,000 had been transferred from it into a US bank account. It was the interpretation that was in question. The prosecution was alleging that the payments had been a scam to avoid Redknapp having to pay PAYE on a bonus due for the sale of Peter Crouch; the defence was saying that the contractual bonus had been paid through the proper channels and that this payment was a private arrangement between two friends.

Mandaric was first in the witness box. Time and again over the course of more than six hours, Mr Black suggested that the money was a bonus and, time and again, Mandaric told him he was mistaken. 'I know I'm sounding like a broken record, Mr Black,' he said at one point, 'but I can only tell you what happened.'

To Mr Black's credit, he had perfected the barrister's sangfroid of looking as if every answer Mandaric was giving was utterly incriminating and just what he expected, but it was obvious he wasn't really getting anywhere, as Mandaric was the model of consistency and politeness. Yes he, Mandaric, had originally been against buying Crouch: 'I thought he was more of a basketball player than a footballer.' Yes, Harry had pestered him for the full ten per cent bonus to which he had been entitled under his original contract: 'Most people want more money if they can get it and Harry is a moaner. But he knew what he was due and accepted it.'

The Monaco money had been entirely unrelated, he said; he and Redknapp had spent many hours together in the car travelling to games, they had become good friends and he wanted to give Redknapp the benefit of his investment expertise and make him some money. So he had told Redknapp to set up the bank account in Monaco – for Mandaric's benefit rather than Redknapp's – as he didn't want to be liable for any tax on monies coming into the UK, and then transferred $145,000 into it as seed money for future investments. A short while later, he got Redknapp to sign a fax, transferring $100,000 of the seed money to his US investment company. 'I was going to give Harry all the profit on anything I made and he was to return the stake.'

Except there was no profit as Mandaric lost the lot. So, feeling embarrassed, he transferred a further $150,000 into the Rosie47 account to make up the shortfall, with a view to investing that money instead. Then he and Redknapp fell out – Redknapp left Portsmouth and took over as manager of nearby rivals, Southampton – and everyone forgot about the arrangement and the account until Redknapp remembered and declared it during the Quest inquiry.

Redknapp looked on intently, though it became clear his mind wasn't wholly on the case. The second Tuesday of the trial was 31 January, transfer deadline day. It was a day Redknapp as an inveterate buyer and seller of players would normally spend with his mobile phone clamped to his ear.

'What's going on?' he asked the football hacks during a break.

'Apparently, you've bought Louis Saha,' someone told him.

'Really?' Redknapp replied. 'That's news to me.'

It couldn't have been, of course. The idea he would have had no idea that Spurs were in the market for the Everton striker and the chairman had gone ahead and bought the player without even bothering to consult the manager was laughable. Rather it was just an endearing Harryism, a perfectly harmless, if not quite true, quote to lift the football pages out of the banality of the run-of-the-mill transfer speak – 'The boy will give the squad a real lift' – that might guarantee him top billing the following day.

Redknapp was on equally good form later that night as his Spurs side took on Wigan in a Premier League fixture at White Hart Lane. He had every excuse to give the game a miss and leave the team in the hands of his deputies, Kevin Bond and Joe Jordan, as he was due to give evidence himself the next day. A night in at the London hotel where he had been staying throughout the trial to gather his thoughts and rehearse his answers might not have gone amiss.

Not a bit of it. Redknapp led the team from the dugout and waved happily to acknowledge the support of the crowd who chanted his name appreciatively throughout much of the game. Whether he heard all the chants was another matter. '*He pays what he wants . . . he pays what he wa-a-ants . . . He's Harry Redknapp . . . he pays what he wants . . .*' wasn't quite the ringing endorsement of the belief in his innocence Redknapp might have wanted, but there was no mistaking the affection. His Spurs side even seemed to have read the script, cruising to an easy win to go a long way clear in third place in the league table.

Football was also clearly on Redknapp's mind first thing the next morning. When he took his place in the dock before the judge and jury arrived, he gave a big grin and made a 3-1 sign with his fingers, a reference to the scoreline the night before. You couldn't help but admire him – here was a man with the focus to engineer a comfortable league win and still have a laugh when he was due to give what could turn out to be the most important performance of his life later in the day. Even Mandaric, who had remained polite if reserved throughout the trial, seemed to be infected by the party spirit. When he returned to the dock, his cross-examination complete, he pretended to throttle Redknapp. Redknapp slapped him on the back and grinned.

There were more laughs – albeit muted – from the press gallery, when Kelsey-Fry called Redknapp to the stand.

'Why were you all laughing when my dad was called?' Jamie Redknapp whispered to me.

'Because Mr Black had told us all in the adjournment that the defence wouldn't call your dad to give evidence,' I whispered back.

'Why wouldn't he?' replied Jamie, genuinely perplexed.

Why indeed? It didn't feel like quite the right time to explain to Jamie that the laughter was all directed at Mr Black, a man who may well have been an extremely competent barrister, but who appeared to have read almost every nuance of the trial rather differently to everyone else in court.

Once in the witness box, Redknapp didn't disappoint for a minute, delivering a one-man show rich in both comedy and stream-of-consciousness passion. In response to Mandaric's barrister, Lord Macdonald, describing Redknapp as an average footballer, the chirpy defendant kicked off in fine style, saying, 'He would say that – he's an Arsenal supporter.'

When asked why he had called the Monaco bank account

Rosie47, Redknapp replied, 'Because Rosie was my dog . . . she was a lovely dog . . . you would be a lucky man to have a wife as lovely as Rosie . . . and 1947 is the year of my birth. It was like a security code. Like I have to say my mother's name, Violet Brown, to get access to my HSBC account over here.' Oops – that was another security code that would now need to be changed.

Had he thought he was due a ten per cent bonus for the sale of Peter Crouch? 'Well, morally, yes, because Mr Mandaric had said Crouchie was a basketball player and I'd be owing him ten per cent on the money Portsmouth lost. But my new contract said five per cent so that's what I got.'

Did he remember signing the form allowing Mandaric to transfer money out of his account to America? 'No. He must have typed it up and I just signed it. Everyone will tell you, I can barely read or write. To be honest, we were playing Man United later that day and I was more worried about marking David Beckham.'

Did he ever ask Mr Mandaric how the investment was doing? 'Once, after we won at Blackburn. Disaster! He told me it had been a total disaster. Everything had been lost and he'd try again. The lads thought it was really funny when I told them; they said that would be the last I ever saw of the money. To be honest, I never thought about the account again until years later.'

Why had he lied to Rob Beasley? 'Why should I tell a *News of the World* reporter the truth? He didn't tell me the truth. All I was interested in was getting him off my back. We were playing Manchester United in the Carling Cup Final the next day and I could do without a whole load of distractions in the paper on the morning of the game. I was more interested in telling him that it wasn't a story, that the money wasn't a bung. Explaining the legal difference between a loan and a bonus was the last thing on my mind.' And so it continued.

The only time Redknapp cracked was when he snapped at the police officer who had led the dawn raids on his house – along with a photographer from the *Sun* – and was sitting with the prosecution team. 'Mr Manley, will you stop staring at me,' Redknapp said. 'I know you are trying to cause me a problem.'

How a photographer from the *Sun* came to be tipped off about the exact time of the raid was just one of the questions that went unanswered during the trial. But whatever the problem Redknapp thought the police were trying to cause, it was soon dealt with as Detective Manley was nowhere to be seen in court the following day.

The picture that emerged of Mandaric and Redknapp wasn't just of a happy-go-lucky, disorganized business arrangement between friends; it was of another world, the world of professional football, where large sums of money are the norm for the very successful. This wasn't a particularly easy defence to sell to a jury – many of whom may have been struggling to get by on £20,000 or less a year – and so this point was never once laboured or spelled out. But it was implicit throughout the proceedings. Mandaric was worth £2 billion, Redknapp earned more than £5 million per year and £100,000 was a relatively inconsequential amount that can be easily forgotten. In the year Mandaric had invested and lost the money for Redknapp, he had lost £17 million in other deals. In other failed transactions, Redknapp had suffered an £8 million loss on a property development and had lost his son a considerable amount of money on a dodgy stock market tip.

This idea of attempting to avoid paying an 'inconsequential' sum was the unspoken essence of the defence closing speeches. Why on earth would either man go to all that risk and effort just to save about £30,000 in tax? Mandaric had paid £100 million in taxes over the previous ten years and had paid much more than he had needed to for Leicester City and Sheffield Wednesday. They'd been bought after he'd sold Portsmouth, but before, rather than after, they had gone into administration.

Redknapp himself had paid more than £8 million in tax and, if he was really so financially opportunistic, why had he given the £140,000 compensation he was due on leaving Portsmouth in 2004 to a football youth development scheme?

None of these arguments was conclusive one way or the other, as a number of wealthy individuals over the years have been found to have fiddled the equivalent of loose change to them. But they were still relevant questions to ask in response to the prosecution's closing remarks that the *News of the World* tape was 'perhaps the most important and compelling evidence in this case'.

Judge Leonard had missed the mark with his pre-trial prediction of the proceedings being wrapped up inside two weeks – he probably hadn't counted on the pedestrian style of the prosecution case – and it was well into the third week that the jury were asked to retire to consider their verdict.

During the day or so they were out, the media played the usual game of trying to appear professional and resist second-guessing the result, while doing precisely that among themselves. Some were convinced Mandaric and Redknapp would be found guilty; others dreamed up a nice sideline in conspiracy theories. 'A London jury will never convict a London manager who is tipped to be next England manager,' one reporter told me. He may even have been right, but to me it all seemed rather more straightforward. While I couldn't have put my hand on my heart and sworn I believed they were both definitely innocent, nothing I had heard in court would have enabled me to find them guilty beyond any reasonable doubt.

The jury had been asked to consider four separate counts – two each of tax evasion against Mandaric and Redknapp – but it was all over after the first. The judge had said in his summing up that it wasn't an option for the jury to find Mandaric not guilty and Redknapp guilty, so when the first charge against Mandaric received a clear 'Not guilty' from the foreman, then the other three verdicts were a formality; if the first payment by Mandaric into Redknapp's Monaco bank account wasn't an attempt to avoid tax on a 'Crouchie bonus', then the second could hardly be either.

As the first verdict was announced, Jamie Redknapp's eyes reddened as he struggled to hold back his emotions. But Redknapp gave little away. A hug with Mandaric, a shake of the hand with the guard sitting next to him in the dock, a mouthed 'Thank you' to his defence team and the jury and he was out of the court. On the steps outside, surrounded by a phalanx of reporters, cameras and microphones, Redknapp said the whole ordeal had been a nightmare and a terrible strain on his family, but you wouldn't necessarily have guessed it just by looking at him. He was a little more subdued out of deference to the occasion – strictly no one-liners for this lunchtime press conference – but it was another brilliant Redknapp performance. Despite a probable mixture of relief, anger, ecstasy and exhaustion, he held it all together perfectly. 'That's all I want to say for now,' he concluded. 'I just want to go home and relax with my family.' And with that, he got into the back seat of a taxi and was off.

As the crowd dissipated and the journalists scuttled away to file their reports, it occurred to me that this was the end of a very long story about corruption in football, one that had begun as whispers over twenty years ago and had developed into concrete charges just over a decade ago. One of the benefits of a ringside seat at the trial had been the privilege of sitting next to my friend and colleague David Conn, the *Guardian*'s award-winning sports reporter, who probably knows as much about the murkier recesses of the finances of English professional football as anyone. He was the first to point out just how much of a disaster the trial had been for both those tasked with 'cleaning up football' and the police. 'Stories have swirled for years that bungs were common-place in a national sport drowning in cash since the breakaway by the First Division clubs from the Football League to form the Premier League in 1992,' he said. 'The Premier League set up the Quest inquiry in 2006 after agents themselves, including Jon Holmes, one of the first and most respected, described football's player transfer business as "like the wild west". Mike Newell, then Luton Town's manager, said publicly that bungs were rife. The former England manager, Sven-Göran Eriksson, was also caught in a *News of the World* "fake sheikh" sting on a yacht, saying, among several other indiscretions, that Premier League managers "put money in their pockets".

'The claims had credence, because even before the billions from Sky TV and the Premier League's commercial revolution, bungs were indeed proven to have been paid. A previous, much more dogged Premier League inquiry – ultimately signed off in 1997 by Robert Reid QC and the league's then chief executive, Rick Parry – found that after Arsenal signed the Danish midfield international John Jensen, and the Norwegian full-back Pal Lyd-ersen in 1991 and 1992, Arsenal's manager, George Graham, was paid £425,000 in kickbacks or 'bungs' (payments to football managers from agents as 'thank-yous' for signing their players) by the players' Norwegian agent, Rune Hauge. They also concluded that £50,000 in cash had been handed to Ronnie Fenton, assis-tant to Brian Clough, one of English football's greatest managers, after Clough sold the striker Teddy Sheringham to Tottenham Hotspur in August 1992. Graham was sacked as Arsenal's man-ager and suspended from football for a year. Clough and Fenton were charged by the Football Association with misconduct for other alleged transfer kickbacks, but Clough was spared due to his deteriorating health, and Fenton retired to Malta.'

That practice – of managers wanting a bung out of transfer fees – is often explained by football managers having always been insecure and not well paid in pre-Premier League days; it might now be termed 'old school'. Quest was tasked with examining all 362 transfers of players in and out of Premier League clubs between January 2004–06, 'specifically to identify . . . unauthorized or fraudulent payments'. Its investigators produced a report in June 2007 which named some high-profile football agents for alleged lack of cooperation and said seventeen of the deals could not be 'signed off'. But on close reading, the Premier League's report exonerated every manager and club official in the Premier League of taking bungs. Redknapp's revelation in court that 'quite a few' managers did not volunteer their bank details to Quest, as he had done – including, fatefully, his Monaco account – cast the rigour of the Premier League's self-inquiry in a new light.

Conn went on to explain that the City of London Police also hardly came up smelling of roses. 'The City of London Police is the UK's lead force for financial crime, a status some experts describe as its justification for remaining independent of Greater London's Metropolitan Police. The force is part-funded by the banks themselves in the City's square mile; £4.9 million in 2010–11 came from its police authority, the Corporation of London. Throughout the serial multi-billion-pound collapses of banks around it, which have cost the taxpayer trillions, the City of London Police has arrested no senior banker for any suspected offence. The force has, though, become expensively involved in horse-racing and football.

'In December 2007, the trial of former champion jockey Kieren Fallon and five other men for alleged race-fixing collapsed, their lawyers accusing the City of London Police of a flawed investigation.' By then, Conn explained, in 2006, Operation Apprentice had begun and had been broadly reported, following several sensational dawn raids, as targeting 'corruption' in football. It ran alongside the other inquiry by the investigation company Quest, commissioned in January 2006 by the Premier League itself, into alleged bungs. These were strongly rumoured to be routine, and would, if proven, constitute a serious corrupting of football's integrity, which relies on managers recruiting players on their sporting merits. When the raid was carried out at Redknapp's house by around 30 police officers at 6.06 a.m. on 29 November 2007, Redknapp bitterly recalled that only his 'terrified' wife was in and that a photographer from the *Sun* happened to be on hand. The police investigation at the time was assumed to be a forceful follow-up to intelligence about bungs.

In fact, as Redknapp's successful 2008 challenge to the legality of the search warrant later revealed, Operation Apprentice was not related to bungs at all. The offices of Portsmouth, Glasgow Rangers and Newcastle United were also raided, attended by massive publicity; Mandaric was subsequently arrested, as was Peter Storrie, the former Portsmouth chief executive, as well as the football agent Willie McKay (a photographer from the *Sun* had also happened to be at McKay's Doncaster home at 6.00 a.m.), and David Sullivan and Karren Brady, then the owner and managing director respectively of Birmingham City. Two Premier League players – the midfielder Amdy Faye and full-back Pascal Chimbonda, formerly of Portsmouth and Tottenham Hotspur respectively – were also arrested.

The investigation centred not on bungs but on tax, specifically whether Portsmouth had paid Faye a fee when he signed for Portsmouth in 2003, disguised it by routing it through McKay, and therefore evaded PAYE and NI due on it. Neither Faye nor McKay were ultimately charged with any offence, and Sullivan, Brady and Chimbonda were cleared of any wrongdoing. Storrie was prosecuted, charged with cheating the public revenue in relation to that Faye alleged payment, and he and Mandaric were also tried for tax evasion over an alleged termination fee paid to the midfielder Eyal Berkovic via a company, Medellin Enterprises, registered in the British Virgin Islands. Both were found not guilty.

So the net result of ten years of investigations into corruption – at a cost of millions of pounds to the public purse in the case of the prosecution brought against Redknapp – was a big fat zero. Not a single conviction. Not a single allegation proved. And after the humiliation of the Redknapp acquittal, you couldn't really see the CPS or the police initiating proceedings against anyone else. They had given it their best shot with Redknapp and failed. If they had had more compelling evidence against someone else, they would surely have already shown their hand. So, as Conn rightly suggested, the Redknapp case looked likely to be the last word on the matter as the CPS was unlikely to risk another high-profile failure.

This obviously raised questions about the competency of both the Stevens inquiry and the City of London Police; if corruption in football was as endemic as everyone had always claimed, how was it possible that they couldn't come up with one case that would stand up in a court of law? I had my own suspicions – as, no doubt, did everyone else – but I was happy to let others follow that paper trail.

My particular interest was Redknapp himself and it seemed that, far from drawing a line under everything, the case had actually raised many more intriguing areas of discussion; not so much about any illegality – that had been decided – but about his personality, his attitudes and his relationships. What was it about Redknapp that had made the investigators and police go after him not once, not twice, but three times? It was as if he was the modern-day Al Capone of football. Surely he couldn't have been the worst – or indeed only – player, agent or manager in their sights?

Redknapp had always maintained that the authorities had got it in for him because he was an 'East End, working-class Cockney'. This didn't seem entirely plausible, either; not because the police are above making judgements based on lazy stereotypes, but because football is full of other characters similar to Redknapp. They may not all be quite as talkative, but they're just as working class and open to regional prejudice.

There again, Redknapp does have an uncanny knack of acting as a magnet for prejudice. Within hours of writing an article supportive of Redknapp's qualities, my inbox was deluged with emails, almost all of which suggested I must be mad. What was fascinating about them was that the most vitriolic came from those who had no interest in or knowledge of football. One from a woman named Helen was a typical example: 'How could you be so nice about Redknapp?' she wrote. 'He's obviously a crook. He should be in prison.'

I was surprised, to say the least, because I knew Helen well. She wasn't a Middle England Tory; she was a left-wing, football-indifferent friend and former National Union of Journalists activist who in the past had always stood up for the underdog and the right of everyone to a fair trial. Yet here she was, having read little more than the headlines of the proceedings and heard none of the evidence, apparently certain there had been a major miscarriage of justice. I was less interested in whether she was right or wrong than in why she cared so much. Redknapp wasn't one of her typical hate figures; he wasn't a David Cameron, Nick Clegg or Rupert Murdoch. He was just a working-class football manager, the sort of person who didn't normally even register on her radar. So why the moral outrage?

It might have been because 'gobby' people tend to attract extreme responses, and Redknapp is nothing if not gobby, a man not given to using one word when three will do. That made some kind of sense, though not enough. Perhaps she had a gut feeling that Redknapp was being welcomed back all too smoothly into the football family and that his acquittal was going to be used as an excuse to sweep the rest of the game's dirty financial secrets under the carpet. That made even less sense. Redknapp had hardly been persona non grata in football's inner circle when he was awaiting trial and, if the Football Association did want to use his acquittal to tidy away other – as yet unreported – grubbiness, it was hardly Redknapp's fault. So why blame him? Once again, Redknapp was proving enigmatic. The closer I got to trying to understand him, the more elusive he became.

The trickiness had been apparent in his relationship with money, but neither the prosecution nor the defence had gone into it in any depth as it had no bearing on his innocence or guilt. 'I'm not a greedy man, Mr Black,' Redknapp had said while being cross-examined by the prosecution. 'You can ask anyone . . . I'm the least greedy person you could meet.' And there were ample demonstrations of his generosity: his refusal to accept the £140,000 severance payout he was due when he left Portsmouth for the first time; and the many charities and friends he had supported in his spare time.

Redknapp was also at pains to paint himself as someone who is a bit financially naïve. He described how he and Mandaric used to drive to away games together and how the Portsmouth owner's efforts to explain the basics of financial investment used to fall on deaf ears; how almost every investment he had done on his own, either in property or the stock market, had gone wrong; and how he had no real idea what he was doing when he was setting up the Monaco bank account and treated the experience as a fun away-day with the super-rich. 'Milan told me to fly over and do it, so that's what I did,' he said. 'All I remember was that the bank was at the top of the hill and Sandra [Redknapp's wife] sat on the wall outside while I went and signed the forms. I was only in there for about five minutes.'

Even the naming of the bank account shrieked of naïvety. If Rosie47 was, as the prosecution alleged, a deliberate attempt to conceal the existence of the account's identity from the tax authorities then it was an extremely feeble one, the link to

Redknapp being so evident it was tantamount to waving a red flag that said, 'Harry's Secret Stash'. And if Rosie47 was, as the defence claimed, just a security password, then it was one any hacker could have cracked in seconds.

Yet it was clear Redknapp was also a man with a keen sense of his own financial worth. The 2012 *Sunday Times* Rich List in Sport ranked him in eighty-fourth place with a salary at Tottenham Hotspur of £4.4 million per year and assets of £11 million, although those who were familiar with Redknapp's financial arrangements considered that to be a very conservative estimate. And for all Redknapp's courtroom protestations that he 'couldn't really read or write', he seems to have always had a very shrewd idea of what was – and what ought to be – in the contracts his agent negotiated.

The $245,000 that Mandaric placed in the Monaco bank account on Redknapp's behalf may, in reality, have been a generous investment opportunity extended by the Serbian billionaire to his friend and manager, but, on Redknapp's own repeated admission, it was always related to the five per cent of the Crouch transfer he felt he had signed away when he changed jobs from director of football to manager at Portsmouth, and to which he was morally, if not legally, still entitled. No matter that his new contract offered him a substantially higher salary in compensation. Or, to put it another way, that five per cent was a debt of honour. This made Mandaric's efforts to make him a few extra quid via the Monaco bank account less an act of generosity and more a matter of duty. Where did knowing one's precise worth end and greed start?

Then there was Redknapp's home in Sandbanks, a small exclusive peninsula that juts out into Poole Harbour. The house has been valued at £8 million, but decoding what that says about Redknapp is less straightforward. Anyone who had watched Piers Morgan's three-part 2008 ITV documentary about Sandbanks might well believe the area was – square metre for square metre – one of the most expensive pieces of real estate on the planet. The projected image was one of a millionaire's playground of seafront gated palaces and chic wine bars stuffed with Russian oligarchs and their trophy wives.

The reality is a long way from that. 'To tell you the truth,' says Paul Dredge, who has worked as an estate agent in the area for the past sixteen years, 'I didn't recognize the place from that TV programme. None of us did. I think Piers Morgan got a bit carried away after talking to a property developer who has long since gone out of business. There are one or two very expensive homes, of which Redknapp's is one, but there are many, many more purpose-built flats available in the £300,000–£450,000 price bracket. Most of the properties are bought as second homes, with families either coming down for the summer or renting them out. Come the autumn, there's not many people around at all.'

A day spent in Sandbanks in late October rather bears this out. There is very little going on, the one wine bar is nearly empty and a drive along the road that loops round the peninsula reveals a great many properties that aren't particularly lovely. A mixture of drab 1930s and bog-standard, new-build architecture. There's even a terminal at the tip of the peninsula – not far from Redknapp's house – where cars line up for the Poole–Swanage car ferry. It's not most people's definition of glamorous and exclusive.

'I love the area,' Dredge continues, 'but it's not the sort of place where you buy a property if you're looking to make a big "I've made it" statement. A couple of miles away from here there's an area called Branscombe with large detached properties that are not overlooked and are surrounded by woods, which much more clearly fits that description. That's much more the kind of place I would expect to find a successful football manager.'

Redknapp likes his creature comforts: the sea views, the fine wines, the beach to walk the dogs. But he's not so obsessed with status that he would go and live somewhere just for the kudos. He has no anonymity and he isn't that bothered. The police aren't the only people who know where he lives. Almost everyone in Sandbanks does, and, on the mornings Redknapp is in the news, there are a dozen or so newspaper reporters and TV crews parked outside his home. More often than not he will come out with a pot of coffee for everyone and a chat. And on those days when there's nothing going on, he'll nip out to the shop for a paper. The *Sun*, usually.

This isn't the lifestyle of someone who values his privacy or uses his wealth to keep the world at arm's length. Redknapp is a part of the Sandbanks furniture, as much of an attraction as the sand dunes. Neither is it the lifestyle of a man who wants to shout his success from the rooftops. If that was what money meant to Redknapp, then there are plenty of other much flashier places he could have chosen. It is, undeniably, though, still the lifestyle of someone who can afford to live in an £8 million house; there's no getting away from that. Making sense of the Redknapp finances is as tricky as making sense of the man himself.

There had also been a great deal of talk about loyalty and friendship at the trial, how Redknapp was a great family man, how his players loved him and how he and Mandaric had been the best of friends, their relationship transcending the normal formal boundaries of club owner and manager. Even his bulldogs adored him. There didn't seem much doubt about Redknapp's closeness to his family and his dogs; his marriage to Sandra has been one of the few in football that has remained rock-solid and his devotion to his sons – and them to him – has always been self-evident.

But loyalty to all his players? That seemed a bit of a stretch. Just take Peter Crouch, a player whom he had bought and sold on several occasions while manager of both Portsmouth and Spurs. The transfers might have been in the best interests of the clubs

– and they were certainly on at least one occasion in the best interests of Redknapp – but were they always in the best interests of the player? Crouch had definitely appeared less than thrilled at being transferred to Stoke from Spurs at the beginning of the 2011/12 season.

Every footballer enters the game knowing he is a tradeable commodity, so perhaps sentiment shouldn't come into it. In which case, why does football so often still insist on priding itself on old-fashioned values, such as loyalty? Most modern players have as little sense of loyalty to the club they are playing for as the club does to them. Loyalty is strictly a market transaction that holds good for as long as it financially suits both parties, as Redknapp himself made clear when he said of Crouch, 'I've done all right by the boy. I've made him a lot of money.' And so he had, as Crouch had made millions in signing-on fees and contract renegotiations. But did it count as loyalty? For Redknapp – possibly even for Crouch, too – the answer was yes. Yet it wasn't necessarily a description of loyalty anyone outside football would recognize.

His friendships also appeared more complex than the happy-go-lucky surface caricature with which the court and the media were more often than not willing to run. Sitting next to each other throughout the trial, Redknapp and Mandaric looked like old muckers; they smiled at one another, chatted during the lulls and, from time to time, openly joshed with one another. Yet when I thought about it later, I had no idea if the two of them really were still good friends, or whether they would still have exchanged two words with one another if they hadn't found themselves contesting the same charges.

That they had once been extremely close was indisputable, as was the fact that there had been a significant breakdown in their relationship when Redknapp walked out of Portsmouth to take over as manager of their arch-rivals, Southampton. By any reading of the situation, that move hadn't just been 'one of those things', the right job coming up at the wrong time. It had been a very definite 'Fuck you' to his old employer. But the cause of the deterioration in their relationship remained a mystery. Spectators wondered whether it been Mandaric or Redknapp who had initiated the ill feeling, whether it was a row about football or a clash of personalities, and how it was possible for them to patch things up less than a year later when Redknapp returned to Portsmouth. Had that been a marriage of convenience or a genuine rapprochement?

So the trial may have shone some light on the Redknapp enigma; many people might still think he was a bit of a geezer, but no one could now say he was a dodgy geezer. But much about the man remained fascinatingly opaque, not least the fact that he had somehow emerged from a two-and-a-half-week ordeal, in which his personal and business life had been exposed and sometimes ridiculed, even more of a national treasure than he had been before.

Within hours of the 'not guilty' verdicts, the Redknapp story had moved to yet another level, as the news broke that the England manager, Fabio Capello, had resigned. This didn't come as a total surprise. There had been rumours among the football writers at the trial that Capello's resignation was on the cards, ever since the FA had sacked John Terry as England captain the previous week, while his court case for allegedly racially abusing the QPR defender, Anton Ferdinand, was still pending. It wasn't the sacking of Terry that had annoyed Capello – that had seemed the only reasonable response given the circumstances and the seriousness of the allegations – so much as the fact that he hadn't even been consulted about the decision.

Capello's pique was totally understandable; it was almost as though the FA had gone out of its way to insult him so that he had no choice but to walk out of the job. There hadn't been much love lost between the FA and Capello for some months; Capello had already made it clear he intended to quit after the Euro 2012 finals. He had never shown much enthusiasm for England or anything English, and he couldn't wait to return to live full-time in Italy.

It was the timing of the resignation that felt significant. Having danced gently around each other for some time in an uneasy truce designed to limit the damage to the England squad until the Euros were played out, it felt as if the FA had seen which way the wind was blowing at the Redknapp trial and had decided to force the issue. At least that's the way Capello looked to have read the situation, as he had announced his resignation within hours of the one obstacle to Redknapp's appointment as his replacement being removed. If it was all just one big coincidence, then it was the sort of coincidence that only happened to Redknapp. His legend was growing by the minute.

'You must be feeling gutted,' said an email from one of my editors at work. 'No sooner has Harry been cleared than he's going to leave [Spurs] and be England manager.' As it happened, I wasn't that gutted since it didn't feel as if very much had actually changed. Capello's departure may have been brought forward but it had been an open secret for about a year that neither Capello nor the FA had any desire to renew his contracts after the Euros and, like most other fans, I had always assumed Redknapp would walk into the England job during the summer. Just as it had never occurred to me that he would still be Tottenham manager the following season, so I also didn't believe Redknapp would walk out on the club mid-season. So while the Capello–Redknapp story made both the front and back pages of the following day's papers, it felt pretty much like business as normal at White Hart Lane.

But it did make me think. How, when and why had the 'Harry for England' bandwagon become so loud and insistent that everyone had come to accept it as a sacred truth? There wasn't a doubt in my mind that Redknapp would get the job; not because he was so obviously a brilliant manager and the right man for the job – although, at the time, I didn't think he was the right man, as I thought he could do better than wasting his time managing a second-rate international side – but because it seemed to be as much of an historic inevitability as a royal succession.

A Redknapp sceptic later claimed that a Jamie Redknapp column in the *Sun* several years earlier, following another disappointing England performance under Capello, was the original source of the 'Harry for England' campaign. Even if this claim was true – it couldn't really be verified one way or the other – it didn't feel right. This was partly because Jamie has written a lot of stuff in his *Sun* columns over the years to which no one has paid any attention, so there was no reason why the collective subconscious of England's footerati should have latched on to this one in particular. But it was also because 'Harry for England' had overtones of a Shakespearean rallying cry that had been lying dormant for centuries, awaiting the man who would rise up and lead us to the promised land of football glory – in the Ukraine or Brazil, if not at Agincourt.

So why Redknapp? His Englishness was certainly part of it. The country – and, in particular, its football writers – had become fed up with a foreign manager being in charge of the national side. Sven-Göran Eriksson had been good for a few off-pitch stories but had been fairly dull on it, and Fabio Capello had never even bothered to learn the language, which wasn't necessarily a problem for the players but was a major no-no for reporters expecting good quotes and the inside track. So Sven and Fabio had both been judged useless and had to go. In football terms alone, the calls for their removal had been quite harsh; both managers had steered England to the finals of every major competition they had played, and their failure to progress beyond the quarter-finals of any tournament had more to do with the ability of their raw material than with managerial lapses. Any sensible FIFA list would have put England somewhere between sixth and tenth in the world rankings, so the team had merely been playing to its potential.

But fairness has sod all to do with football, especially the England team, where all perspective is forgotten the moment any tournament starts, as many pundits invariably talk up the squad to make us favourites to win. Or, if they are being exceptionally impartial, second favourites. So when the team is knocked out early – as it almost always is – the inquests are invariably bloody. And Sven and Fabio had both long since run out of white knights to champion them.

What was needed, according to the general will – or what approximated to it – was an English manager to lead the England side. Poncy foreigners in smart suits might be good at managing Premiership clubs because they all had loads of foreigners in their squads anyway. But only an Englishman could really get a team of Englishmen to play like Spaniards. How quickly the legacy of Graham Taylor and Steve McClaren had been forgotten.

Redknapp was an English manager through and through, one of barely a handful in the Premiership, among a disproportionate number of Scots. He was also a football writer's dream. Always ready to chat, good company and with a natural gift for the one-liner, he could be relied on for regular stories and brilliant headlines. So he naturally became the runaway favourite – make that certainty – to replace Capello even before he had gone.

The BBC sports reporter, Gary Richardson, did a short, telling interview with Redknapp's former West Ham colleague Geoff Hurst on the morning after Capello's resignation, with both men taking it as read that Redknapp would be the next England manager.

'So tell me, Sir Geoff,' said Richardson, 'when you played

alongside Harry, was there anything about him that made you think he would become a brilliant football manager?'

It was the perfect set-up question, one that in sports interviews invariably invited the full benefit of hindsight to be brought into play with a 'Yes, Gary, there was something about him . . . he was always thinking tactically, that made me think this bloke could go all the way as a manager.' Only Hurst didn't say that at all. What he said was, 'You know what, Gary . . . out of all the footballers I played with back then, Harry was the one I would have said was least likely to go into management. He really didn't seem to have any interest in it whatsoever.'

Richardson laughed, as did a million or so listeners, no doubt. It was funny. And very Harry Redknapp. How much more exciting and entertaining was it to have a manager who had never even thought about being a manager, than some geeky, four-eyed European with a degree in chalkboard 4-4-2 and a charisma bypass? No one really cared that Redknapp's twenty-five-year career in football management had hardly been decked out with trophies. Just one FA Cup, a Champions League quarter-final and a couple of promotions – with a relegation thrown in for good measure. All these achievements weren't so much water under the bridge as entirely irrelevant; Redknapp understood footballers. That's all that mattered. He could get under their skin. What he may have lacked in tactical nous, he more than made up for in powers of motivation. Above all, his teams played an attacking, attractive game. With Redknapp at the helm, English football wouldn't just put the smile back on its face on the pitch – the smiles would be seen on the terraces, too, along with a few belly laughs.

There were also laughs on the day before Spurs played Newcastle at Redknapp's first press conference back at White Hart Lane after the trial. When Redknapp was asked the inevitable, 'Are you going to take the England job?' he straight-batted in typically dry style. 'I know what you lot are like,' he said, 'so

I'm keeping my mouth shut, 'cos if I'm not careful I'll go and say something that loses me the job before I've even got it.' You didn't need to read between the lines to see it wasn't just the rest of England who thought he'd get the job. It was Redknapp, too.

If the press conference had felt like a celebration, the Newcastle game was as good as the coronation. Newcastle had been one of the surprise form teams of the Premiership and nobody had found them easy. But Redknapp's Spurs simply took them apart 5-0 with one of the exhibitions of the season. The passing was slick, the pace devastating and the finishing clinical.

Everything Redknapp touched turned to gold. Many pundits had predicted that the purchase of Louis Saha would be waste a of money as he had failed and got bored at every other club. Saha, though, looked strong and keen and had scored twice on his home debut. Arsenal fans had said Emmanuel Adebayor would go AWOL before Christmas; in mid-February, he scored one and created four other goals. Intermittently, throughout the game, the fans would chant, '*We want you to stay . . . we want you to stay! Oh Harry Redknapp, we want you to stay . . .*' and each time Redknapp would get up from the dugout and wave to his people.

On the way out of the ground, I said to Mat Snow, the former editor of *Four Four Two* magazine, 'I thought I'd seen it all with the Inter Milan game last season, but this was even better. I had no idea we could play so well.'

'Me neither,' he replied. 'And I doubt the team did either.'

As an audition for the England job – if one was still needed – it had been nigh on perfect. There can't have been anyone who watched that game live, or saw the highlights later on television, who didn't believe that Redknapp was the England manager-elect. Even Alan Hansen, the *Match of the Day* pundit who would generally rather slit his own wrists than say something complimentary about Spurs, was drooling over Redknapp.

3

Just About Managing

1981

Harry Redknapp and Bobby Moore had left Oxford United within a year. Their time in charge hadn't been a great success; the team had underperformed, the club's wage bill had rocketed and almost everyone involved was miserable. Moore might have been driving a Daimler, but Redknapp had been running on empty, working out of a temporary Portakabin office. He made no secret of not missing the daily commute, but he was short of both a job and money. In the sanitized version of Redknapp's life story, the transition from Oxford back to Bournemouth was seamless.

But it wasn't quite like that. 'He later told me just how desperate that time had been for him,' said Pete Johnson. 'His money was running out, the phone wasn't ringing and he was seriously considering forking out his last £17,000 on a taxi and licence.' It was another Londoner, the former Chelsea player David Webb, then managing Bournemouth, who saved Redknapp from a career driving a cab round Bournemouth – and his passengers an earful – by offering him a coaching job at the club that had slid into the Fourth Division.

Football has never operated in the same way as other industries when it comes to employment law. And back in 1981, it was like the Wild West. Few posts were ever formally advertised and many jobs were almost arbitrary, with appointments – and sackings – decided on a 'who you know' basis, together with moveable selection criteria, rather than a formal recruitment process. Sometimes no one even knew there was a vacancy until the right man turned up to fill it. So it's hard to know whether Webb was actively seeking a new coach for Bournemouth, or whether he just ended up chatting to an old mate who was short of work and reckoned he might be a useful addition to the set-up. Either way, it was a win-win situation as the cost of one more less-than-generous salary could easily be absorbed into the club's overall wage bill without the chairman, local solicitor or millionaire Harold Walker batting an eyelid. And if it worked out, all well and good; if it didn't, then the arrangement could be ended at a moment's notice.

The partnership worked well, apart from Redknapp allowing his arm to be twisted into making a final appearance as a player in a league cup tie against Manchester United, during which his most incisive contribution to the defeat was an own goal. Despite that minor setback, Bournemouth were promoted to the Third Division in Redknapp's first season. The fans were thrilled, if not always quite able to understand just why Webb and Redknapp were such a successful combination. 'Webb had always seemed great at getting the players fired up,' said Keith Rodgers, a Bournemouth regular throughout the 1980s, 'but he didn't have that good a reputation among the players on the training ground. And in some ways, Harry was quite similar – he was good at the technical stuff and well liked by everyone, but neither he nor Webby were tactical geniuses. It was all fairly basic 4-4-2, but somehow it worked. What we lacked in nous and planning, we more than made up for in team spirit.'

Within a year, though, the partnership came to an end when

Webb was sacked. The trouble started when Webb began to think he was too big for the club, that Bournemouth had no ambition and that he ought to be in charge at Chelsea. Redknapp tried and failed to talk him out of his megalomania – not least because he was concerned that if Webb was fired then he'd be out, too. When the chairman began to believe that there was evidence that Webb had been plotting to oust him, the point of forgiveness had long passed. Webb was fired in December 1982. This put Redknapp in a dilemma. He liked working at Bournemouth and he needed the job, but there was football's unwritten code of honour that said if Webb was sacked – no matter how out of order he had been – then Redknapp should resign as a matter of principle.

'Webb definitely expected Harry to walk out with him,' says Pete Johnson, the veteran reporter on the south coast, 'and he was surprised and disappointed when he didn't. He felt that he had given Harry the job and Harry should stay loyal to him, no matter what.'

Part of Redknapp undoubtedly felt the same way. 'I didn't want to be manager. I was very happy with Webbie,' he said, but when he was offered the job of caretaker manager after several players had petitioned the chairman to offer it to him, he couldn't turn it down. Webb may have seen this as a stab in the back – he's certainly never had a good word to say about Redknapp since. In a very strict sense it was a betrayal, but it wasn't about ambition, as is so often the case in football.

'Harry never had any great ambition to be a manager,' Pete Johnson continues. 'He was very happy just taking a back seat doing some coaching. "There's only one thing that ever happens to a manager – he gets sacked," he said to me. "And I don't need all that grief." '

Just as much as the regular income, Redknapp wanted stability for himself and his family. He didn't want to go looking for another job; he'd had enough of all that. In all probability, if

Webb had been in demand, and had been offered a bigger job at a bigger club with Redknapp part of the deal as his number two, then Redknapp would have walked out, too, and been happy to talk up the virtues of loyalty. But only Torquay eventually came calling for Webb, so Redknapp stayed put at Bournemouth. The need for stability, security and self-preservation won the day.

There was no great honeymoon period in his new job, either. In fact, the 9-0 defeat to Lincoln in his first match in charge has become part of the Redknapp legend, the epitome of the man who can look adversity in the face and laugh. 'The Lincoln pitch was like concrete,' he later wrote in his autobiography. 'No way could you play on it. But the ref somehow gave the go-ahead. Kirky, the physio, got the boots out and I asked him where the ones with rubber studs were. "We haven't got any," he said. All we had were boots with long nylon studs, almost suicidal on a rock-hard pitch. I couldn't believe it.

'The Lincoln players came out with those boots with little pimples for studs, playing one-twos in the kick-about, pirouetting about like ballet dancers. We trundled out and right away three of our players went arse over tit. It was a joke. Crash, bang, wallop, we were 3-0 down at half-time. I said to Kirky, "If we're not careful, this could end up six or seven." That was a bit optimistic as it turned out. Lincoln scored their ninth with eighteen minutes to go, so it could have finished twelve or thirteen. But luckily they eased off. We were lucky to get nil!'

This is Redknapp at his media-friendly best – funny, self-deprecating and always ready with highly quotable anecdotes. Listening to most managers give a press conference is enough to make anyone feel as if they have been slipped a Mogadon. Dull, dreary and defensive, their abiding principle is 'Say nothing interesting . . . see nothing interesting . . . hear nothing interesting'. It's as if they've received their media training from the three wise monkeys – and missed out on the wisdom. Redknapp lights up a room; a minute with him feels like a minute, not an hour. And if he sometimes goes on a bit no one cares, as he's writing the story better than you could yourself.

What often goes unnoticed is that Redknapp is also a master of misdirection. While everyone is busy having a good time, various inconvenient truths can be overlooked. Take the Lincoln game: it was played in the middle of a cold spell on the last weekend before Christmas. Several other league fixtures had been called off, so a rock-hard pitch can hardly have been unexpected. Yet no one in the Bournemouth back-room team had given the correct footwear a moment's thought. Once the players had arrived at the ground on the morning of the game there was even time for someone to nip out to a sports shop to kit out the team with the right trainers, or borrow some, if money was really that tight. But no one apparently noticed. The team was underprepared and the manager ultimately has to carry the can for that.

The same could be said for Redknapp's tactics. He joked that the reason Lincoln didn't win by even more was because they eased off, not because he tried to alter the formation to limit the damage. It was as if he was bewitched by the situation and unable to react. Even if a manager feels powerless and the situation is out of his control, he has to act as if there is something he could do differently and do it. Do something ... anything. If Plan A isn't working, then there must be a Plan B, if only to prove to the fans that you understand Plan A is a failure. But Redknapp didn't have a Plan B at Lincoln. You could forgive him for this; it was his first game in charge as caretaker manager, he was inexperienced and didn't know better. Yet it's worth bearing in mind because, for many Harry-watchers, it's a fault that often goes unnoticed to this day.

One of the reasons Redknapp's misdirections work so well is that they feel uncontrived. Sam Delaney is a journalist who once ghosted a magazine column for Redknapp and has also worked extensively with celebrities and politicians. 'Of all those I've observed at close quarters,' he says, 'only Harry is right up there with Tony Blair and Katie Price as someone who understands his own brand. He has the gift of being able to perfectly communicate the message he wants to put across. He can get you to believe what he wants you to believe. There's nothing calculated about this. Unlike Blair, who would spend hours going through a speech, checking for nuance and practising his inflection and plausibility, I don't believe for a second Redknapp prepares what he's going to say in advance. What he does isn't an act, it's an innate talent; he just goes out there and says the first things that are in his head.'

That's partly what makes him so lovable; Redknapp is believable because, unlike other managers, he does actually believe what he's saying. It's just that what he believes is often not the whole story; it's the one that will get him the most laughs and show himself up in the most sympathetic light. Which makes keeping track of all those things he doesn't say every bit as important as the things he does when trying to understand Redknapp. Keep the text close and the subtext closer.

Redknapp might be a media natural, but it still took him a while to realize just how useful the press could be to him. 'He was always good company, the life and soul,' says Pete Johnson, 'but when he first took over at Bournemouth he didn't seem to appreciate how the relationship with the media could work to his advantage. It was only when I pointed out to him there were actually a couple of local journalists who were interested in what was going on at the club and that if he kept us in the loop he would have a much better chance of getting his point across. Once he understood that, there was no stopping him and he would call me frequently. And I was more than happy to talk to him at any time, because he had an instinctive nose for what kind of story I was after.'

There wasn't much of an improvement in the game following

the Lincoln fiasco, with Bournemouth losing 5-0 to Orient, but results began to pick up and Redknapp was on the verge of being offered the full-time job of manager when Walker sold the club. The new chairman, Anton Johnson, an erstwhile nightclub owner and full-time wheeler-dealer, and managing director Brian Tiler appointed Don Megson in his place. Redknapp considered an offer to be assistant manager at Brighton before deciding to stay at Bournemouth.

'Meggy was a good bloke and I liked him,' said Redknapp. 'But things didn't go so well for him at Bournemouth. The team was struggling and he fell out with Brian and Anton. Brian used to give him some grief. I don't think he thought Meggy was up for the job. After about eight months, Meggy got the bullet and, in October 1984, I was back in charge, this time not as caretaker.'

As so often with Redknapp, this apparently straightforward account of Megson's time in charge of the club – he got the job . . . the team did badly . . . he got sacked – bears a second reading. For what it doesn't say is whether Redknapp felt any personal responsibility for what was going wrong at the club. Sure, it was Megson's neck on the line, but a good number two should also be watching out for the number one. We get no idea if Redknapp was a loyal lieutenant to Megson, pointing out the things he thought were wrong with the team, or if he had actually got the hump at not being given the job in the first place and being quite happy to adopt a passive attitude by sitting back and letting Megson fail. Or, indeed, whether he was even aware that there might have been a possible subconscious conflict of interest.

Redknapp's appointment as Bournemouth manager owed as much to his friendship with Tiler and with him being a relatively cheap option – the club was short of cash at the time – as to a genuine belief in his managerial talent. At the time, the jury would still have been out on that; the feeling might have been that he couldn't do any worse than Megson as he knew the team and stood as good a chance as any of keeping them in the Third Division. And if he didn't, then the club could get rid of him at the end of the season.

It's hard to get an accurate idea of what Redknapp's managerial style was like in his first season. Some former players described him as tactically naïve; others said that he had a very definite idea of how he wanted the team to play. His man-management skills were also up for interpretation. For some, he was the touchy-feely type, being one of the few managers whom players called 'Harry' or 'H' rather than 'Gaffer' or 'Boss'. Others simply felt frozen out.

'Players often feel that the manager has favourites when they aren't playing,' says John Williams, the former Bournemouth central defender who now works for Radio Solent. 'Harry wasn't the best at making me feel as if I was really important to the side when I was out injured and I did find it hard to deal with. But he wasn't the worst either. That's just the way it was back then. There wasn't the back-room staff to look after us. I'd just go in to the club to see the physio in the morning and then go home. I wouldn't necessarily see anyone else all week.

'Harry wasn't the most brilliant tactician. More often than not, his instructions to me would be, "We've got some good players in midfield. Just give them the ball." But I knew exactly what he meant. And he was quite fair. If you made a genuine mistake, he could live with it, but if he thought you weren't giving a hundred per cent, he would get stuck in and have a row. What he was good at was assembling a team to do a job. At Bournemouth, he put together a resilient side, capable of getting out of the Third Division. We weren't all the best ball players, but Harry could spot players with other strengths. Having said that, Bruce Rioch, the Middlesbrough manager, once said to me that the difference between Bournemouth and the other teams in the league was that we were a lot better off the ball. So there was some degree of organization.'

'I'd put him into the category of the old school-type manager
. . . it is all about the football, it's [all about] getting the result on
the Saturday,' says Steve Claridge, who signed for Bournemouth
as a seventeen-year-old in 1984 and now works as a BBC football
pundit. 'Harry is not going to go out of his way to man-manage
or mollycoddle you. You are either going to be a proper person,
stand up to it and be a man about it or go under, and if you go
under he will get rid of you, that's the type of person he is. I can't
say I always knew what I had to do to get his attention; he's the
sort of manager who uses you when he needs you and forgets
about you when he doesn't. He's got that ruthless streak . . . and
along the way, you are going to upset people, but ultimately it
will be for the good of the football club.'

Despite only playing eight times for Bournemouth before being
sold on to Weymouth, Claridge has no bad feelings about how
he was treated. 'As you get older, you become more introspective
about the reasons your career didn't pan out as you had hoped.
When you're young, you don't really know why you're playing
well or badly. If you're playing well, you assume it's down to
you and, if you're not, you blame the manager. You've got no
perspective. I enjoyed my time at Bournemouth. Harry was very
settled, there wasn't a lot of pressure and we had a lot of fun.
But there were limits to what we could all achieve. Sure, it was
a come-down returning to non-league football, but the bottom
line was Weymouth were in the top three of their division and
Bournemouth needed the money.'

Whatever his technical or interpersonal deficiencies, Redknapp
always had two vital things going for him: he knew a decent footballer when he saw one and he wasn't lazy. At his trial in 2012,
Redknapp made a great deal of how he could 'barely read or
write', but those with long memories at Bournemouth remember
that he was seldom without his well-thumbed copy of the *Roth-
mans Football Yearbook*. 'He knew virtually every stat of every

player in every division,' says Pete Johnson. 'He could tell you exactly how many appearances he had made, how many goals he had scored, what position he had played. It was amazing. He was a walking encyclopaedia and would spend every spare minute out scouting players. Nor, like many managers, did he ignore the non-league clubs; quite the reverse. He went out of his way to go to the places, such as Maidstone and Weymouth, to snap up talent on the cheap that everyone else had missed.'

In a post-match television interview after Spurs had lost to Wigan, Sky's Rob Palmer jokingly referred to Redknapp as a 'wheeler-dealer'.

'I'm not a wheeler-dealer. Fuck off!' Redknapp snapped before storming out. The conversation continued off camera. 'Don't say I'm a fucking wheeler-dealer. I'm a fucking football manager.'

Redknapp's hypersensitivity to the word 'wheeler-dealer' was no doubt explained by his having recently been charged with tax evasion. Taken in a certain context, wheeler-dealer can be short-hand for a wide-boy. But in its other sense of a person who loves the thrill of buying and selling, who can't resist a deal, Redknapp is most definitely a wheeler-dealer, and a very capable one at that.

Back in 2003, Michael Lewis wrote the bestselling *Moneyball*, a gripping account of how the 2002 Oakland Athletics baseball team (known in the US as the A's) – with a payroll of about $41 million – took on and beat much higher-rated teams, such as the New York Yankees, that could afford to pay their players three times as much, by ignoring the conventional methods of assessing the value of a player to a team. Instead of using the same statistics as every other team – batting averages and stolen bases – to judge a player's ability, the A's' analysis, known as 'sabermetrics', led them to believe that other criteria, such as on-base percentage and slugging percentage, which were undervalued by everyone else, were a far better guide to potential. As a result, the A's were able to recruit a number of players in whom the bigger teams had no interest at a salary level the club could afford. They became competitive as a result by setting an American league record of twenty consecutive victories and winning the American League West in the process.

Following the success of the A's and the publication of *Moneyball*, some baseball traditionalists dismissed sabermetrics as a fluky piece of back-room bullshit. But just as many, including, significantly, the big spenders such as the Yankees and the Red Sox, who had lost out when the A's out-smarted them in the draft and transfer market, thought there was something in it and employed their own sabermetricians. The geeks had finally found a place at the high table of the all-American game.

The potential for *Moneyball* analysis wasn't lost on other sports, either, although football has yet to come up with a definitive measure for ranking the effectiveness of player stats. If it had, you can't imagine Liverpool paying £35 million for Andy 'He's big . . . he's English' Carroll or Chelsea forking out £50 million for Fernando 'He's quick . . . he's Spanish' Torres. But many clubs now employ people to spend days in front of a screen replaying old matches, searching for the holy grail of those features of players' performance that have previously been disregarded and mark them out as something special. Used properly, *Moneyball* cuts both ways; not only does it help you to pick up potential match-winners on the cheap, it helps to prevent you from paying over the odds for duds.

Redknapp is a long way off being a football geek, or any type of geek for that matter – he likes to give the impression he can barely operate a DVD player. But there is a sense in which he instinctively grasped the principles of *Moneyball* long before the boffins turned it into a science. He had a feel for the kind of player he was after and scoured the country to find them on the cheap. You could argue that he had little choice, as Bournemouth didn't have the resources to pay a few million for the big stars;

but then neither did any other manager in the lower divisions and Redknapp consistently outplayed them in the transfer game.

'Some of it wasn't rocket science,' says Pete Johnson. 'There's a fairly standard formula for getting promotion from the lower divisions. Get two big centre-backs, a playmaker in midfield, a big strong centre-forward to knock in the goals and build the rest of the team around them. And Harry knew that better than anyone as he'd had lumps kicked out of him at Bournemouth as a player, which is why he often made a point of signing precisely the type of players who used to terrify him.

'But other managers in the division worked the same system and were looking for similar players and Harry was a bit of a genius at getting the players others had missed. If he fancied a player, he would go all out to get him. He would chat to him, charm him, do whatever was necessary to get the signature. One tactic that always worked well was to pounce early at the end of May when the rest of the football world was only thinking about going on holiday. He picked up both Efan Ekoku from Sutton and Ian Bishop from Carlisle ahead of the opposition in that way.'

One of Redknapp's first acquisitions, the striker Colin Clarke, who was signed from Tranmere for £20,000, was a typical example of Redknapp's financial nous, and one he has always been happy to shout about from the rooftops. Curiously, perhaps, he remembers that deal as much for the money he personally lost as for the value he bought to the club. When he'd originally approached the chairman for Clarke's £20,000 fee, he'd been told there was no money available. Whereupon, Redknapp suggested putting together a syndicate in which he and three others would personally put up £5,000 each and – in a forerunner to the Peter Crouch arrangement that would later be the subject of his court case – split any profits on Clarke's subsequent sale. The chairman turned this suggestion down and finally came up with the money himself.

'So Clarkie played for a season,' Redknapp said, 'got 36 goals and then we sold him to Southampton for £500,000. My syndicate was gutted – that would have been a profit of almost half a million pounds – but at least it confirmed to me that I could spot a player and had a big future in the management game.'

The Clarke deal is yet another of the great 'loveable Harry' stories, pitched artfully somewhere between bigging himself up for having been so clever and taking the piss out of himself for having missed out on a bumper payday. It diverts us from thinking about what was really going on in any depth. We're meant to think, 'That Harry . . . what a geezer. Gets a player the chairman doesn't even really want for next to nothing and then flogs him for a fortune in next to no time.'

This is really only half the story, though, because what gets left out is that, in the summer of 1986, Clarke was picked for the Northern Ireland World Cup squad in Mexico and was one of its few stars, scoring a consolation goal in the defeat to Spain during the group stages. Most pundits reckoned that showcase goal more than doubled his eventual transfer fee. So while Redknapp deserved credit for spotting and developing talent, the size of the profit owed a great deal to post-World Cup hysteria. Good as Clarke was, Redknapp can never have imagined he was a half-million-pound player.

More significantly, though, the deal glosses over Redknapp's failure sometimes to distinguish between the private and the public good. It's as if his default position is that anything that benefits him automatically benefits those around him and, yet again, it raises questions about where his loyalties ultimately lie – to himself or the club? This is a recurring theme with Redknapp. The Clarke transfer might suggest that, on that occasion, Redknapp was rather more concerned about his own lost opportunity, as what he seems to remember most clearly is that he missed out on the chance of making a quick and easy £120,000. There is no record of him ever having said, 'Thank God the club did so well as it was struggling a bit at the time.'

The aftershock ripples of the Clarke transfer didn't end there. Had the money stayed with Redknapp, it would probably have been put towards buying a bigger home or invested in a local business; he would later buy an Italian restaurant in Bournemouth. And the club might have stayed in the Third Division. As it was, the half million proved to be the financial launchpad for Redknapp to acquire the team that was to win Bournemouth promotion to the Second Division in the following season. It bought John Williams, a centre-back from Port Vale whom Redknapp has often described as his best-ever signing; defender Tony Pulis from Newport; strikers Dave Puckett from Southampton, Trevor Aylott from Crystal Palace and Carl Richards from Enfield; and goalkeeper Gerry Peyton from Fulham. All of them turned out to be shrewd acquisitions by Redknapp, and they would never have been possible without the Clarke windfall.

The John Williams deal shows just how cannily Redknapp operated. 'I didn't really want to leave Port Vale,' says Williams. 'I had just bought my first house in Holmes Chapel and I was feeling settled. But Clarkie [Colin Clarke] had tipped Harry off about me and he wouldn't take no for an answer. Eventually, I agreed to go down to Bournemouth and Harry took me straight out on to the beach. After Port Vale, I thought I was in Magaluf. He then chatted to me and my wife about the best private schools in the area . . . he later told me his trick was to sign the wife, not the player.

'Anyway, it worked on me. I think I agreed to the move on the spot. I got a small signing-on fee, but it wasn't about the money. My weekly wage only went up from £250 to £300. I signed because I liked Harry.'

Redknapp began his career as full-time manager at Bournemouth on a tide of goodwill from the supporters; he wasn't Megson and he was a former Bournemouth player, someone who understood the club and had demonstrated his loyalty by buying a house and settling in the town. Within a month, he had become a local hero when his team beat Manchester United 2-0 in the third round of the FA Cup. 'That was the thing about Harry,' said Glenn Rodgers, a Bournemouth season ticket holder. 'He could deliver these fantastic days, when the impossible seemed to become possible, that you knew you would remember for the rest of your life. It was a bit like having the most fantastic sex with your girlfriend; you instantly forgot all the times she had played hard to get or ignored you. Memories of defeats that shouldn't have happened quickly melted at the prospect of another good time just round the corner.'

And the good times did continue, at least for a while; Bournemouth avoided relegation and won the Associate Members Cup (now the Johnstone's Paint Trophy) in Redknapp's first season. Two years later, Bournemouth won the Third Division Championship and were promoted to the Second Division. Within three years, they were relegated and no one was exactly sure why. Redknapp was still talking a good game to the local press, he was still active in the transfer market, bringing in high-profile and high-value players, such as Gavin Peacock from Gillingham for £250,000, George Lawrence from Millwall for £100,000, Bobby Barnes from Swindon for £110,000 and Luther Blissett from Watford for £50,000, but the team just didn't gel on the pitch.

'There was a lot of head scratching,' says Pete Johnson, 'because on paper the team looked easily strong enough to stay up, despite a long late-season injury list. So had Harry just found his level? Was he a good manager for the lower divisions but didn't have the tactical nous for the higher ones? Had he become so focused on buying and selling players that he had taken his eye off the day-to-day running of the club? Did the players think they were on to a cushy number at Bournemouth and were not as committed as they should have been? Was he just too matey with the team, too quick to join in with the daily trip to the bookie's after training? No one could work it out.'

For John Williams, the immediate blame for relegation rested with an injury list that took out the entire back four. But he also wonders if the team wasn't as professional as it might have been. 'There was a big drinking culture at the club,' he says, 'and we could be a bit of a handful at times. Harry tried to keep one step ahead of us, but he didn't always manage it. It was the same at a lot of clubs, mind. I also think it must have been awkward for Harry, as a few of us were good friends with his son Mark. He probably didn't always know whether to talk to us as the boss or a family friend.'

Within months, no one at Bournemouth was thinking much about football. During a holiday in Italy with Brian Tiler to watch the 1990 World Cup, the minibus in which they were both travelling was hit by a car travelling at 90 mph on the wrong side of the road. The three Italians in the oncoming car and Tiler were killed instantly. Redknapp, who had been sitting next to Tiler, suffered a fractured skull and was in a coma for two days. Initially, the doctors didn't expect him to live, but after three weeks in an Italian hospital he was well enough to be flown home to convalesce. Or rather, that was the idea. He had been warned not to go to any matches, but in a matter of weeks he was back at Dean Court, disguised in sunglasses and a baseball cap, watching Bournemouth play Aldershot in a pre-season friendly.

'When I look back on the accident now,' he later wrote, 'it hasn't altered my outlook on life although I suppose for a while it put things into perspective. I thought at the time that there was no way I'd allow football to be the be-all and end-all of life for me, that I would be able to switch off. But within a few months I was just like I'd always been – still getting the hump when we get beat, and taking everything too personally. I'd be lying if I said it radically changed my life. For a while, I completely lost my sense of taste and smell; I wouldn't have a clue what I was eating. The taste came back, though not fully, after about six months but even today I can't smell anything.'

Spoken like a man. More than that, spoken like an English professional footballer brought up in the school of hard knocks. But should we believe that he hadn't really been affected by the accident? 'Those of us who did observe Harry close up reckoned the accident did change him,' says Johnson. 'He had always had his favourites and he wasn't afraid of showing it; if a player wasn't one of those he really valued, he wouldn't go out of his way to put an arm round him and make him feel good about himself. If he was angry about something, he would let him know it. The onus was always on the player to get back in Harry's good books.

'But after the accident, his mood swings did get more extreme and he could suddenly lose his temper over next to nothing. It definitely affected the players. There was one lad, Wayne Fereday, a winger whom Harry had signed from Newcastle, who turned out to be absolutely hopeless. Harry regularly humiliated him in public by getting him to come in and do extra training, running round the pitch, on a Sunday. It wasn't Harry's judgement that was off – Fereday regularly features in the top two or three of any poll for the worst footballer to have played for Bournemouth – it was his handling that was off. Fereday's confidence was clearly shattered; what he needed was some TLC, not humiliation.

'He also had a go at me for no reason whatsoever. All I'd done was write in the local paper that Jamie's [Harry's son] transfer to Liverpool from Bournemouth for £350,000 was a big move for a seventeen-year-old . . . which it self-evidently was. There was nothing controversial about it whatsoever, but Harry rang me to shout at me for about half an hour and, for a while, I was persona non grata.'

John Williams also thought the accident took its toll. 'Harry would almost never talk about it,' he says. 'It was as though he kept that bit of him to himself, and would only let us see the same fun and jokey side of him. But I think it did make him a bit harder, a bit more determined. As if he realized he had come so close to losing everything and that he now owed it to everyone to make the absolute best of every opportunity that came his way.'

Clearly, such a serious accident must have had some effect on Redknapp. He'd experienced a severely traumatic event, his skull had been fractured, and who knows what peripheral damage may have been caused to his neural pathways? Indeed, he may even have suffered post-traumatic stress disorder; mood swings are a classic symptom. And then there was survivor's guilt. Tiler had been one of his best friends and the two of them had been sitting next to each other. If Redknapp had got into the minibus first he might have been the one killed. As it was, his friend was dead and he was alive. Left untreated or unacknowledged, that kind of guilt, however irrational, can gnaw away at a person indefinitely. All things considered, it would have been more remarkable if Redknapp hadn't been changed somehow by the accident.

Tiler's death certainly had one very concrete knock-on effect. Together, Tiler and Redknapp had been a powerful, virtually unassailable, double act at Bournemouth. They looked after one another, affording each other protection. If someone wanted to knock one of them, they had to be prepared to take on the other. But with Tiler's death, Redknapp was that bit more vulnerable. And he was even more so as Bournemouth showed no signs of making a return to the Second Division.

Having had a set-to with the Bournemouth chairman, Ken Gardiner, for being disrespectful about Tiler's death, Redknapp then fell out with Norman Hayward, a local businessman, who had joined the club board and wanted a more hands-on role. At the end of the 1991/92 season, Redknapp handed in his resignation. Did he jump or was he pushed? Both, probably. Hayward must have been aware that treading on Redknapp's toes would eventually provoke the inevitable resignation letter and, when it duly arrived, no one at the club tried to persuade him to stay.

By the time Redknapp left, Bournemouth found themselves in a financial crisis with debts of £2.6 million; at one point that summer, the club was within fifteen minutes of going into administration and, with the team not making much headway on the pitch, Redknapp was an expensive overhead. And not just because of the salary and bonuses written into his own contract. As with all managers, Redknapp was quick to point out his transfer successes, such as Shaun Teale, who had been bought from Weymouth for £50,000 and sold two years later for £500,000; and Ian Bishop had been bought from Carlisle for £20,000 and sold to Manchester City a year later for £465,000. If the club's finances were rocky, then it was nothing to do with him, surely.

Except Redknapp had everything to do with Bournemouth's financial woes as the straightforward profit and loss account on the buying and selling of players only ever tells half the story. It's the wage bill that tells the other half and Bournemouth's was out of control. 'Harry was brilliant at persuading footballers who might not normally have considered dropping down to the Third Division – Paul Miller, Kevin Bond, Jimmy Case and the like – to come and play for him at Bournemouth,' says Pete Johnson. 'Part of the persuasion was pure charm; Harry would make them feel special, as if moving to Bournemouth would showcase their talent and make them a target for the big clubs within a year. The other part was money. Harry would offer them salaries that were far higher than other clubs in the division were paying. By the end of the 1992 season, the wage bill was running an unsustainable 100 per cent of the club's turnover.'

You could argue this was a case of 'chairman beware'. It's the manager's job to get in the best players he can and, if the chairman is stupid enough to sign off unaffordable salaries, then it's his and the club's lookout. Nothing to do with me, guv. But even if you go with this line of argument, it doesn't say much for Redknapp's sense of financial awareness or responsibility, because another important part of a manager's job is to build a team for the mid- and the long-term future, to preserve the club for the fans and the community. Walking blindly into a situation where a club would either require a massive injection of capital or fire-sell its best assets to survive is folly. If Redknapp didn't know that the club was nearing financial breaking point, he ought to have made it his business to find out; and if he did know but didn't think it was in some way his responsibility, then he lacked judgement.

Whichever it was, Redknapp doesn't seem to have been willing to work out a solution with the club. When Hayward wanted more say in the day-to-day running of the club, Redknapp got the hump. His role was being compromised. If Redknapp had just walked away at that point, then the Bournemouth fans might have waved him off and wished him well.

'Whatever his down sides, he had been a good manager,' says Glenn Rodgers. 'He'd given us some great times and, even though the club was in a financial mess, no one really blamed him for it – though looking back at how he's managed other clubs since, maybe we should have. It was the fact he insisted on taking £100,000 in compensation with him. He might have been legally owed the money, but it just felt as if all those times he had gone on about how much he loved the club and how Bournemouth meant everything to him had just been bullshit really. The bottom line was that what really came first for Harry was Harry. He didn't mind if the club went to the wall so long as he got the money he was owed. We appreciated he might have gripes with the chairman and the board, but taking the money was a classless slap in the face for the fans.'

Redknapp didn't see it that way. He felt he had given the club eight years' loyal service, adding he had turned down approaches from West Ham, Aston Villa and Stoke to manage them, though just how advanced these conversations had ever become was not made clear. He had also made the club money on transfer deals and said he'd opted not to take a salary for four months to help the club's cash flow, which rather suggested he did know precisely how precarious Bournemouth's finances really were. But he took the £100,000 pay-off anyway.

'If those cynical fans still believe I shouldn't have been paid that hundred grand,' he said, 'then I give you the name of Jamie Redknapp, signed for nothing and sold for £350,000 with another £350,000 eventually reaching the club after Jamie had made so many appearances for Liverpool. A man's entitled to £100,000 if a club gets £700,000 for his own kid.'

Jamie's transfer to Liverpool did work to Bournemouth's advantage, but it wasn't entirely through the altruism that Redknapp chose to portray. Even as a young kid, Jamie had shown exceptional football talent and Harry had never hidden the fact that he regarded his son's career as his own special, long-term project, and it's become another landmark of the Redknapp legend that he used to tell Sandra he was taking Jamie to school when he was actually driving him to extra football coaching.

By the age of fourteen, Jamie was considered to be one of the best prospects in the county – so much so that the local FA had to step in to limit the number of games he could play to make sure he didn't get injured, as on some weekends he was in demand to play for his school, the Bournemouth youth side and the Dorset county side. 'He was remarkable,' says Pete Johnson. 'He would join the Bournemouth first team for a training exercise where everyone would get points for which part of the goal target they hit – the corners being worth the most – and he regularly came out as one of the best. Even the pros were impressed.'

Jamie made his debut for Bournemouth as a sixteen-year-old in 1990 and, at the beginning of the 1990/91 season, was loaned out to Spurs. He was recalled to the club before Christmas and the following January was sold to Liverpool for £350,000, making him one of the most expensive seventeen-year-olds in English football at the time. Pete Johnson had been on the wrong end of Redknapp's tongue for suggesting it was a big move, but he wasn't the only one to be surprised by the deal. 'As far as I remember,' says one Spurs insider, 'the reason Jamie was recalled to Bournemouth from us is that he was feeling homesick. So it did come as rather a shock to see he'd gone to Liverpool just a few months later. I guess he'd got over his homesickness by then!'

The lasting impression of Jamie's transfer to Liverpool is that it has Harry's fingerprints all over it. Harry and the then Liverpool manager, Kenny Dalglish, had been friends since the Scottish striker had had a brief trial spell at West Ham in the late 1960s before signing for Celtic, and both Harry and Sandra had been to stay with Dalglish the year before Jamie joined Liverpool. 'I think he was a little bit too young to leave home then,' Dalglish told Liverpool TV in 2011, 'and his mum didn't want to let go of him. The meeting that we had at West Ham all those years ago wouldn't have done any harm with that. The fact that it was Liverpool that Jamie was coming to, a club Harry has a great deal of respect for, wouldn't have done any harm either. He's a good guy and there is a bit of a friendship there.'

There was nothing coincidental or fortuitous about Jamie's move; it was the maturation of the long-term investment that Harry had made in his son's career ever since he'd given him his first coaching lesson. The transfer may have been good for Bournemouth, but it would never have taken place if it hadn't suited the plans of the Redknapp family as a whole. So to cite his son's move as a symbol of everything Redknapp had done for the club and a justification for taking the £100,000 is – not to put too fine a point on it – disingenuous.

This, then, makes the reason for Redknapp taking the money

all the more fascinating. Calling him greedy is just too glib. As Redknapp said at his trial, he had refused the offer of the payout he was due when he left Portsmouth for the first time, suggesting the club donate the money to a youth charity. This wasn't the action of an inherently greedy man who would satisfy his selfish aims regardless of circumstance. Neither does the suggestion that he took the money because it was a matter of principle really stack up; he had been owed the Portsmouth money and he had been owed the four months' wages he had declined, which was hardly the act of a man who insists that every last contractual obligation has to be paid in blood. Indeed, four or five years later, when he was settled at West Ham, Redknapp made an interest-free loan to Bournemouth to help them through another financial crisis. Again, this isn't the action of someone who is by nature greedy, rather it's the action of someone big-hearted – albeit, possibly, a big-hearted person who wasn't entirely comfortable with how he had behaved when he left the club, but was still living in the area and wanted to make some kind of amends.

The only thing that does make sense is that Redknapp must have felt that he actually needed the £100,000 severance payment. He could make do without four months' wages when he still had the guarantee of a job and the promise of a regular salary in the future but, when the plug was pulled, he felt insecure. Like most of us, Redknapp appears to be happiest making the big gestures when life is sweet – or sweet enough – but when the pressure is on, self-interest kicks in.

Remember what it was like in the early 1990s. Property and share prices had crashed in the late 1980s and were still struggling to recover. If Redknapp's investment portfolio, such as it was, was in good shape it would have been a miracle. Remember also that Redknapp was probably not quite so confident about the future as his happy-go-lucky public persona might have suggested. He might have hoped – or indeed been promised – that his old friend, Billy Bonds, would come running to his rescue to offer him the job of assistant manager at West Ham, but he couldn't be sure. People make a lot of promises in football and not all of them come true.

In May 1992, Redknapp was forty-five years old and hadn't exactly taken the football world by storm. He'd done relatively well at Bournemouth and had acquired a reputation both for lively one-liners in press conferences and as a manager whose teams played decent football and could pull off the odd remarkable result. But Bournemouth were pretty much in the same position in the Third Division as they had been when he had taken over. Redknapp had got them promoted and he had got them relegated, and they were now in a much worse financial state. This wasn't a CV to set the hearts of potential employers racing, and it must have occurred to Redknapp that it was just possible his time in football – the one thing he loved doing above all else – was coming to an end. The prospect of driving a yellow cab around Bournemouth must have been even less enticing than it had been ten years previously.

And that's almost certainly why he took the £100,000.

4

England Expects

February 2012

In the week following Spurs' 5-0 victory over Newcastle, football's aristocracy queued up to pay homage to the England manager in waiting, who had gone to Dubai for four days' R&R with his wife to unwind from the stress of the trial. 'There's only one candidate in my mind . . . and a lot of people's minds,' said Mark Hughes, manager of QPR. 'They will get the man they want in the end.'

'Harry has the experience, the knowledge and also the support of 90 per cent of the people in England because he is the one,' said Paolo Di Canio, who had played under Redknapp at West Ham and was now proving himself a more than capable manager at Swindon.

'If Redknapp decides to stay and they give me a call, I wouldn't be available,' said Alan Pardew, Newcastle's manager and one of the few others notionally in the frame for the England job. 'Six or seven years down the line, maybe I would be. I think Harry is the right age and has the right experience.'

The West Ham manager Sam Allardyce was similarly unequivocal. 'It's obvious. He hasn't just been talked about now, he's been talked about since he started to become successful at

Tottenham. It's not unusual that Harry is the number-one choice in the country.'

Most emphatic of all in his endorsement was Sir Alex Ferguson, the most successful club manager in English football history. 'There's no doubt Harry is the best man,' he said. 'He's got the experience and that's important. He's got the personality, the knowledge of the game, and he's changed the fortunes of every club he's been at. It's the right choice.'

It had all the feel of a political party's leadership election, with the grandees having checked which way the wind was blowing and making sure their nomination for the clear front-runner was duly heard and noted. Even Gary Lineker, the BBC *Match of the Day* presenter, who usually grabbed the opportunity to sit on the fence on any given issue, came out in support of Redknapp. Get your favours in early; that way, there's a greater chance of them being returned some time later. If anyone had any doubts about Redknapp, they were keeping them to themselves. After all, why risk making a potentially extremely powerful enemy?

England international footballers were also rushing to get their congratulations in first. England striker Wayne Rooney tweeted, 'Got to be English to replace him [Capello]. Harry Redknapp for me.' The Manchester United defender, Rio Ferdinand, was quick to agree. 'Everyone wants Harry to be the next England manager,' he said – a tweet he would have some cause to regret several months down the line. And just to prove he had no hard feelings at being left on the substitute's bench by Redknapp for much of the season, Spurs striker Jermain Defoe also joined in the Redknapp love-in – although some people might have detected the faintest evidence of gritted teeth.

Redknapp took it all in his stride on his return from Dubai. There had been no official confirmation of the FA's thinking – or even any sign it was 'thinking' at all, although that in itself was not unusual – about whether a shortlist had been drawn up for the England job or if a time frame for the appointment had been decided. Redknapp abhors a vacuum and he happily filled in the blanks with the confidence of a gambling man who could spot an odds-on favourite when he saw one. No diplomatic silences for him.

First, he insisted he was committed to staying at Tottenham until the end of the season and urged the FA to delay making any announcement until the end of May. 'I wouldn't want the players to think, "Is he going . . . is he staying?" I've got to be here until the end of the season, whatever happens. I owe that to Tottenham,' he said, apparently unaware of, or different to, the fact that just by making that statement he had guaranteed his players would spend the rest of the season thinking, 'So he's going then.'

Redknapp then went on to talk through the complications arising from England's participation in Euro 2012 in Poland and the Ukraine that summer. Initially, he appeared to have ruled out one suggestion that had been floated of the FA making a short-term appointment just for the tournament. 'If somebody takes it to the end of the Euros and it does not go well, where do you go then? Back to your club with your tail between your legs? I think it's a job that somebody has to do full-time. You have got to make a decision on somebody and give it to them.' Redknapp then raised the possibility of his becoming the England manager on a part-time, job-share basis for the duration of the Euros in the event that the FA wanted to delay making a permanent appointment until afterwards.

As with most of Redknapp's streams of consciousness, his was a decidedly disjointed narrative. Indeed, it left things even more vague and unsettled than if he had said nothing. He'd be staying at Spurs . . . he wouldn't be staying at Spurs; he'd accept the England job . . . but only on a full-time basis; he'd manage England for the Euros . . . he wouldn't manage England for the Euros; he'd consider a part-time job . . . he wouldn't consider a part-time job.

To add to the sense of the surreal, Redknapp was highlighting precisely the issues you would have expected a spokesman for the FA to be raising; and in the FA's silence, it was hard not to assume that Redknapp had become the de facto voice of the FA, that what he was saying had their approval.

Redknapp might have been a bit demob happy following his acquittal, but he was no mug. If he'd thought he was stepping out of line and jeopardizing his chances of getting the England job, he'd probably have shut up sharpish. It's stretching things to imagine Redknapp's press interviews had been Machiavellian brinkmanship to force the FA into giving him the job before they were ready, so the only logical conclusion was that, while no official approaches to Redknapp had been made, the unofficial channels were taking care of business to the satisfaction of both parties.

That's certainly the way the football press seemed to read the situation. There were a few highly speculative reports that the FA were considering Barcelona's Pep Guardiola and Real Madrid's José Mourinho – they should have been so lucky – but the overwhelming consensus was that the next manager had to be English. And, when the names of Roy Hodgson, Sam Allardyce and Alan Pardew – all of whom were more-than-competent club managers but hardly men who gave the impression they could inspire a team to take on the Spanish or the Germans – were offered as possibilities, that manager had to be Harry Redknapp.

Many papers went so far as to report confidently that the FA were prepared to wait until the end of the season before making an approach for Redknapp. The only uncertainty was the exact amount of compensation the Spurs chairman, Daniel Levy, would be able to extract from the FA for allowing Redknapp to break his contract. Spurs had paid Portsmouth £5 million to secure Redknapp's services in 2008 and the club would definitely want that back, and Levy would almost certainly demand every penny of the fifteen months left on Redknapp's Spurs contract, so a figure of £8–£10 million seemed likely. A significant amount of money, but not one that anybody suggested might be a deal breaker.

What nobody gave any real thought to was whether Redknapp actually wanted the job. After the trial had finished, Redknapp had made a lot of the right noises: 'Who wouldn't want to be England manager if everyone thinks you can do a good job?' But he had also raised one very obvious drawback. 'Everyone who's had the job has been slaughtered at some stage, haven't they? Terry [Venables] is the only one since Alf [Ramsey] who hasn't had any grief. We've seen Ron Greenwood, a great manager of mine at West Ham, and Bobby Robson, a fantastic football man, get terrible stick as England manager.' He might just as well have added Kevin Keegan, Steve McClaren, Glenn Hoddle and Graham Taylor to that list.

Neither was he under any illusions about the difficulties that lay in wait after Euro 2012. 'Going to the next World Cup in Brazil [in 2014] isn't going to be easy, is it? Not even for Spain, as good as the reigning world champions are,' he added. 'If one of the South American teams doesn't win that World Cup, it would be a shock, wouldn't it? Even so, you look at all that, then realize that someone has to manage England. As an eternal optimist, why wouldn't you think, "I can do that"?'

Because the England team wasn't very good might have been one answer. The so-called golden generation of Rooney, Gerrard, Lampard and Ferdinand hadn't exactly covered itself in glory at the previous few international tournaments, and now that most of them were coming to the end of their careers there weren't any obvious superstars-in-waiting to take their place. So there was no expectation of improvement. Misplaced optimism – the belief that you are the one who can overturn historical inevitability – is a necessary part of any manager's make-up, so you can understand Redknapp's qualified bullishness. But there was still something crucial missing. Where was the gung-ho 'This is the job I've always wanted since I first started out in management' that was supposed to be seared on the tongue of every new England manager?

'There's an assumption that often comes with any high-profile job that the person in line for it must really want it,' says Martin Perry, a sports psychologist and confidence coach who has worked with a great many football managers and players. 'The ambition for a particular job is seen as one of the requirements for getting it. We don't always like obvious signs of ambition, but we have come to expect them. The idea that someone might just slip into an important job almost by accident and without having dedicated themselves to getting it just doesn't feel right.

'This expectation is passed on to, and understood by, every candidate. It feels wrong to be half-hearted or ambivalent about a job you know thousands of others would dearly love to have. You feel unworthy, as if you have let yourself and everyone else down, by not being utterly focused and desperate for it. So there can be a temptation to pretend that you care more than you do. Only the individual himself can truly know just how much he wants something, but asking yourself just how ambitious you think Redknapp really was for the England job seems to me to be a very interesting question to start with.'

It was a question almost no one had given any proper consideration, having been swept along by the mantra that being England manager was a job to which any right-thinking English football manager must have automatically aspired. It was also one that drew out some unexpected answers. Redknapp was forty-five when he resigned/was forced out as Bournemouth manager, the age by which many men will have hoped already to have made their mark. He had also already turned down supposed offers to join West Ham, Aston Villa and Stoke. He then went on to West

Ham as number two to Billy Bonds before inheriting the top job at Upton Park a couple of years later. After that, he returned to the south coast to manage Portsmouth and Southampton, both clubs – like West Ham – with no great expectations of instant success. He had turned down the job at Newcastle and the Spurs job had also rather landed in his lap. He hadn't been actively seeking it and a significant factor in his accepting it seemed to be that London was close enough to his home in Sandbanks for him to commute daily.

This may have been the career of a hard-working and talented manager, but it wasn't one driven by the vaulting ambition of a Fergie, a Wenger or a Mourinho, the alpha males of football for whom anything less than 110 per cent, heart-on-sleeve commitment to being the best is an intolerable admission of weakness. Redknapp's ambition appears to fall somewhere well short of theirs, somewhere comfortably and recognizably classifiable within the well-adjusted band of the spectrum. He wants to do well, he's prepared to work hard to succeed, but the bottom line is that there are other things that mean more to him than football. Redknapp's main aim had always been to make a living out of football, to earn enough money to provide for his family while doing something he enjoyed.

His ambition had been measured in his career's longevity rather than its trajectory and he'd long since been satisfied with what he had achieved. Doing a job he liked and being able to return home to Sandra and the dogs and stare out across the harbour through the telescope he had mounted in his living room was all he had ever dreamed of when he first went into management. Redknapp had been perfectly happy at Portsmouth the second time around when the Spurs job landed in his lap and he had been perfectly happy at Spurs – despite the odd bust-up with Daniel Levy – when the England job was apparently being handed to him on a plate. He had to pretend the England job meant the world to him, though; to have done otherwise would not just have appeared ungrateful – disrespectful, even – it would have revealed a side to his personality that was not for public consumption in football circles.

It's also tempting to imagine that Jamie was keener on his dad taking the top job than Harry was himself. Jamie was still a youngish man, making his name in a second career as a TV pundit; he was also close to his dad and loved him a great deal. Under those circumstances, ambition is easily displaced. 'Go on, Dad, you've got to take it,' he might well have said. 'It's the chance of a lifetime. You'll be brilliant.' It's the kind of conversation many sons would dearly love to have if their fathers were in line for a big promotion.

It would have been hard for Harry to resist that kind of influence. He had always enjoyed being Jamie's hero and role model, and the family dynamic would probably have demanded that he was suitably enthusiastic. And who knows? After telling everyone he really wanted the job, maybe he even came to believe it. Sometimes, you are only aware of how much you want something when it is placed directly under your nose. But if Redknapp was really keen on taking the England job after all, everything about his previous career and his immediate responses in the aftermath of the post becoming available indicated that the ambition was very recently acquired.

No one had also given much thought to whether Redknapp would be psychologically suited to the England job. As with the question of ambition, it was just generally assumed that if someone was offered the job then he must be able to do it; all that was required was to replicate what he had brought to club management at international level. 'It's not just the psychological stresses of meeting a whole nation's unrealistic expectations that make managing the England side a radically different proposition,' said the psychologist Martin Perry. 'It's also the very structure of the job that requires a change of mindset. Being England manager is essentially a part-time job in which you get together with your squad for about two days a month; it can be tough getting used to that.

'I know Capello's time in charge wasn't widely well regarded, but he did cope well with the down time. By contrast, Sven-Göran Eriksson wasn't well suited to having time on his hands which is partly why, I'm sure, he got side-tracked into various sexual dalliances. So what needs to be asked is: How well would Harry cope with the boredom of being England manager?'

Put that way, the only adequate response is: Not very. Redknapp likes to be busy, he likes tinkering. The idea of him spending days on end attending meetings with FA apparatchiks before sitting in the stands with a deadpan expression on his face, checking out the form of a possible fourth-choice England centre-back playing in a match in which he has no interest, feels laughable. There was a joke doing the rounds at White Hart Lane following the Newcastle game. 'What's the first thing Harry is going to do when he becomes England manager? Answer: Buy a couple of Croatians to play in midfield.'

It wasn't that funny, but it raised a few smiles because it recognized a central truth: one of Redknapp's favourite managerial responsibilities is buying and selling players. He loves the chase, the deal, the bargain. Yet trading players was going to be the one thing he couldn't do as England manager; he would have to make do with what he had got and shuffle the available resources into a team. If there was an obvious gap in a certain position, then it was just tough. Even worse, his selections would always be subject to the prior demands of a player's club. He couldn't ask for a key player to be rested ahead of an important game. Or rather, he could, but he'd most likely be ignored. Was this a situation that Redknapp would enjoy, in which his managerial talents would thrive? Hardly. Yet still there wasn't a single voice even seriously questioning his credentials. Why challenge a done deal? It was a foregone conclusion that Redknapp could do the job. He was Harry Redknapp, wasn't he? He could do anything.

Back on the field, a 0-0 away draw to Stevenage in the fifth round of the FA Cup that Spurs had been fortunate not to lose was quickly written off as one of those things; an off day, a poor pitch and a highly motivated, well-disciplined underdog up for a fight in front of their own fans. A replay wasn't an ideal addition to the fixture list, but no real harm had been done. The team was still in the competition and the slick Spurs machine would surely roll over the Second Division side in the return at White Hart Lane.

It was less easy to write off the 5-2 away defeat to Arsenal the following week, especially as Spurs had been 2-0 up within half an hour, but that was also effectively what happened in the post-match press conference. 'We've got to come back like we did earlier in the season,' Redknapp said. 'We need to bounce back and recover. We came in at the break feeling sorry for ourselves having been 2-0 up and pegged back. We seemed to buckle after they scored, which isn't like us. We don't do that often. It's going to be tight, but we're in a great position. If we can finish third, that's a great season for us.'

Redknapp's match analysis was less readily accepted by the Spurs Harry-watchers than it was by the professional football media. 'No Spurs fan likes losing to Arsenal at the best of times,' said Trevor Jones, a long-time Spurs season ticket holder, 'but this defeat felt catastrophic because we'd thrown the game away. At 2-0, Arsenal were there for the taking as the home crowd had even started booing their own players. Harry didn't seem to accept any responsibility for the fact that we had blown the game; he just looked on powerlessly as our midfield was overrun and our defence torn to shreds. He couldn't motivate the players to lift their game, neither did he try to alter the formation to cope with the threats.'

There again, Spurs fans do like a good moan and every manager has days when he looks like a rabbit caught in headlights. By the following Wednesday, Redknapp's claim on the England job was stronger than ever without him needing to go anywhere near a touchline, as England, under the guidance of caretaker-manager Stuart Pearce, were beaten 3-2 by Holland at Wembley in a friendly. The scoreline made it sound close, but it wasn't. The Dutch had cruised to a 2-0 lead and then dropped their intensity to little above walking pace; England scurried diligently to equalize before Holland bothered to up their game again. Afterwards, even Pearce wasn't bothering to put himself seriously in the frame to stay on in the job full-time. 'I'm pretty lightly raced,' was how he described his management career to date.

Once again, Redknapp was the only story in town and, as attention now turned to what kind of England team Redknapp might pick, there were, as so often with him, as many variations of the story as there were writers. Typical of this was Gary Neville, who had surprisingly proved himself to be one of the best analysts on television in his first season as a Sky pundit. Writing in the *Mail on Sunday*, he had argued that Redknapp was the best candidate for the job and that the way forward was for England to be prepared to write off Euro 2012 and blood new, young players as the first step to building a strong squad for the next World Cup in 2014.

This sounded great until you gave it a moment's thought. Even a cursory look at Redknapp's team selections over the previous ten years would have told Neville that he almost always chose experience over youth. If Redknapp was in charge at Euro 2012, he would be far more likely to try to persuade Neville himself to come out of retirement than he would to pick a youngster, such as Jordan Henderson. So Redknapp being the best man for the job and England following a youth policy were much more likely to be mutually exclusive propositions. Even Neville, a man whose judgement was normally so sound, was behaving as if he had been bewitched by Redknapp. Normal thought processes had been suspended; the aura around King Harry was all-pervasive.

The interregnum between England managers is usually open season for everyone with an opinion to rubbish the credentials of every possible candidate, to riff on why they are almost certainly going to be useless, why they are bound to fail and why whoever lands the job will be a compromise candidate – the best of a bad lot. With Redknapp there was just one long wave of optimism. Where were the doubts? And what would it take for them to surface?

5

Hammering Out a Deal

1992–2001

'You know what the most revealing section of Harry's autobi-ography is, don't you?' Pete Johnson said to me over lunch. 'It's the chapter where he talks about replacing Billy Bonds as West Ham manager. It's not what he says, so much as where he says it, because the Bonds saga comes right at the very start and he goes on and on at such length about how he didn't stitch Billy up – "I could never have done that . . . Billy was my best friend" – that you end up feeling he must have a guilty conscience. If he didn't, he'd surely have gone into the whole affair in much less detail later on in the book.'

Not for the first time – and certainly not for the last – there were questions to be answered about Redknapp's ambition and sense of loyalty.

Harry Redknapp had first been approached to return to West Ham in 1989 when John Lyall had left after fifteen years in charge of the club. How far the negotiations got is characteristi-cally vague, with Redknapp saying he didn't really fancy leaving Bournemouth at the time and the West Ham board letting their actions speak for them by appointing Lou Macari instead.

Macari's tenure was a one-year disaster. The fans hated him

– 'He wasn't a Londoner and he made us play a long ball game' – and so did the directors, although when Macari resigned after just seven months, Redknapp was not considered as his replacement. Instead, the job went to Billy Bonds, a die-hard Hammer who had played for the club from 1967 until his retirement in 1988, after which he had become the youth-team coach.

Bonds and Redknapp went way back; they had become good friends during their playing days at West Ham – Bonds had even been best man at Redknapp's wedding – and had remained close ever since. And after Bonds had followed up securing West Ham promotion to the old First Division in his first season in charge, only to see them relegated the next, and Redknapp had been given the elbow by Bournemouth, they were both in need of a little help and were perfectly placed to do one another a favour. It was an alliance made in the boozers of Bethnal Green. Helping out a mate was something you just did.

Who was doing whom the favour depended on who was doing the talking. In an interview with the West Ham retro fanzine, *EX*, Bonds remembered, 'I'd had a few phone calls from Harry Redknapp telling me that he was fed up at Bournemouth, fed up with management itself and that he would be happy to come and work with me on my own terms. Harry wasn't a top-drawer coach but he was good out on the training ground and good with players.'

Redknapp recalled it rather differently. 'When they were relegated, Bill gave me a call,' he said. 'I thought something must be up because he never phoned anyone. He told me he could do with a bit of help. I'd had enough of managing. I'd had nine years at Bournemouth and that was plenty. When Bill rang me that summer and started talking about someone assisting him at West Ham, I thought I wouldn't mind some of that.'

At the time when Redknapp became Bonds' assistant in 1992, such differences of interpretation were largely immaterial and could easily be overlooked. Two old muckers having a laugh and working together for a club they both loved . . . what could be better? The pair got off to a great start with West Ham continuing to act like a yo-yo by gaining promotion back to what was now the Premier League in their first season in tandem – and it was very much 'in tandem'.

The players certainly weren't put out by Redknapp's arrival. 'We all loved Billy Bonds,' says Trevor Morley, the striker who had been with the club for three years and was player of the year in 1994, 'but he did have his limitations. If anything, he was too nice a bloke. We needed someone a bit more street-wise and, since Billy and Harry got on so well together, Harry was the perfect fit in many ways. Harry is a very shrewd man . . . he didn't say much when he first arrived. He just eased his way in and gradually made his presence felt.'

Redknapp's arrival looked a little different from the outside. 'Harry was always brilliant at getting himself noticed,' says Sam Delaney. 'Right from the time he arrived, he gave the impression he was on an equal footing with Bonds because he had a much higher profile. West Ham had always been one of those clubs about which people were respectful but which were usually largely forgotten. Under Ron Greenwood and John Lyall, the mantra had always been to say as little as possible . . . no publicity was good publicity. Bonds was very much in the same mould, but Harry was completely the opposite. He loved talking to the media, so naturally the media quickly started coming to him first, which made him look as if he was running the show more than he really was.'

That could be an understatement, because if you were only to listen to Redknapp, you might be forgiven for thinking that Bonds had made hardly any contribution at all. 'I knew right away serious changes had to be made for the good of the club,' Redknapp wrote. 'Dead wood had to be shifted. I think if Bill was honest, he would say he didn't have a lot of time for the players. He'd been such a good player himself, a whole-hearted servant of the club, and I think deep down the thought of some of them earning high-grade salaries for low-grade performances disgusted him. That attitude was understandable, but it didn't help when you had to get players to turn it on for you. I saw it as one of my first tasks to lift the players, to instil confidence, to tell them constantly how good they were. At the same time, stricter discipline was essential. There's no doubt that one or two of them had been on the booze and let themselves go. I decided we had to train them harder, and get them to lose a bit of weight.'

Alongside this, Redknapp was also in charge of training, saying, 'He [Bonds] let me get on with training and, after the first couple of months, I really enjoyed the coaching aspect without the aggravation of being manager.' It was also left to Redknapp to take the lead role in his particular area of expertise – the transfer market. In his first season, West Ham had twelve players coming in and out; during the second, that figure had almost doubled to twenty-three, including the controversial sale of the fans' hero, but club liability, Julian Dicks to Liverpool. 'I was the instigator of the Dicks transfer,' he said, 'so I suppose observers may have suspected at that time that I was taking on an increasingly high-profile role, but wheeling and dealing [a description he wouldn't be so keen on in 2010] was what I was good at and Bill let me get on with it.'

On the basis of this evidence, it sounds as if Redknapp was doing everything except select the team. He was taking the training sessions, doing the touchy-feely Mr Motivator stuff, was in charge of nutrition – a bit of a turnaround for the man whose motto had been 'win or lose – on the booze' – and was dictating transfer policy. If Redknapp was overstating his input, it wouldn't have been the first time a manager had done so, but the real issue is one of intent. Was Redknapp on a deliberate land grab to try to undermine Bonds, or was he just a hard worker, happy to get stuck in wherever he could?

Everything points to the latter. The relationship between Bonds and Redknapp remained – by and large – sweetness and light. The club was doing well and so were they. It was just that Redknapp was the brighter star and Bonds wasn't the first – nor would he be the last – to be dazzled and become a little overshadowed by his brilliance.

'I don't think anyone at West Ham really minded Redknapp taking a bigger and bigger role,' says Delaney. 'Bonds was just relieved to be spared the effort and the fans loved it. For the first time in ages, West Ham became a club that people were talking about; you could turn to the sports pages and find something about us.'

The extra attention Redknapp was attracting didn't do him any harm because, during West Ham's pre-season tour to Scotland in the summer of 1994, Bournemouth – presumably having noticed that Redknapp had kept his home on the south coast and was commuting to London – asked him if he would like to return. Redknapp was tempted. 'OK, it would have been a step backward leaving a Premiership club,' he said, 'but my home was still Bournemouth. I thought to myself, "Well, Harry, you're pushing 50, why not settle for an easier life?" When I told Bill about the offer during our pre-season trip in Scotland, his attitude was, "I don't blame you, Harry, it's your home. But I don't know what I'll do without you." Then, after a pause, he said without warning, "If you go, I'll go." I couldn't understand it.

'"Don't be stupid, Bill. What do you want to do that for?"

'"Ah, I don't want to do it any more," he said. I told him that if he was taking that attitude then I was staying put. I certainly didn't want to be responsible for Billy walking out of his beloved West Ham. "No," he said. "You do what you want to do. I may not go. We'll see what happens." '

Thereafter, things become steadily less clear. According to Redknapp, what happened next is that West Ham got wind of

Bournemouth's interest and he and Bonds were summoned to a meeting with West Ham chairman, Terence Brown, and managing director, Peter Storrie, during which Brown cross-examined Redknapp about his management ambitions before offering him the job of West Ham manager on the spot. Redknapp turned it down, pointing out that the club already had a manager in Bonds. At which point, Brown suggested creating a job for Bonds as director of football. Having been silent so far during the meeting, Bonds then said, 'It's quite obvious you want Harry to take over from me. I'm not stupid. You think he's better at it than me. You want Harry as manager.'

'I told Bill that I genuinely didn't want the West Ham manager's job. Maybe I was lacking in ambition or something, but I just didn't feel comfortable with all the aggravation. And, of course, there were two other factors playing on my mind: first, the tempting offer from Bournemouth; second, the growing realization that, if I was to take over from Bill in the circumstances I've just described, it wouldn't take mischief-makers too long to put two and two together and make five.'

Within a few days, Redknapp had taken the job . . . or been bounced into it. Bonds had quit and the chairman had called a press conference to announce Redknapp's appointment. 'I managed to get hold of Bill again and told him of the chairman's offer,' Redknapp said. '"Take it, Harry, you'd be a fool not to," he said. "It's a good job. It's well paid, Take it."

'"But Bill, what about . . .?" I began.

'"Don't worry about me," he said. "I've had it off. I've been well looked after."

'With that I was almost bundled into a press conference announcing me as the new manager. Yet it wasn't something I'd wanted to happen. I allowed myself to be pushed into it too quickly and that was a mistake.'

But he had taken the job, and with Bonds' blessing. Which just leaves the awkward question hanging: Why has Bonds – one of Redknapp's closest friends for nearly thirty years – never spoken to him again since? Bonds has said little in public about his exit from West Ham apart from one interview with the fanzine, *EX*, almost ten years later in 2003. But what he did say rather challenged Redknapp's version.

'Harry came in with talk that Bournemouth wanted him but whether that was just to try and bump up his wages, I don't know,' said Bonds. 'He was always talking about being wanted elsewhere. Before Bournemouth it had been Oxford. I used to say to him, "Well, if they want you – go. I'll miss you but if you want to leave, then do it." I think the board got wind of the fact that Bournemouth were after Harry and they clearly wanted to keep him.'

Reading between the lines, Bonds appears to have partially misread the situation. He was so used to Redknapp talking about everything and nothing – Redknapp and silence are not natural bedfellows – that he failed to realize that this time the chat about Bournemouth's interest had more substance than usual and, as a result, he wasn't alert to the seriousness of the possible implications. Equally though, Redknapp was an old and trusted friend, the West Ham board had given no hints they were in the market for a replacement and Bonds, according to his account, had never given any indication he was ready to chuck it all in, so why should he have been on his guard?

The most crucial difference between the Redknapp and the Bonds versions concerns the meeting with Terence Brown and Peter Storrie. Redknapp remembers it as a collegiate, friendly chat in which the idea of him taking over from Bonds emerged as a surprise. Bonds recalled it very differently. 'When I got to the room at six o'clock on the dot, the whole of them – the board members, Peter Storrie and Harry – were already sitting around. I'm not a mug and I got the strong vibe that they had already discussed everything and that Harry wanted to have more say in team matters. I didn't feel needed or wanted any more. I don't think the directors wanted me to leave the club, but I would imagine that they wanted Harry to take on a more senior management role. I told them that I knew where I stood and that I'd resign, but they wanted me to go on the board. I would have been the first manager to go into a director of football-type role but I'm not really one for staying around if I'm not wanted. I suppose I was hurt by it. That's life. It happens.

'Don't get me wrong, no one should be guaranteed a job for life. It's [being manager] the biggest job you can have at a football club and you know that one day you will get the bullet. I'm just sorry I left West Ham in the circumstances I did. All I will say is that I was a very bad judge of character where one person was concerned.'

What actually happened, and whose version should we believe? Once again, the enigma that is Harry Redknapp refuses to provide a straightforward answer.

The idea that Redknapp set out to stab Bonds in the back by cultivating an offer to return to Bournemouth seems far-fetched. Redknapp was still living in Bournemouth, he was popular there and had maintained close links with many people at the football club, despite the manner of his leaving. A conversation in which a former chairman, Geoffrey Hayward, said he was contemplating buying back the club on the condition Redknapp managed it, would have been neither particularly unexpected nor unwelcome – not least because he was being offered the same salary. Money had always been more attractive to Redknapp than prestige, so the temptation of an easier life in a lower division without the hassle of a daily commute should be taken at face value.

What might have taken Redknapp by surprise was the panic with which the West Ham board responded to the possibility of him disappearing back to Bournemouth. The board had been happy enough to have Bonds in charge with Redknapp as his number two so long as there was no threat to the status quo. The question of who was actually doing what was an irrelevant complication; as long as the team was doing well and Bonds and Redknapp were happy, then why rock the boat? It only became an issue when it looked as if Redknapp might be off, because everyone understood that Redknapp was the heartbeat of the team. Bonds might not have been too bothered if his old mate upped sticks, but everyone else was. At which point, it's reasonable to assume that the board went on a Redknapp charm offensive to get him to stay.

Now look at the position from Redknapp's perspective. He'd been trundling along at West Ham, working hard, enjoying himself and not giving too much thought to any career move when – BANG! – out of nowhere the chairman love-bombs him with an irresistible offer. It's one thing to consider trading in the job of assistant manager at a Premiership club for a return to managing a club that you know and love in a lower division; it's another to trade in the chance of managing a Premier League club. The chance of managing West Ham was a serious game changer. This wasn't about ruthless ambition so much as having a golden egg thrust in his face. Who wouldn't give it serious thought? So long as Bonds was not hurt in the process, then it was a win-win situation for everyone.

And that's what Redknapp must have reckoned was on offer when the chairman suggested the idea of Bonds moving upstairs with the promise of a job for life as director of football. In Redknapp's mind, a job for life in an insecure business was about as good as it could get: no driving taxis, no running a pub like so many other ex-players and managers whose football careers had outstripped their shelf life. Billy would be looked after in the game he loved until he chose to retire. Director of football might be a bit of a non-job, but Billy would be OK with that as he'd always been quite laid-back about Redknapp doing aspects of his job anyway. Once you began to think about it properly, he was actually doing his mate a favour ...

What Redknapp hadn't counted on was that Bonds might mind and would get the hump. It is here that the discrepancies between the two men's stories almost certainly arose and Redknapp glossed over a few awkwardnesses to cover his back, because Bonds' account of walking into a room where Redknapp and several members of the board were already gathered is also the one given by one of the board members present.

'Yes, we did discuss the situation with Harry first,' one of the board members who had been present told me on the proviso he could remain anonymous. 'So he did know we were going to offer him the job as manager and move Bill upstairs beforehand. The way we let Bill down is one of my biggest regrets about my time with West Ham. We should have talked to him. If we had, it's possible he might have been happier about taking it on as he would have felt included in the process. At the very least, we would have had an inkling he would refuse and have the breathing space to try to come up with another proposal which he could accept.

'Harry is right on one point, though. He never actually came out and said, "Make me manager or I'm off to Bournemouth." That's not the way he does things.' The board member said that Harry did not explicitly state he wanted the manager's job, but the board nevertheless thought he did. 'So Harry can say with hand on heart that he didn't stab Bill in the back, but all of us on the board knew that once the possibility of him being manager had been raised, he really wanted the job and colluded in finding a way to make that happen.'

Aware that the Bonds and Redknapp affair was in danger of turning into a PR disaster for the club, Peter Storrie issued a statement aimed at damage limitation. 'It wasn't a case of taking the managership away from Bill,' he said. 'We wanted him to stay as a director. But he wanted a break. There are no hard feelings. It was difficult for both Bill and Harry but their friendship is as strong as ever. If Harry had gone to Bournemouth, there was a good chance Bill would have resigned anyway, so we were in a no-win situation. We're sad that Bill is going and it's a big blow, but it's time to move on and we have appointed a great manager.'

Storrie's words went unheard, for, as Steve Blowers recorded in *Nearly Reached the Sky*, his history of West Ham, the next day's back-page headlines were all about how Bonds had been shafted by the club he had served so loyally. In the long term, though, the only lasting damage was to Bonds' and Redknapp's friendship. 'Had this all taken place now,' says Delaney, 'then the fallout would have been much worse. All the fans knew that Billy had been treated very shabbily but there weren't the Internet message boards of Twitter for that feeling to gather momentum and make itself heard.

'It was also much easier for the club to keep control of information back then, so it took time for the whole story to come out, by which time its moment had passed. I also feel there was a certain amount of collusion between the club, the players and the fans. No one wanted to see Billy go, but we all knew that Harry was the better manager and that the club was likely to do better under him, so it was as if there was an implicit pact not to make too big a deal of it. We all basically just wanted the whole situation to go away.'

Not that it ever would entirely, not least because Redknapp handled the transition spectacularly badly with his players. 'When he called us in to explain what was going on,' one ex-player remembered, 'Harry told us that he'd been out for a drink with Billy the night before, that they were still good mates and that he was taking over with Billy's blessing. So we were all OK about it until Tony Gale talked on the phone to Billy a day or so later and discovered that was all nonsense. Billy and Harry hadn't been out for a drink and Billy hadn't given Harry the OK. At that point a lot of the squad lost a bit of respect for Harry as we knew he hadn't been straight with us.'

This isn't the definitive proof – the smoking gun – that Redknapp did stab Bonds in the back, but it is indicative of the self-destructive side of his personality. If he'd simply told the players, 'I haven't spoken to Billy about all this but I know he isn't very happy . . .' he'd have had the squad pretty much on his side. Most footballers understand the game can be brutal, with managers and players frequently expendable, and they would have quickly adjusted with little lingering resentment towards Redknapp. As it was, Redknapp's desire to be liked – even to the extent of telling an account that was almost bound to be found out within hours, if not days – made a bad situation worse.

With his legs under the manager's desk, one of Redknapp's first back-room moves was to get his brother-in-law and fellow ex-Hammer, Frank Lampard senior, in as his assistant. It was an appointment that raised a few eyebrows among the fans as Lampard had no track record in management or coaching since retiring as a player in 1986, but, as he was considered to be one of the West Ham family, most were prepared to give him the benefit of the doubt.

As important to Redknapp, one might imagine, was that Lampard was a member of his own family; having seen how easily close friendships could go pear-shaped with Bonds no longer speaking to him, Redknapp might well have seen the virtues in an assistant with blood ties. If not a sign of the guilty conscience to which Pete Johnson referred, then it was certainly one of a good understanding of the nature of football *realpolitik*. Over the years, Redknapp has been careful to make sure his assistants' first loyalty has been to him rather than their own ambition; none has ever exploited a downturn in his fortunes and popularity to try and replace him.

Redknapp's most pressing on-field problem was Joey Beauchamp, a winger, whom West Ham had bought from Oxford
United in the summer for £850,000, yet who showed a remarkable reluctance to play for his new club. After numerous set-tos
with Beauchamp, who made no competitive appearances for
West Ham, Redknapp sold him on to Swindon just fifty-eight
days after buying him. 'It was like a black cloud had been lifted,'
Redknapp said when Beauchamp was finally shown the door.

In some ways, though, the Beauchamp saga was a miniature
portrait of Redknapp's management style throughout his time at
West Ham. While Redknapp had managed to contrive a solution
to the Beauchamp problem, he was less willing to acknowledge
that he had, in large part, been responsible for creating it. During
the Bonds regime, Redknapp had taken the lead role in buying
and selling players so, to all intents and purposes, Beauchamp
had been signed on his watch and on his say so. For an outlay
of £850,000, you might have expected a little more preliminary
work before the deal was done; watching a player gives you an
idea of his talent and fitness, while talking to him reveals his state
of mind – his ambitions, anxieties and desires – which are every
bit as important. Beauchamp's neuroses and homesickness didn't
appear out of thin air the moment he moved fifty miles east of
Oxford. They would have been there for all to see if only anyone
had bothered to look for them. Redknapp only saw what was
in front of him, part of which was a capable footballer, part of
which was also the deal.

Much as Redknapp may now dislike his reputation for a knack
in buying and selling, it appears to have been hard-wired into his
blood as a manager. 'Harry just loved the thrill of a deal,' says
the former West Ham board director. 'It was almost as if it was
a drug. Almost every week he'd be going on at me about how "so
and so is a brilliant player and we've got to buy him before anyone
else does" and every week it would be about a different player.

With Stan Lazaridis it was that he'd seen him doing keepy-uppies on a tour of Australia. Harry doesn't stop. He wears you down.'

And he frequently got his own way as the West Ham team of the mid- and late-1990s often gave the appearance of operating on a revolving door policy: one player in, another out. If a player wasn't performing as well as Redknapp expected, he wouldn't waste too much time trying to understand why or tinker with the formation to help him improve. He'd get rid of him and bring in another player he thought could do a better job.

It was a policy that misfired as often as it worked and occasionally exasperated the West Ham fans. 'We'd get some brilliant players in – John Hartson and Paolo Di Canio did fabulously for us,' says Sam Delaney. 'But Harry also brought in some real shockers, most of them from the European mainland. For a while, it was quite exciting. There weren't so many foreign players in the Premiership back then, and those there were didn't want to come to West Ham. But under Harry they did and it made us all feel good to bask in the kudos as he would big them all up on their arrival as World Cup stars. And then we'd see them play . . . Some barely lasted a season, they were that bad, and it made us into a bit of a laughing stock.'

Even Redknapp couldn't gloss over just how disastrous some of his acquisitions had been. Marco Boogers had been bought from Sparta Rotterdam for £1 million before the 1995 season, with West Ham proudly announcing they had acquired the player who had been voted third best in the whole of the Dutch league the previous season. As Steve Blowers pointed out, this wasn't quite true. 'It now transpired he had only been voted into third place in the Sparta Rotterdam player of the season poll,' he wrote.

With Boogers having been sent off after just eighteen minutes of his first game, Redknapp came under scrutiny. 'Of course he's the kind of player I expected,' he said, back-pedalling in response to criticism. 'I knew exactly what I was getting. People are saying that I bought him off a video. I don't know who dreamt that one up!'

No one, as it happened, for it wasn't a dream. A while later – with Boogers having apparently gone AWOL in a caravan in between fitting in ninety-eight minutes' playing time in his four appearances, before being shifted on to Groningen along with a mental-health sick note – Redknapp came clean. 'I could tell after three or four weeks that I had dropped a "rick" with him,' he said. 'His attitude stank. Someone sent me a tape of Boogers in action and urged me to watch it. I was very impressed and, for the first time in my life, I signed a player purely on what I'd seen on video. The season was upon us and we didn't have time to check him out any further.'

The least that could be said was that it was a cavalier way of spending the club's money and one that cost the club £800,000 in transfer costs along with Boogers' wages.

The signings of the two Romanians – Ilie Dumitrescu and Florin Raducioiu – weren't quite as catastrophic as that of Boogers, but not far off. Dumitrescu had been bought from Spurs in 1995 for £1.5 million, but, as he had played fewer than a quarter of the games for the north London club for which he had been eligible, the British government was reluctant to issue him a work permit. So he also sat out a fair few games for West Ham and, when he did become available, was either injured or disappointing and was transferred for £1 million to the Mexican club, FC de America, at the end of the following season.

Raducioiu lasted even less time. Bought for £2.4 million from the Spanish club Espanyol at the beginning of the 1996 season, he was sold back to the same club for £1.5 million long before the end of it. 'It was a toss-up between Raducioiu and Marco Boogers for my worst ever signing,' was Redknapp's philosophical take on West Ham's £900,000 loss.

Redknapp didn't lose on the signing of another foreigner as

Paulo Futre was acquired on a free transfer from AC Milan, but neither did he gain. The forward decided to retire in the same season as his arrival, leaving Redknapp to observe ruefully after an away game at Roker Park, 'There was a howling wind and Sunderland were swarming in on our goal and Futre, Dumitrescu and Raducioiu were standing there on the halfway line looking on. I knew then it wasn't going to work . . .'

It was the overseas signings that attracted the most interest – and criticism – but Redknapp was as busy as ever in the home transfer market, equally as happy trading in low-value players from his old club Bournemouth as in high-value ones, such as John Hartson, Trevor Sinclair and Paul Kitson. But then as long as he was trading, Redknapp was usually happy. And for the most part, his signings all did a decent job for a season or two; Redknapp may have made the odd howler during his career, but he has a nose for a good footballer.

What he doesn't have a nose for is stability. When Redknapp invites his critics to judge him on his transfer track record, the only subject up for discussion is the profit and loss account – the amount each player cost set against the fee the club recouped on his eventual sale. This way he more often than not emerges in credit. The element that gets lost here is the hidden, invisible costs. Treating players as mere commodities – functioning objects who either do their job well or badly – is an inefficient and expensive way of doing business. Most players – people – want to feel loved and valued; they want a sense of belonging. They don't want to feel as if they are being judged on a game-by-game basis and, if found wanting, are going to be shipped out to the highest bidder at the first available opportunity.

But that's precisely the atmosphere that Redknapp tended to create in his West Ham teams as the players knew they could be in favour one week and on their bike the next. And that type of atmosphere can be extremely demotivating – not just for those who are insecure about their status within the team but also for the players who have good reason to believe they are semi-permanent fixtures. The most successful teams may now be the ones crammed with the best and most expensive players, but they weren't always in the 1990s. Back then, mutual understanding and cohesion were just as important and Redknapp seldom allowed his teams the time to develop those qualities. This, in turn, often made his teams less than the sum of their parts and goes some way to explaining why they stumbled along near the bottom of the Premiership in the first few years of his tenure at West Ham.

Giving Redknapp's managerial style a more positive spin, you can argue that he treated his players like adults. He told them what he expected and left them to get on with it, without any excessive interference or micro-management. That approach might have worked better if his players had also behaved like adults. In his autobiography, Redknapp wrote of his exasperation about a Christmas party that got out of hand in 1994. 'There was a little group of players who couldn't behave themselves,' he said. 'They were forever having booze-ups and causing aggravation. Dale Gordon was head of the club's entertainment committee and for Christmas he wanted to hire an open-top bus to trawl through London's West End. "Are you out of your mind?" I said to him. "We're struggling in the league and you want to go around looking like you've won the FA Cup!" Instead, they hired a minibus to take them to the Phoenix Apollo in Stratford. One or two of them had too much to drink and set alight to the seats on the bus at the end of the night.' Steve Blowers suggested the seats were also both slashed and slashed upon.

Redknapp might have given the team a bollocking afterwards, but what really matters is that the players got trashed in public anyway, even though he had given them a prior warning. Why? Because they thought they could get away with it. The bottom line was that they just didn't respect Redknapp enough. He was too much one of the lads – 'H' rather than 'Gaffer' – and he wasn't someone they necessarily trusted.

'There were times we felt we were being spied on,' said one former player, 'that Harry was trying to listen in to dressing-room conversations rather than asking us for our opinions outright.'

It didn't help that his 'win or lose – on the booze' mantra still followed Redknapp around. And Redknapp often didn't seem in much hurry to lose it. Several years later, when asked why his team wasn't playing particularly well, he suggested the problem lay with the foreign players who preferred to stay at home rather than go out drinking with the rest of the squad. At best this was inconsistent, at worst crass. It gave the drinkers licence to go on boozing and the overseas players a reason to think they were better off packing their bags and returning home.

'If I'm honest,' says Trevor Morley, 'there were a number of us that were the last of football's drinking culture. These days, players wouldn't dream of going out on a Thursday night but, back then, the only day we all stayed in was the night before the game. Looking back, that wasn't particularly professional of us, though we were by no means the only club behaving like this. Harry knew exactly what was going on but never interfered as long as our performances on the pitch weren't affected. Occasionally, though, he did get the strop. Every year he'd take us on a mid-week break down to Bournemouth. After one party got out of control, we found ourselves downgraded from a five-star to a two-star one the following year.'

'Some of the fans used to quite like all these kinds of Harry shenanigans,' says Sam Delaney. 'They thought it was funny and made us different from other clubs who took themselves far too seriously. And there was that feeling that Harry was a real person in comparison to the uptightness of a Sir Alex Ferguson. But it also began to wear me down, because there was often a feeling of chaos about the club, as if no one was really in charge or knew what was going on.

'There was the time when our team were at the airport at the same time as Arsenal. The Arsenal team were all kitted out in matching club suits and were waiting in the business class lounge to board; we were all dressed in jeans and jostling with the public to board an easyJet flight. There was the time the team was supposed to be boarding the coach to play Stockport County away in the League Cup and Raducioiu was out shopping in Harvey Nichols. And then there was the time we fielded a cup-tied player [Emmanuel Omoyinmi] in a match against Aston Villa and were ordered to replay the tie. How could anyone at the club make such an idiotic mistake? You just couldn't imagine it happening to anyone but West Ham.

'Individually, all these things probably seem quite amusing, but taken together they were just embarrassing. They made us look unprofessional. There were often occasions during this period when supporting West Ham felt more like watching a circus act rather than a football club, with Harry being only one step away from being the Barry Fry-like, novelty-act ringmaster.'

These comic, quasi-slapstick tales have become part of both West Ham's and Redknapp's legend. There isn't a Hammers fan from the 1990s who doesn't have instant recall of them – usually accompanied by a curious, hybrid grin-cum-cringe. Seldom does anyone ask why they happened but, if they do, the answers tend to go no deeper than 'that's Harry and West Ham for you'. But why should it have been that way? Redknapp may not be a well-educated man, but he is extremely quick-witted and nobody's fool. Neither is he the slightest bit lazy; he puts in more hours than most managers. So why did he and the club so often end up looking a bit stupid?

The easiest answer is that he was looking in the wrong direction at crucial times. Everyone who has worked with Redknapp says he is something of a control freak, a man who likes to have a finger in every available pie. And with so many different things going on at a football club at the same time – and with Redknapp invariably giving priority to which players he was planning to buy and sell – it was inevitable that something was going to give from time to time.

But this analysis only gets you so far. Redknapp was nearly 50 by this time and the strengths and weaknesses of his personality couldn't have been any surprise to him. You therefore have to question his choice of management team. Most of the off-field disasters were ones that shouldn't have got anywhere near the manager. The Christmas party, Raducioiu's shopping expedition and Emmanuel Omoyinmi's ineligibility; they were all complications that should have been dealt with by the back-room staff. So why weren't they?

There are two possibilities: either Redknapp had hand-picked a management team whose most important quality was loyalty to him rather than administrative competence; or the level of his constant interference in the way his staff went about their daily jobs resulted in them feeling disengaged. It's easy to imagine someone thinking, 'I can't be bothered with this as Harry will only come along and change it all.'

You also have to question what the club thought it was doing. Even if Redknapp wasn't self-aware enough to assemble a management team who could compensate for his weaknesses and were good at the details which didn't interest him, then the West Ham board ought to have been. Fifteen years ago, football clubs may not have been the slick corporate machines they are now, but there was enough money and expertise around to have kept some sort of eye on what was going on. A single phone call to the Bournemouth board of directors would have told them all they needed to know about where Redknapp was likely to need help. If Redknapp wasn't going to make the right appointments, then

(*above*) The Academy of Football: West Ham United, 1964. Harry is in the top row, 12th from the left.
(© R. Fortune/Daily Mail/Rex Features)

(*left*) The nippy right winger …
(© Getty Images)

(*below*) For the team that never quite delivered on its potential.
(© Mirrorpix)

© Mirrorpix

Treading water on the south coast at Bournemouth.
(© Offside Sports Photography/Rex Features)

Family man: at home in the 1970s with Sandra, son Mark, and the first of several bulldogs.
(© Offside Sports Photography/Rex Features)

Finding his niche: Manager of the Month at Bournemouth.
(© Getty Images)

'He loves me, he loves me not …'

Part 1: Best man at Bonds' wedding, worst of enemies since Bonds was sacked as manager of West Ham and was replaced by Harry.
(© Frank Tewksbury/ Evening Standard/ Rex Features)

Part 2: With Portsmouth owner Milan Mandaric. At least these two managed to kiss and make up after their falling out.
(© Andy Hooper/Daily Mail/Rex Features)

Part 3: With Peter Crouch, whom Redknapp has bought and sold seven times while in charge of three different clubs.
(© Getty Images)

'Not his finest hour ...'

Part 1: Southampton were relegated
during his only year in charge and ...
(© Getty Images)

Part 2: Having signed Jamie to help keep
Southampton in the Premiership, his son
spent more time in the physio room than
on the pitch.
(© Getty Images)

His finest hour: leading Portsmouth to their first FA Cup win in 2008 in nearly 70 years.
(© Getty Images)

On the beach at Sandbanks with Rosie, the UK's only dog with a Monaco bank account.
(© Mike Walker/Rex Features)

With Kevin Bond – known as 'The Driver' by Spurs fans - Harry's faithful Number Two.
(© Getty Images)

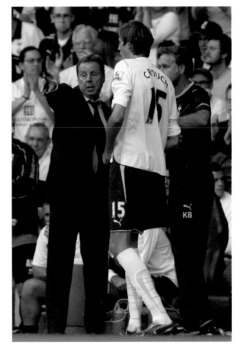

An unforgettable night at the San Siro stadium, Milan, when Spurs played in the Champions League for the first time.
(© Getty Images)

'You're on your bike to Stoke now, Crouchie.'
(© Akira Suemori/AP/Press Association Images)

(*above*) Not guilty: on the steps of Southwark Crown Court after his acquittal on charges of tax evasion (check out the bloke just behind his right shoulder).
(© Getty Images)

(*left*) End of the pier …
(© Rex Features)

End of the road … Redknapp's relationship with Spurs' chairman began as a love in and finished in acrimony.
(*left* © Martin Rickett/PA Archive/Press Association Images; *right* © Mike Egerton/EMPICS Sport)

Turning his back: following his acquittal, Spurs' form nose-dived and the club failed to qualify for the Champions League.
(© Getty Images)

Sacked by Spurs, but still smiling for the cameras.
(© Rex Features)

'Great club. I've always loved QPR.' In December 2012, Redknapp takes over as manager of bottom of the leaguer QPR.
(© Getty Images)

the board could have stepped in and insisted on making them for him. But they didn't. Exactly why they didn't is something to return to later.

For now, what matters is that Redknapp was left exposed. Unlike in government where ministers can use their special advisers as fall guys, in football the manager always gets the blame. So when things went wrong, Redknapp was in the firing line and, as someone who does not always engage his brain before opening his mouth when under pressure, he was left to make contradictory statements – 'we're not a drinking club' . . . 'the players don't drink enough together' – that only ever made a bad situation look worse.

Even at the best of times, though, when he wasn't being asked awkward questions, Redknapp was prone to lapses of tact and judgement, especially when the opportunity for a one-liner presented itself in a room full of appreciative reporters. It's a hard temptation to resist sometimes.

For Redknapp, the consequences were sometimes rather more serious. Asked why Stan Lazaridis had yet to join the club from Australia, Redknapp said he was probably still shagging sheep. Talking about Ian Dowie's aerial threat, he said, 'Judging by the look of Dowie's face, I'd reckon he's headed a lot of balls.' After signing Dani, a Portuguese striker with boy-band good looks, Redknapp joked, 'Dani walked into the dressing-room and all the lads said they're not bringing their wives to the games any more. He looks like a film star. The other teams won't know whether to mark him or fuck him!' And so it went on . . .

Taken individually, none of these gags was totally out of order; the damage came in the cumulative effect, which was to make Redknapp appear abusive. Unless he is a big star, a player has little comeback against a manager who takes the piss out of him in public. Make a fuss and he looks thin-skinned, someone who can't take a joke. Worse still, he could find himself in the reserves for a spell. It's largely a one-way power relationship, with the player having little choice but to roll with the punches. But the crime does not go unforgotten and, on a cold February afternoon, the team finds itself with a player disinclined to put his body on the line in the last twenty minutes when only absolute commitment is enough to hang on for a draw.

It's not only those players who find themselves on the wrong end of Redknapp's humour who are affected. The whole team knows that if it can happen to one of their number, then it can happen to any of them. No one knows who is going to be next, and the insecurity spreads – possibly as far as a player trying to goad Redknapp into having a laugh at another's expense, merely to deflect attention away from himself. Much as Redknapp might try to pass off his gags as 'spur-of the-moment, harmless fun' – a way of relaxing the team and bringing it together – in many cases his humour will have the opposite effect. It will make the players treat him less seriously and, more crucially, trust him less. There's a time and a place for a manager to give a player an earful, and if you're hoping to provoke a positive response, that time and place is not in front of a room full of journos.

Trevor Morley never got on the wrong end of one of Redknapp's gags but he did know what it was like to be both in and out of favour. 'Harry has the gift of making you feel really special,' he says. 'After he'd been at the club for six months or so, he took me aside to say that he's been told that I might be trouble but that he'd been really impressed with my attitude. That kind of thing made a difference. He also noticed things. In those days, many players used to report back for pre-season training overweight and unfit, but I used to go and play for the Norwegian side Brann over the summer and he used to comment on how sharp I was looking and that I was guaranteed a place in the starting line-up.

'The downside of this is that it's much harder when things

aren't going well. In my last season at the club, I got badly injured, tried to come back too soon, got injured again and knew my days were numbered. I was never a big one for going to bang on the manager's door, so I just felt I was left in limbo a bit. It's the same with most managers, I suppose. When you're in, you're in – when you're not, you're not. The manager just hasn't got the time to reassure players who aren't in line for a game at the weekend. But because Harry had once made me feel so good about myself, being ignored by him was hard to take psychologically.'

There were also knock-on effects to the image of West Ham as a club on the edge of chaos with a joker for a manager, as outsiders came to look for the worst in any possible situation. One case in point was the final game of the 1996/97 season at Old Trafford when the ball was passed to Paul Kitson at the kick-off, whereupon the striker launched an optimistic kick down-field that went straight into touch. The crowd laughed, but the bookies blanched as some punters reportedly made a killing on a spread bet for the time of the first throw-in.

In his autobiography, Redknapp was adamant that nothing crooked had taken place. 'Looking at replays of his attempted pass,' he said, 'I'd have to admit it wasn't Kitson's most elegant ball. That match, or at least the poxy kick-off, would have been long forgotten had it not been for a story in the *Racing Post* the following week. Spread-betting firm Sporting Index apparently reported a large number of sellers at sixty-five seconds, forcing the line down to 50–65. The inference was clear. Someone had cleaned up at the bookies' expense. And the finger of suspicion was pointing at West Ham United. Kitson's misplaced pass looked worse and worse the more you saw it.

'I suppose you have to admit the circumstantial evidence was pretty strong but, believe me, that's all it was – circumstantial. But if you looked at all the characters involved in the supposed coup you'd realize it was a cock-and-bull story. There were no

punters at West Ham except John Hartson who wasn't even playing and Kitson knows about as much about betting as I do about
nuclear science. I didn't even have a spread-betting account. And
who won this small fortune? Sporting Index claimed they saw a
large number of sellers but they later said little damage had been
done. Our kick-off that day was one we and, indeed, most clubs
in the Premiership followed regularly. It just didn't come off.'

He then added a curious coda. 'The betting riddle made a good
story, sure, but there was nothing in it. And even if there was, do
you think I'd ever admit it? They'd lock me up!' In other words,
you shouldn't rely on him to tell the truth. In which case, you
might ask, why should we trust that he'd done so now? Nothing
was ever proven and no charges were ever brought, so there is
no reason to think that Kitson was guilty of spot match-fixing.
But you can't help thinking that the reputation of the club at the
time went a long way to creating the air of suspicion that something iffy had taken place. Redknapp has to take his share of the
blame for this, and not just because he was known to fancy the
odd flutter himself. If Kitson's attempted pass had gone straight
into touch when Ron Greenwood or John Lyall had been in the
dugout, the chances are that no one would have given it any further thought.

What's more, the rumours have persisted. Talk to the West
Ham players of that era about the incident and you are met
with a knowing smile. And if Redknapp and his players weren't
involved in a petty betting sting, then, if the *Guardian*'s Secret
Footballer (a veteran Premiership player writing anonymously
for the newspaper) is to be believed, they were among the few
who weren't. In his book published in 2012, the Secret Footballer wrote, 'When I started playing professionally, in-play betting had just come to the market; nobody really knew if it was
going to take off but that didn't stop every bookmaker from
offering his own version. The service has been refined in the

intervening years to maximize the bookies' profits but there was a small window of opportunity where the punters and the players were able to take advantage.

'An old team-mate of mine was one beneficiary. Throughout the season, a team will usually win the toss fifty per cent of the time, but away from home, even if a captain loses the toss, the home team will forfeit the kick-off so that they can kick towards their own fans in the second half. If you intentionally go after the kick-off and you don't care which end you kick towards first, then you could easily end up with seventy-five per cent of the kick-offs over the course of a season. And if that happens, then it becomes ridiculously easy to bet on which team will win the first throw-in.

'As a young, naïve kid, I simply thought that this player was hopeless. We'd take the kick-off, pass it back to him and every time, without exception, he'd hit the ball towards the touchline and out of play. It was so easy that nobody noticed, and it wasn't until years later when a few of us from the team were talking about the old days that it dawned on me what had been going on. Whenever I tell that story to a player who was also plying his trade back then, his reply is usually the same: "Oh yeah, we had a lad who used to do that, too. He made a fortune." I have heard of the same being done with corners, goal kicks, fouls and even yellow cards.'

Redknapp's judgement had also come under scrutiny earlier that season when Michael Tabor, an East End bookie and racehorse owner, had made a hostile bid to take over West Ham with promises of a large cash injection into the club's finances. The board rejected Tabor's bid, with managing director Peter Storrie pointing out, 'The offer is not as straightforward as it seems. Of the £30 million, £22 million would be in the form of loans which would, therefore, put West Ham largely in his debt . . . He has, perhaps, given the impression that he is a white knight riding in to save the club, but the supporters should know that there are a lot of strings attached.'

As Steve Blowers reported, sometime later it became general knowledge that it was Redknapp who had brokered the original meeting between Tabor and Storrie at the Cheltenham races, leaving everyone to wonder what exactly was in the deal for Redknapp and when had it become part of the manager's remit to set up a possible deal to sell the club he was running. Redknapp, as ever, had a positive spin on the situation. 'It is possible that Michael Tabor's interest indirectly saved us from relegation,' he said. 'I think the fans clamouring for Tabor's money, and my offer to resign, perhaps forced the chairman's hand. He knew we'd go down unless drastic action was taken and, all of a sudden, he found the money to buy Hartson, Kitson and Lomas, three signings which kept us up.'

Redknapp might well have been right in his assessment. Tabor's interest may have kicked the board out of inertia. But there are other significant aspects to the bid which aren't so readily apparent. Such as, by appearing to get involved in the boardroom deal, Redknapp's concentration on how the team was performing on the pitch may have been less than total. Perhaps this partly explains why West Ham were battling to avoid relegation. And even if Redknapp was right in his summing up of the Tabor bid, his response reaffirmed his style of management. You don't try to play your way out of trouble by getting the best out of the existing squad: you buy your way out of trouble by adding to it.

When Redknapp had offered his resignation in the early months of 1997 during the Tabor takeover bid, West Ham had already been embarrassingly knocked out in the third round of the FA Cup at home to Wrexham, and were in the relegation mix in the Premiership table. It's an offer that many chairmen might have accepted, given that the club could hardly be said to have overachieved in Redknapp's first two seasons with fourteenth- and tenth-place finishes. So why didn't the West Ham board replace him?

Pragmatics came into it. The available gene pool is significantly reduced mid-season, with most managers tied in to their clubs until at least the end of the season, and the ones that can be tempted to make themselves available often come with an inflated price tag – a price tag that West Ham's stretched finances couldn't meet. So the board may well have looked around and decided there was no one better than Redknapp for the money they had.

But there were also more positive reasons for keeping him. Redknapp was fun to be with, well liked (by most people) within the club and he did know what he was doing. Cut through his wheeler-dealing tendencies and there was a man who understood the game, could identify good players and had the potential to make the team successful.

Within a matter of months, the club's faith in Redknapp had been rewarded as West Ham finished the season in fourteenth place, having managed to avoid relegation. The next three seasons would prove to be their best ever since the mid-1950s, with successive Premier League finishes of eighth, fifth and ninth and victory in the Inter-Toto Cup – not something that most clubs would choose to make much noise about these days if the competition still existed but, for fans more used to trips to Liverpool and Birmingham, the opportunity to play Jokerit of Finland and Metz of France was not to be passed by.

'I was there when we won the Inter-Toto Cup in Metz,' says Sam Delaney, 'and the game still stands out as one of the highlights of my life as a supporter. We had lost the first leg at home and to win away in France and qualify for the UEFA Cup was just incredible. It wasn't what was supposed to happen to West Ham. Up till then we had always been condescendingly referred to as "the neutrals' favourite" – the team that played attractive football but for ever came up short. We'd have great days out, such as winning away at Manchester United, but then fall on our arses by losing to Coventry the following week.

'The Inter-Toto was the first cup we had won for almost twenty years and we had done it with a team that included Di Canio, Kanouté, Wanchope and Ferdinand – players of genuine star quality – so it didn't feel as if we had got a bit lucky and sneaked a win against the odds. It felt deserved. Like the team had made the transition from underachievers to genuine contenders. It was a great time to follow the club.'

As Delaney points out, the West Ham teams of 1998–99 had real talent, with Redknapp as active in the transfer market as ever, acquiring Paulo Di Canio, Freddy Kanouté, Paulo Wanchope, Ian Wright, Marc-Vivien Foe and Shaka Hislop . . . and not forgetting Neil 'Razor' Ruddock. For all the plaudits and, from time to time, criticism, Redknapp attracted for playing expansive football, he never forgot the lesson he had learned as a player that a brick shit-house at the heart of the defence never did any harm. Redknapp also proved to be as able a salesman as he was a buyer; getting Wimbledon to hand over £7.5 million for an overweight and out-of-form John Hartson has to be one of the best pieces of business he ever did.

Ian Wright didn't turn out to be quite the landmark acquisition Redknapp had hoped. His £750,000 transfer fee netted just nine goals (and an infamous sending off against Leeds) in twenty-two appearances before moving to Celtic on a free transfer, and there's a suspicion his purchase had more to do with sentiment than acumen. Redknapp has never tired of telling the story against himself about how he missed the chance while managing Bournemouth to sign Wright as a teenager before he went to Crystal Palace. Mind you, the story has changed over the years. The first of a couple of versions has it that Carl Richards, the player Redknapp had signed from Enfield, told Redknapp there was a great player he should take a look at.

'Is he any better than you?' Redknapp asked.

'No,' said Richards.

'Then I don't think I'll bother,' Redknapp replied.

In the other version, Redknapp was watching Richards play before he bought him and one of Richards' mates said he shouldn't bother with Carl and go and watch a player called Ian Wright instead. Either way, missing out on Wright was not something a man like Redknapp could easily forget.

If Wright turned out to be a mixed blessing, Di Canio most definitely wasn't, as the Italian striker quickly became the club's talismanic figure, not least with the fans who adored him for his style as much as his goals. Di Canio wasn't quite so well loved in the dressing room, as he was a player who adored himself every bit as much as the fans did and quickly acquired a reputation for being extremely high maintenance. One of Redknapp's greatest pieces of man-management at West Ham was to keep the rest of the squad – more or less – happy and to keep Di Canio at the club.

Di Canio recently described Redknapp as 'one of the most intelligent managers I have ever worked with' in an interview with the magazine, *Four Four Two*, although not even the Italian may quite have appreciated just how skilful Redknapp had been in handling him. 'Paulo was a strange character,' said a former member of the West Ham board, 'who always used to refer to himself in the third person. He'd say things like, "Paulo Di Canio thinks . . ."

'It was very odd and made dealing with him on a one-to-one basis quite tricky. So when Manchester United openly expressed an interest in buying him, there was a lot of soul-searching about the best way of persuading Paulo to remain at a much smaller club. It was Harry who cracked it by suggesting we should call him into the boardroom for talks, having put up photographs of

Bobby Moore and Paulo side by side next to each other on the wall. Harry opened the conversation by saying, "Bobby Moore is the greatest footballer ever to have played for this club. You are the second greatest." After that, it was never really in doubt that Paolo would stay with us.'

It wasn't just the bought-in superstars who were catching the eye at this time. For some years, West Ham had been running one of the best football youth academies in Britain and the dividends were beginning to be returned in the shape of Rio Ferdinand, Frank Lampard junior, Michael Carrick and Joe Cole. Redknapp was not slow to spot their potential and was happy to ease them into the first-team squad where they soon became established regulars. This three-year 'youth policy' window – combined with the close attention he paid to his own son's junior career – has become another permanent fixture of the Redknapp legend and goes a long way to explaining why a pundit as smart as Gary Neville might be led to believe that Redknapp would embrace a new generation of young players if he were to become England manager. It's also another aspect of the Redknapp stories that bears closer examination.

Tony Carr had been West Ham's director of youth policy since 1973 and there was an established network of talent scouts throughout the East End, Essex and south-east London long before Redknapp arrived on the scene. So the idea that the Redknapp regime was the catalyst for a major hunt for emerging talent is a non-starter; rather, the opposite is true. 'It was widely felt within the club that Harry wasn't particularly interested in the youth team,' says Sam Delaney. 'When Harry is interested in something he tends to want to meddle, and he didn't meddle at all with the youth team. He let everyone get on with their jobs. All he really did was listen to the advice of Frank Lampard senior and others that some of the youth squad were ready to be tried out at a higher level.

'To be fair, he does deserve some credit for that as he could have just said no or not given them enough time to settle, but you rather feel that any decent manager would have spotted the potential of players such as Ferdinand, Lampard, Carrick and Cole. The fact that the four of them came through at the same time while Harry was manager was just a fortunate coincidence that has carried on working to his advantage ever since.'

The youth-team player who was to make the greatest impact in the West Ham side was Rio Ferdinand, and it was his sale that ultimately set in motion the chain of events that led to Redknapp leaving West Ham at the end of the 2000/01 season. How Ferdinand came to prominence at West Ham is open to debate. There is the dull account, in which Ferdinand had been spotted at an early age by talent scouts in Peckham and nurtured by West Ham until he was ready to make his senior debut. And then there is Redknapp's, in which it was his father, Harry Redknapp senior, who happened to notice Ferdinand's true potential in a South-East Counties League Cup Final in 1995.

Redknapp recalls his dad saying, '"What a player you've got there . . . I've never seen anyone like him," he told me. For the life of me I couldn't work out who he was talking about. "You know," he said, "the big lad . . ." fumbling for the match programme, ". . . Ferdinand."

' "Oh yeah," I said, thinking my dad had gone a bit nuts. I'd watched Rio in training for some time on Tuesday and Thursday nights and, while we all thought he was OK, we'd seen little hint of the enormous talent to blossom.'

The circumstances of Ferdinand's departure from the club would turn out to be equally disputed. By the middle of the 2000/01 season, Ferdinand was one of West Ham's biggest assets, a central defender whose price seemed to be increasing weekly after becoming the transfer target of several big clubs. 'Why should we sell Rio Ferdinand?' Redknapp had said around

Christmas time. 'Are we a Premier League club or are we just a feeder club for bigger clubs? If we start selling players like Rio, where is the club going to go?'

Within a month, Ferdinand had been sold for a record fee of £18 million to Leeds, with Redknapp claiming the credit for a last-ditch act of brinkmanship that forced the price up another £3 million.

'Rio was special to us and he was happy here,' said Redknapp. 'But £18 million was just an amazing offer. What can you say to that? We just couldn't turn it down.' Redknapp's take on the transfer was regarded as the last word on the subject by the football press and the fans. No one really wanted Ferdinand to go, but £18 million seemed like silly money at the time and was a lifeline for a cash-strapped club. For that price tag, West Ham would surely have no problem buying an equally good defender as Ferdinand's replacement and have plenty of money left over in the bank.

One suspicious mind saw the deal rather differently and, in his book, *Broken Dreams*, the investigative journalist Tom Bower revealed that Redknapp had personally made £300,000 as his share of the deal. Countering Redknapp's suggestion that he had been an innocent bystander in the Ferdinand sale, Bower claimed he had been the one to talk West Ham chairman, Terry Brown, into it.

'Terry Brown was watching cricket at the Oval,' wrote Bower, 'when Redknapp telephoned. "I've just had a bid for Ferdinand from Leeds," he said. "They're offering £15 million." Brown was puzzled, not least about why the manager and not the chairman should receive the offer.

'"What do you think?" Brown asked.

'"I know you can't reject it because it's best for the club."

'Brown expressed his astonishment that Redknapp was suddenly so willing to lose a key player. "This doesn't sound like you to let Rio go."

'Redknapp sounded unusually measured. "No, I think this is best for the club." '

And, by implication, best for Redknapp.

'That's pretty much the way I remember it, too,' says a former West Ham director. 'I can't be sure who instigated what, but once Rio's price had got up to £15 million, Harry became a lot keener on the deal. He said he needed the £300,000 because his mum had cancer and he wanted to make sure she got the best treatment.'

For Bower, this was proof that Redknapp was guilty of taking a bung, but a subsequent enquiry showed the £300,000 payment to be no such thing. Under the terms of his contract with West Ham, he was entitled to a percentage of the profit on any player sold, and the £300,000 had been paid to him net of income tax and National Insurance contributions. Nor was there anything particularly unusual about Redknapp having such a condition within his contract; he was just the first manager about whom it became public knowledge.

Nowadays, it's almost standard practice at many clubs, as Blackpool manager Ian Holloway explained in an interview with the *Daily Mirror* in January 2012. 'When the details of my contract with Blackpool were laid bare for public consumption last year, I was made to feel like someone who had been caught with his hands in the till,' he said. 'There were an awful lot of raised eyebrows when it was revealed that I receive a bonus payment every time the club sells a player for profit. One of the things I believe I am good at is spotting a player. I like to think that I can take a player another manager can't work with, restore his belief, polish him up, and make him an asset for my club. Mr Oyston [Blackpool chairman] agreed. He said it was only right that I should be rewarded appropriately if I improved the squad at Blackpool.

'At first, I was only paid a bonus if a player I had signed was sold. Now I get paid if any member of my squad is sold on. I am at a club that refuses to pay big wages and it is still a source of some frustration that I don't get the kind of basic salary that most of my peers take for granted. But my chairman does offer incentives. If we're doing well towards the top of the league, or we get into the play-offs, or get promoted, then I benefit financially. And I think you will find it's the same with every single manager in the world. The only difference is there's also an incentive for me to improve the club's playing squad.'

In his enthusiasm to nail Redknapp on criminal charges, Bower rather missed the broader moral questions raised by such sell-on clauses. Namely, how can you be sure that a manager – and anyone else at the club personally profiting from a transfer deal – is acting in the club's interests rather than his or her own? And how are the fans supposed to know whether the prime motivation for one of their best players being sold is commercial or private gain? After all, the fans pay the same amount regardless of what team the manager fields. Football's stock answer to this is that managers and clubs are all honourable and that the bonuses on offer for team performance far outstrip the incentives of a sell-on clause and therefore it wouldn't make sense for anyone to asset-strip a team. The flaw in this logic is cash flow and short-term greed – the promise of a definite gain now against a potentially bigger one later.

Untangling whether the Ferdinand deal was driven primarily by commercial or personal concerns – or perhaps a combination of the two – is a fruitless exercise. Everyone, including those involved, will almost certainly see only what their own prejudices allow them to see. But it did mark the moment when the 'dodgy' part of 'dodgy geezer' began to carry more currency than the 'geezer' part in many people's minds whenever Redknapp's name came up in conversation. And this was a word that would follow him from job to job over the next decade. Redknapp didn't do himself too many favours in all this by making remarks such as

'Don't rip anyone off . . . but if there's a chance to earn a few quid, take it,' but, in reality, he was only echoing the attitudes of everyone else involved professionally with football. His sin was to voice it out loud, to dispel the desperately held illusion that the beautiful game was still beautiful – or ever had been to those on the inside.

The more immediate effect of the Ferdinand transfer was Redknapp losing his job. When Ferdinand left West Ham, the team was in sixth place in the Premiership, playing well and in the running for European football the following season; by the end, it was fighting to avoid relegation, eventually finishing fifteenth. The focus wasn't so much on the Ferdinand sale itself, but with what the proceeds of that sale were spent on. Had Redknapp signed a big-name replacement – Gareth Southgate was often mooted as a possibility, though no deal ever materialized – then it's possible West Ham's season might have stayed on course. And, even if it hadn't, Redknapp might have escaped some of the blame by appearing to have done the right thing.

As it was, Redknapp brought in Christian Dailly, Rigobert Song, Hayden Foxe, Ragnvald Soma, Titi Camara, Litex Lovech, Svetoslav Todorov and Kaba Diawara – all less than inspirational players on more than inspirational wages who failed to make any positive impression. For once, Redknapp's luck had run out. In the past, his scatter-gun approach to acquiring other teams' cast-offs and undiscovered talent had paid off with at least thirty per cent of his purchases coming good, allowing him to overlook the failures. But this time his squad of misfits lived down to their reputations and Redknapp came under fire from all sides for wasting £8 million of the Ferdinand inheritance. The other £9 million – less the lawyers' fees, bonuses and spiralling wage bill – was retained by the club, either to pay for the ground redevelopment or to prevent Redknapp from spending it. The truth might well lie somewhere between the two.

Redknapp claimed to be gob-smacked when he was sacked. In an interview with the *Independent on Sunday*, he said, 'I'd agreed a new four-year contract with the club, but then I did an interview with a fanzine that the chairman didn't like . . . and he took the hump. So the following week, after we'd beaten Southampton, I walked in to see him about my contract and he says, "I'm not happy with you, Harry. I'm going to call it a day." '

Terry Brown saw it rather differently, as did other members of the board. 'We had already decided not to renew Harry's contract well before the end of the season,' says one board member. 'What Harry did or didn't say to the fanzine was a complete distraction. The only reason we hadn't announced we were going to sack him earlier is that the club was struggling to avoid relegation and we didn't want to do anything that would unsettle the team until we were either safe or down.

'We felt that Harry had probably taken the club as far as he was going to and we didn't share his vision of the future. Harry likes to talk about the money he has made on transfer deals but he forgets the wage bill which had risen to an unsustainable level by the time he left. So we had to do something. Harry has said that it was as much the chairman's fault as his that we signed off so many transfers and salary increases, and he's right about that. After he left, the first thing we did was change the arrangement so that three board members had to sign off every deal rather than just the chairman. Maybe if we'd done that earlier, then Harry wouldn't have had to go. Many of us came to regret his leaving; appointing Glenn Roeder as his replacement was an utter disaster.'

Fans are rarely noted for being in sync with the board. This time, though, they were. 'We were all pissed off about the way the money the club had made from the Rio deal appeared to have just been squandered,' says Sam Delaney. 'We felt it [the club] – and Harry in particular – had wasted what could have been a great opportunity to build on the success we had had by bringing in a whole load of below-average players and we would inevitably resort to being a bit rubbish again. So I was in favour of Harry going. But within a year, I found myself really longing for him to be back in charge. That's the thing about Harry: when he's around, he infuriates the hell out of you . . . and when he's not, you miss him.'

6

Going, Going . . .

March 2012

As Spurs slipped to a second successive league defeat, this time at home to Manchester United in the first week of March, speculation that the England job might be adversely affecting both Redknapp and his team got louder the longer the silence from the FA was maintained. The FA was in a no-win position – it didn't want to appoint a new England manager while so many issues were still to be decided in the Premiership for fear of being accused of unsettling the team whose manager was named, yet the silence in itself was unsettling because the very fact the FA was saying nothing was widely taken to be an endorsement that the public's front-runner was also their own preferred candidate.

With news pages to fill, the media were happy to step into this vacuum. In some papers, the FA was hoping to get José Mourinho; in others, it wasn't. According to some reports, Sir Trevor Brooking, the FA's director of football development and member of the selection panel, had intractable problems with Redknapp dating back to Harry's time in charge of West Ham. In others, Brooking had long since resolved these problems and was said to be happy with Redknapp. The sources for all these stories were FA members briefing journalists off the record, so there must have been a fair few in the FA hierarchy who were either misinformed or were guilty of extremely wishful thinking.

The one story that no one had at that time was whether there was any kind of power struggle going on within the FA over the appointment of the next England manager. It was seldom presented as anything other than a happy family that spoke with a single voice. So, to all intents and purposes, it was still 'Harry, Harry, Harry' all the way, with the FA offering nothing by way of contradiction.

The only real power-play in town was back at White Hart Lane. When the trial had ended, I had said rather gloomily to Donna Cullen, Spurs' Communication Director, 'I suppose this means Harry will now be off to England.' She had replied, with a smile, 'It's not a done deal . . .' and sure enough, within a matter of weeks, there were reports being leaked that the Spurs chairman, Daniel Levy, was in negotiations with Redknapp to extend his contract beyond the end of the following season with an improved pay offer.

Levy is one of the shrewdest and toughest negotiators in football; those who have done business with him say it is an exhausting process. Every time you think you've reached an agreement, Levy will say, 'Just one thing . . .' and you're back where you started. He grinds you down. It's a skill that has, by and large, served Spurs quite well during his time as chairman, as the club is in better financial shape than most other Premiership clubs, although he does give the impression of suffering from a peculiar myopia whereby he overvalues his own assets considerably and undervalues other people's by just as much. Somehow he felt right for the club, though, as frustration has always been one of the team's main gifts to its supporters and Levy had become as much a part of the entertainment as the football. For every Harry-watcher there was also a Daniel-watcher.

And the Daniel-watchers immediately began to wonder if

Levy's contract negotiations were all that they seemed. The club had been immensely supportive to Redknapp during the build-up and course of the trial, but relations between Levy and Redknapp had otherwise been sticky at times. They were very different personalities and had very different attitudes to money – Redknapp's was to spend it, and Levy's to conserve it – and they had clashed over transfer policies, with Levy generally winning, as he usually does. So, despite the Spurs team playing some of the best football in the Premiership and Redknapp no longer at risk of being detained at Her Majesty's pleasure, the idea that Levy would immediately initiate a public romance with Redknapp and love-bomb him with promises of cash seemed a little far-fetched.

'I wouldn't be surprised if what Daniel is really doing is trying to drive up the amount of compensation he can get from the FA when Harry goes to England' was a frequently expressed opinion on the Tottenham fan blogs and in much of the media. It had all the hallmarks of the ideal Levy scenario of appearing to keep everyone happy whatever the outcome. If Redknapp went to England, Levy would be a few million quid richer because, at that stage, there was still no mention that the level of compensation would be a serious obstacle; and if Redknapp stayed, then Levy would be in favour with the fans for having made every effort to hang on to him. Even better, if Redknapp was rejected by England, his price tag could probably be negotiated down again.

Meanwhile, Redknapp was busy playing his own game. It would have been prudent not to discuss openly his position with England and Spurs while everything was still in the balance, and yet he gave an interview with the French sports magazine, *L'Équipe*, in which he said he was unsure about taking the England job if it was offered. 'I'm not sure,' he said. 'I have a good job at Tottenham today and I like it. I do not know. Wait and see. When you have a club and are looking for a striker, you go out and take one. When you're [England] coach, you must make do with the players you have. If you do not have a good scorer, you have no one. You almost never see the players. Two days every month. It's very difficult.'

Redknapp's reservations about being England manager had the virtue of being true. But since everyone knew that, despite the lack of any apparent hunger for the job, Redknapp would take it given half a chance, Harry-watchers immediately began to become suspicious that he was ramping up his own bargaining position. While Redknapp might generally find it hard to resist stopping in front of a journalist's microphone, even he would have been aware of the sensitivities of his position – especially as he had been specifically asked to keep his mouth shut. It was hard to imagine he had been caught off guard by a French magazine, so it seemed reasonable to think he knew exactly what he was doing – and what he was saying – when he gave the interview. And for the Harry-watchers, his game seemed to be playing hard to get. By not looking too keen, he might make himself more attractive to the FA and force them to make their decision sooner rather than later. Who knows, it might also even lead them to offer him a better contract?

It's possible, of course, that the Harry- and Daniel-watchers were generating their own conspiracy theories and that neither the Spurs chairman nor manager had any hidden agenda behind what they were doing and saying in public. It would have been unusual for them both, but possible. But as the FA maintained its omertà about the managerial succession, the devil was more than happy to make work for idle hands. One thing that wasn't really open to interpretation, though, was that Spurs' on-field form was beginning to dip alarmingly.

After an unconvincing win in the FA Cup replay against Stevenage, Tottenham had lost 1-0 away to Everton. Redknapp had been defiant in his post-match interview that Spurs had 'battered'

Everton, deserved at least a point and would still come third in the Premiership, but his audience was becoming increasingly sceptical. This wasn't a game – like those at Arsenal and Manchester United – that Spurs might have been expected to lose, it was one where a draw should have been a bare minimum for a third-placed team and the Spurs fans voiced their displeasure by chanting, '*Gareth Bale . . . he plays on the left*' in response to Redknapp's decision to field his most effective player out of position on the right wing in an unsuccessful effort to fill the gap left by an injury to Aaron Lennon and to maintain a hitherto successful 4-4-1-1 formation. Even the neutrals noticed the team had lost some spark and confidence in front of goal. When asked outright if he thought that the speculation over his future was affecting the club, Redknapp replied, 'It is the biggest load of nonsense I have heard in my life. They [the players] don't care if I'm manager next year.'

Redknapp might have been backed into a corner – openly agreeing that the speculation was damaging would only have made a difficult situation worse, one that he was struggling to contain behind closed dressing-room doors – but he would have been better off saying nothing, because the idea that the effect was entirely neutral was absurd. Even if only at a subconscious level, the speculation must have made a difference because speculation is, by its very nature, unsettling. And to claim the players didn't care if he was manager or not the following year implied a couple of interesting ideas: that the team would play fundamentally the same way regardless of who was managing them and that Redknapp really didn't make much of a difference one way or the other; and also that there was no rapport or understanding between the players and himself and that the squad was entirely indifferent to whether he came or went.

On a very general level, Redknapp may have had a point. Modern players are mercenaries with few loyalties other than to themselves and their bank accounts; the job security of the manager has never been a deal-breaker in players' contract negotiations. Yet it's only natural that every player wants to feel loved and valued by his manager. They want to feel they are an important part of the set-up and guaranteed a place in the starting eleven more often than not. Very few are happy pocketing a salary just to warm the subs bench. Apart from being bad for the self-esteem, it puts you in a worse negotiating position for your next contract. So those players closest to Redknapp would be feeling understandably anxious about the future, while those on the periphery of the squad would have been sensing an opportunity. It could not have been any other way, even if many of the team had suspected for some time that Redknapp was not going to be around for another season. All the rumours must have sharpened the mind and intensified feelings of insecurity or opportunity; either way, the team dynamic had changed significantly.

Redknapp's own psyche is another factor to be considered. The popular narrative was that the trial had been a hugely stressful distraction, that Redknapp had done miracles keeping the team playing so well both before and during it, and that now it was over and Redknapp's entire focus could return to football then the results should be even – if possible – better. When they weren't, everyone started asking why and, understandably, the first thing that came under the microscope was speculation about the England job. The coincidence was inescapable.

Yet the mind does not always follow linear logic. 'It's as, if not more, likely that the reverse was going on,' says sports psychologist Martin Perry. 'People are often surprisingly good at holding things together when they are under extreme pressure. That's not to take any credit away from Redknapp for the way in which he handled himself throughout the trial process, but it's not necessarily as remarkable as one might think. He must have been under huge pressure for many months – the timing of his heart problems was surely no coincidence – but football could have acted as an enormous release for him. Concentrating relentlessly on football allowed his mind time off from worrying about the court case.'

Far from being a distraction, the court case might have been the catalyst for one of Redknapp's most focused periods of football management, when he was alive to nuances in player moods and team tactics over a sustained period of time. Spurs' results over the previous six months would back up that analysis. But it was the other half of this psychological equation that would have the most devastating consequences, as far from being more focused after the trial, Redknapp was more likely to be far less on the ball. It's probably pushing it a bit to suggest he was suffering from post-traumatic stress disorder, but it isn't to reckon he can't have been a bit demob happy.

There's only a certain amount of time that anyone can hold everything together without something having to give. And Redknapp had done a brilliant job keeping himself and his football club on track during a prolonged period of stress. Only very rarely, such as in his courtroom outburst against Detective Inspector Manley, had his jokey, chatty persona cracked, and even then his poise had been regained within minutes. It would have been entirely natural, then, for Redknapp to have relaxed his grip. Once the initial euphoria of the 'not guilty' verdict had worn off, the enormity of what he had been through – that had been hitherto repressed as the only way of coping with it – would have begun to sink in. Juries are notoriously unpredictable, and the possibilities of how close he might have come to a 'guilty' verdict and long-term imprisonment must surely have had their impact at some point. How could a few dropped points or a couple of sulky players in the dressing room possibly feel quite such a matter of life and death as it once had after that? It's like getting a cancer all-clear from the oncologist; for a while, routine worries are put in perspective.

All this would have been taking place at a subconscious level, so it's unlikely Redknapp would have given any of this a moment's consideration; on his own admission, he isn't a man much given to introspection. He was putting in the same long hours, so he must be doing the same job in the same way, right? Except that he wasn't. Like most of us, though, he was unwilling to accept that his performance might have dropped a little.

There are plenty of statistics to measure a player's performance; goals scored, passes completed, yards run, tackles made . . . You name it, someone somewhere will have been quantifying it. How much relevance any of these stats have is beside the point; what matters is that they exist and there are benchmarks against which you can argue whether a footballer is playing well or not.

For a manager, these yardsticks are far less visible. League position? It tells you something, but by no means everything, as it doesn't always reveal the extent to which a team is in that position because of, or despite, the manager's influence. Essentially, it doesn't give you a value-added index. If a team continues to lose, it may be a near inevitability the manager will be sacked – the chairman needs someone to blame and part of a manager's job description is to be the fall guy – but that doesn't necessarily make it a fair outcome.

This creates problems of its own. For even if a manager knows his performance has dropped, he doesn't necessarily know why, or what he can do about it. Blackburn Rovers, by Christmas 2011, had only won two league games all season. Statistically, it would have been hard for anyone with no managerial experience whatsoever to have done much worse than Steve Kean, the Blackburn manager. During his more sleepless nights, Kean couldn't have failed to have been aware of this, but was powerless to do anything about it. Time and again, he would have analyzed those games where his team had been successful, looking for differences between then and now. He would have considered different formations, changing personnel, shouting at players he had previously been nice to and being nice to those he had previously shouted at. And yet . . . nothing. His team were playing just as badly, whatever he did.

Worse still, Kean was in a double bind, because the one thing a manager can't admit to anyone – probably not even himself – is that he doesn't know why his team is playing badly. In March 2012, the Burton Albion manager, Paul Peschisolido, said he was baffled to explain the loss of confidence in the team that was on a fourteen-game winless streak having been battling for promotion earlier in the season. That statement, as much as the run of poor form, cost Peschisolido his job. The moment a manager admits he doesn't have a clue, he's lost the confidence of the chairman, players and fans. Not knowing what's wrong is simply not an option for a football manager unless he wants the sack. If he doesn't know what's wrong, he somehow not only has to convince himself he does, he has to convince those around him, too.

Here was Redknapp's perfect storm. No matter what he said to the contrary, speculation over the England job was unsettling him and his players; his concentration and intensity levels were compromised at the very moment he needed to up his game. And even if he was aware his eye wasn't wholly on the ball, he wasn't entirely sure which part of his team's performance needed tweaking to restore it to its pre-trial consistency. Into this mix, you then have to add the players.

'Footballers do notice these things,' says Perry, 'and they take advantage. It would be nice to think of the players as mature adults, but not all of them are. Some of them are spoilt young men in their late teens and early twenties and, if they spot an opportunity to get away with stuff, they will. The relationship between the leadership and the players grows weaker, and there is a subconscious realization that there are fewer consequences for stepping out of line. Loyalties that are, at best, often, only ever fragile, begin to break down once a manager's hold on his players weakens.

'Sir Alex Ferguson is probably one of the finest examples of a manager who can gather round him a squad of awkward characters and impose on them a desire to win at all costs. He makes them bow to his will through sheer strength of personality. Yet when he announced he intended to retire at the end of the 2001/02 season, even he was powerless to halt a decline in his team's performance. The resolve of players who had been utterly committed to the cause weakened when they thought the manager was half way out the door.' And that resolve returned when Ferguson changed his mind and stepped back in later in the season.

Faced with a manager who was distracted on three separate fronts, it was almost inevitable that the players with a tendency towards laziness in the Spurs squad became just that bit lazier; those with a tendency towards blaming everyone else for their own failings started pointing the finger elsewhere just that bit quicker; and those who were thinking about moving clubs at the end of the season asked their agents to begin making a few more phone calls. Given all this, the last thing Redknapp needed was any extra distractions. But one came along anyway – this time one that nobody could have foreseen – when the Bolton midfielder Fabrice Muamba had a cardiac arrest on the pitch forty-one minutes into a fifth-round FA Cup tie.

Thanks to the swift intervention of the paramedics and a cardiologist who happened to be in the crowd, Muamba's life was saved, but for everyone who witnessed his collapse and resuscitation it was a profoundly affecting experience, a reminder of the precariousness of existence that was all the more shocking for taking place in a location where the only things expected to die were dreams. For a week or so, it was Muamba's near miraculous recovery rather than football that rightly dominated the back pages, but any relief that Redknapp might have ordinarily felt at being given an unexpected, if temporary, respite from being the centre of attention would have been offset by the extra problems he knew would be created. The last thing he needed in a Spurs team low in confidence was any reason for his players to be any less committed to him. Yet after seeing an apparently fit athlete come within moments of death – and, indeed, 'die' for several minutes before being revived – who could blame any of the Spurs players for wondering if the same thing might happen to them? A manager asking them to put their bodies on the line for the cause must have lost its appeal once the demand no longer seemed entirely metaphorical.

A goalless draw away to Chelsea bought Redknapp a little more breathing space from those accustomed to Spurs' long history of dire results at Stamford Bridge. But those watching the game more closely drew less comfort. No matter what Redknapp may have said in his post-match press conference, his Tottenham team was still misfiring badly and the away point owed more to Chelsea playing with as little confidence as Spurs as any revival in form. And if Redknapp couldn't see that, then the FA should have.

The FA might have originally acted with the best of intentions by delaying the appointment of the new English manager until the end of the season but, six weeks later, at the end of March, it was obvious their procrastination was proving to be every bit as unsettling as a declaration of their intent. Now was the time a bold and far-sighted organization would have cut its losses, admitted its selection time frame hadn't worked out as planned, named a new manager and lived with the consequences. But when there's a timid and myopic path on offer, English football's governing body rarely hesitates to embrace it, and so the FA passively allowed itself to become a key player in what was to turn out to be a very English Greek tragedy.

7

Rival Bids

Summer 2001

One of Redknapp's favourite moans towards the end of his time at West Ham had been how badly paid football managers were in comparison to their players. Strictly speaking, he was absolutely right; many of Redknapp's signings were earning a great deal more than him. But the way he talked often made it sound as if he was hard up and badly done by. That was stretching the truth. His basic salary at West Ham had been about £1 million per year before bonuses, and it's reasonable to assume that the Rio Ferdinand transfer hadn't been the only one from which he had benefited financially. So Redknapp was more than comfortably off – he was secure. He was now in his mid-fifties, living in a house worth several million pounds on which his pay-off from West Ham could virtually clear the mortgage, he had business interests outside football, his youngest son, Jamie, was earning a seven-figure salary as a professional footballer and life was sweet. Driving a cab was no longer a career option that needed to be given serious consideration.

Harry Redknapp was also by now a football name; if not 'A' list, then certainly top of the 'B' list, a man who could be relied on to make a few gags and have an opinion on almost anything.

Want a story on why foreign footballers find it hard to get on in English teams, or why they don't, for that matter? Redknapp was your man. He even had a regular column in the *Racing Post*, although hopefully nobody took much notice of his tips. 'Harry was a hopeless punter,' says local south-coast news reporter Pete Johnson. 'He used to tease Alan Ball for betting with his heart rather than his head, but Harry was just as bad. There were days when he'd bet on almost anything from the three o'clock at Doncaster to a baseball game in America he knew nothing about. It used to drive Sandra mad.'

With his high public profile and perfectly respectable track record at West Ham – falling out with the chairman is generally treated as an occupational hazard and rarely warrants a black mark on a manager's CV – there was a general expectation that Redknapp's next job would be with another Premiership team. Instead, he slipped down a division to Portsmouth. There were good reasons for this: he hadn't been flooded with other offers; he wasn't so ambitious about climbing the football management career ladder that he was prepared to hold out until the perfect job came along; and Fratton Park was a very easy commute along the south coast from Poole.

Any of these might have been enough in themselves, but there was one more factor which was the clincher. When Redknapp had been playing for the Seattle Sounders in the 1970s, one of the men with whom he had become friends was Milan Mandaric, the Serbian billionaire who had made his fortune in personal computers after arriving in the US with next to nothing, and then took over the San Jose Earthquakes football team. After leaving the US, Mandaric had moved back to Europe, buying football clubs first in Belgium and then in France, before settling in Britain and buying Portsmouth in 1999, at a time when the club was drowning in debt and had gone into administration. After first saving the club from going bust and then helping to save it from relegation, Mandaric had become the town's local hero. And he was about to become Redknapp's as well, by offering his old friend a job as director of football.

In an interview for Les Roopanarine's biography of Redknapp, Mandaric says that Redknapp's response to being offered the job was, 'By the way . . . can you tell me what the director of football job is?' This was almost certainly a classic piece of Redknapp disingenuity, because he had every reason to know exactly what a director of football was, having seen – or been party to, depending on whose version you believe – Billy Bonds' exit from West Ham some seven years earlier having been offered just that job. For men like Bonds and Redknapp, director of football was the ultimate non-job. There was no getting grubby with the players out on the training pitch, selecting the team or doing any of the fun, hands-on stuff they both enjoyed; the director of football was just another suit, a board member detached from the action whose main responsibility was identifying potential players to buy from other clubs.

Redknapp had always accepted jobs that had been put his way by friends, but why did he accept one that he must have known he wasn't going to enjoy that much? The money must have helped; it came out in the 2012 court case that Redknapp had originally agreed a salary of £1.75 million, a breathtakingly high salary for a job of that description in the First Division (now Championship) at the time. But even so, it didn't make a lot of sense. Mandaric may have been extremely rich but he wasn't a man to chuck money away on salaries unnecessarily, and Redknapp wasn't so desperate he had to accept the first job he was offered.

It makes rather more sense if you allow for the possibility that, right from the off, Redknapp was being lined up as a replacement for Graham Rix, Portsmouth's then manager. Not that there was ever a formal agreement along those lines, more a mutual understanding – a nod and a wink. Mandaric was fundamentally a decent man and he didn't want to get rid of Rix just like that, but his patience must have been running thin. He had invested millions into the club and had got precious little in return except league finishes of eighteenth and twentieth. Rix was a manager who inspired neither the team nor the fans. So a hedge bet on Redknapp must have seemed a good idea.

'Harry is somebody who knows a lot of players and has a lot of character,' said Mandaric. 'I needed that at Portsmouth, because nothing was going in the right direction. That particular year was a breaking point for me. I didn't have room for a manager at that time, but when I found Harry was available I called him immediately. I didn't really know what he was going to do, I just yanked him in to be somebody I could lean on, if nothing more.' Hmm. Perhaps.

On taking up his new job, Redknapp made all the right noises about not wanting to be a threat to the manager. 'It's not easy for Graham and I to understand his situation,' he said in a newspaper interview. 'When someone tells you there will be a director of football coming in, who will suddenly be responsible for buying and selling players, you suddenly think, "Hang on, what's going on?" But I had a meeting with Graham the other night and the one thing he knows is that I don't want his job. I don't want to be the manager.'

How reassured Rix would have been by this is anyone's guess. Under the circumstances, Redknapp could hardly have said anything else. 'Well, you know how it is, lads. The chairman's not too happy with the way the manager is performing at the moment . . .' Even Redknapp wouldn't have gone that far.

If there had been an implicit understanding that the manager's job was on offer if Rix didn't shape up, then Redknapp would have been the man to read the signals. He had inherited David Webb's job at Bournemouth within a year and Billy Bonds' at West Ham within two, so he knew the form. Or at least the possibilities. And it's equally hard to imagine Redknapp accepting the job of director of football at Portsmouth without having some kind of conversation with Mandaric along the lines of, 'I don't much fancy being stuck in a fucking office all day, Milan. It's just not my style . . .'

Maybe there were no prior deals – implied or otherwise – as Mandaric and Redknapp have since insisted, but within nine months of joining the club as director of football, he had his feet under Rix's desk. And no one was surprised or upset by his appointment, as Redknapp had become a firm favourite with everyone in the town. It felt like a home from home for him, a piece of the East End transposed to the south coast, a working-class, one-club town.

'He immediately seemed to "get" the club in a way other managers never had,' says Julian Guyer, a Portsmouth season ticket holder and sports writer for Agence France-Presse. 'He could remember when it had been a footballing force. I had started going to matches in the late seventies and, by then, Portsmouth was a fairly rubbish second or third division club and fans of my generation felt we had missed the boat . . . that we were condemned to listen to the old boys in the pub talking about the glory days and that my grandparents' 1939 FA Cup Final programme was as close as we would ever get to a trophy. Redknapp filled that longing within the fans for the sleeping giant to awaken. None of us thought he was cut out to be a director of football. It was a job description that smacked of European sophistication – something neither Portsmouth nor Redknapp possessed. So we all thought he'd either leave quite quickly or become manager.'

This assessment proved to have been spot on. Redknapp did admit to getting bored. 'I miss picking the team and all the aggro that goes with it,' he said. 'The life I've got now is easier with no aggro or pressure but perhaps I thrive on them. It can get boring. If something comes along, then who knows?'

Something did come along. Leicester City sacked Peter Taylor and offered Redknapp a return to management in the Premiership. A more ambitious manager – one with an eye on the England job – would surely have accepted it, but Redknapp turned it down, reluctant to abandon either Mandaric or the south coast. He was also publicly still backing Rix – after a fashion. 'If Graham left and Milan asked me to be manager then I would take it,' Redknapp said. 'I would be the obvious choice. But I want Graham to stay.'

Mandaric was even more equivocal in his support for his manager. 'Graham stays on the advice of Harry,' he said. 'It would have been the easiest thing in the world to pull the trigger.' If Rix hadn't been paranoid before that, he should have been afterwards.

Redknapp may have been bored as director of football, but he wasn't idle and he did know how to play the fans. David Ginola was never likely to be tempted down to Portsmouth even though he was nearing the end of his career, but that didn't stop Redknapp from publicly linking the French player with Portsmouth. Much as the West Ham supporters had done so before them, the Pompey fans enjoyed the attention of being talked about and being associated with international stars. It made the club look ambitious and feel bigger than it was.

To many observers, Redknapp's habit of publicly expressing an interest in dozens of players who may or may not be available is a form of 'Transfer Tourettes'. And there is an element of compulsion about it; for Redknapp, professional football is a transfer merry-go-round where most players are available at a price, and he can't help himself from thinking out loud. It's like taking a kid to a sweet shop. But there is also something quite canny about this approach, too. Providing he didn't make himself look stupid by linking several of the world's best players with Portsmouth, Redknapp could create a 'no smoke without fire' buzz about the club, so in people's minds it became one to which others gave a second thought. Rather than using a small fish to catch a big one, he was using a big one to catch a slightly less smaller one than he otherwise might. It worked. Portsmouth didn't get Ginola, but Redknapp did buy Alessandro Zamperini (from Roma), Svetoslav Todorov and Robert Prosinecki from Standard Liège – all three players who might have been expected to think twice about such a move.

Redknapp also bought the six-foot-seven Peter Crouch from Queens Park Rangers in a club record £1.25 million move that would later attract the attention of the Inland Revenue after Crouch was sold to Aston Villa for £5 million within a year and would be pivotal to the prosecution case at his and Mandaric's trial at Southwark Crown Court in 2012. The legal aspects of this case were all examined at length in court, but the wider implications of the Crouch transfer for Redknapp's and Mandaric's business relationship escaped scrutiny and they suggest intriguing possibilities.

Mandaric was an unusually hands-on chairman, one who travelled to every away game with Redknapp and who could laugh at himself for his initial assessment of Crouch as being more of a basketball player than a footballer. The relationship between Redknapp and Mandaric went far beyond the normal chairman–manager pleasantries, developing into a proper friendship. And yet Mandaric still changed the terms of Redknapp's contract when he switched jobs from director of football to manager.

At the trial, it was revealed that Redknapp's wage deal was increased from £1.775 million to £3.025 million, while his bonus for selling on players was reduced from ten per cent to five per cent – and it was this five per cent reduction the prosecution alleged Mandaric was trying to make good in the payments made to Redknapp's Rosie47 Monaco bank account. Mandaric's defence counsel quite reasonably pointed out that Redknapp was being rewarded well enough as it was – a near hundred per cent pay rise had been more than generous – so why would the chairman have felt obliged to give his manager any more than was legally required?

What wasn't explored in any depth was why the contractual arrangements had been changed. And there could be only one explanation. The Crouch deal had alerted Mandaric to a possible conflict between Redknapp acting in his own interests and those of the club, and he wanted to recalibrate the deal to make sure Redknapp would be encouraged to do the latter. Nothing else makes sense. If the original deal had been satisfactory, there would have been no need to change it. Mandaric could easily have got away with paying a slightly smaller salary and retaining the ten per cent sell-on bonus. No matter what anyone else might have said, the message from Mandaric to Redknapp in the new contract was that, while he liked him and considered him to be a good manager, he also wanted to keep him on a rather tighter rein. Just in case. And if Redknapp wasn't aware that's what Mandaric was saying, then he ought to have been. It also sheds some light on the bust-up between the two men that was to happen two years later and that might otherwise seem to have come from out of the blue.

Having managed to steer Portsmouth away from relegation during the last couple of months of the 2001/02 season, Redknapp typically set about making such wholesale changes to the squad that only Nigel Quashie made the starting eleven for the last game of the season and the first of the next. In came – among others – the Australian Hayden Foxe, the Dutchman Arjan De Zeeuw, the French-Cameroonian Vincent Pericard, the goalkeeper Shaka Hislop and the former Arsenal midfielder Paul Merson.

'Harry did get a bit lucky,' says Pete Johnson. 'ONdigital, the ITV digital TV service, had finally been wound up in May 2002 and was unable to fulfil its £315 million deal to broadcast

First Division matches. This left a huge hole in many clubs' cash flow, making them temporarily unable to compete in the transfer market. With Mandaric's money behind him, Harry had no such problems and was able to get some players a great deal cheaper than he otherwise might.

'Having said that, Harry still had a wonderfully good eye for players that other managers had either overlooked or thought were past their sell-by date. He could get the best out of a strange collection of different temperaments. For all the big names he brought in at the start of the 2002/03 season, it was the little-known Matt Taylor he picked up for £600,000 from Luton who was the pick of the bunch. He was a decent enough player in the Premiership, but in the First Division he was outstanding. Matt often seemed to be the player who was holding the team together and making things happen in his first season.'

Redknapp's Portsmouth got off to a flying start in his first full season in charge and, after he had strengthened the squad in the January transfer window by buying the Nigerian striker Yakubu, and the Spurs midfielder Tim Sherwood, the team went on to win the First Division title and win promotion to the top level of English football after fifteen years of trying. 'Arthur Hopcraft put it beautifully in *The Football Man*,' says Julian Guyer, 'when he wrote that a football crowd never has to be told when their team is playing well – they know. And at Pompey, we did know. We achieved success by playing attacking football, rather than packing the defence and booting a hopeful long ball up to the strikers. Friends of my dad said it was the best football they had seen the side play since the fifties.'

Not only did Portsmouth get promoted; against all expectations, they stayed up. There was even a brief moment at the beginning of the season when they topped the table. 'The last time we had been in the top division we had gone straight back down,' Guyer continues, 'and most of us thought the same thing was bound to happen again. We weren't that unhappy about it, just resigned to it. There was a feeling we had played above ourselves to get promotion and that we should just enjoy a season in the bright lights while we could. But it was so much better than that. We beat Manchester United at home for the first time in nearly fifty years, a result I certainly never thought I'd ever see. The mood in the city was just brilliant. The club's performances lifted everyone and, even when we were thrashed at home by Arsenal, we were still cheering because it was so wonderful to be watching such fantastic football.'

Success had been predicated on the usual Redknapp strategy of hyperactivity in the transfer and loan market. At times, it seemed as if the club was almost operating a revolving-door policy and the players must have sometimes wondered who was going to show up for training as nineteen squad members were signed over the course of the season. The fans didn't mind; their team was doing well and they assumed Mandaric was good for the money. Besides which, when was the last time you heard a terrace chant of '*We've got the best balance sheet in the world*'?

Despite Redknapp's assertions that he wasn't costing the club a lot of money – he was unquestionably getting some players, such as Alexey Smertin, at knock-down prices – the club's wage bill was beginning to rocket and the first sign of a crack in the hitherto good relations between Mandaric and his manager came towards the end of the 2003/04 season when the chairman suggested a new infrastructure needed to be put in place the following season to make the club less reliant on new signings. The fallout initially centred on the future of the assistant manager Jim Smith.

Mandaric had told the BBC it was Redknapp who had suggested Smith should leave. 'I tried to protect Harry and not go public,' he told Radio 4, 'but he said this in an official meeting in the boardroom in front of others, including the chief executive.

Harry said he could do without Jim and really didn't need him. He said he would like to keep him for the rest of the season because he was doing this favour for Jim. That is not a good reason to keep somebody.' Mandaric went on to say Redknapp had said Smith should really go in December because he was useless, but 'pleaded with me not to make the changes there and then because he was concerned about what Sir Alex Ferguson or some of his friends might say.'

Redknapp was outraged when Mandaric went public with this, accusing his chairman of telling 'filthy lies', and saying it had been the chairman's idea to get rid of Smith and that he would leave Portsmouth if his assistant was fired. 'Milan's record in bringing in coaches is not good. Tony Pulis and Graham Rix were good coaches but not good enough. If Milan wants to bring in a coach to work under me, I've got no problem,' he said. 'I'm all for coaches – that's why I brought in Luther Blissett to help the strikers – but I don't see why there's any reason to break up the current staff.'

This was slightly disingenuous on Redknapp's part. There is no way he wouldn't have had a problem with Mandaric bringing in a new coach under him. Redknapp has always been careful to appoint staff who aren't going to challenge him directly or – possibly with one eye on his own guilty conscience – replace him. Smith and coach Kevin Bond were men who could be relied on to do what Redknapp wanted. Redknapp didn't like threats to his hegemony, and he didn't like not getting his dues. Blissett had been brought in to teach the strikers to score more goals and, when they had done so, Redknapp had not been all that happy about Luther being given the credit in the local press. Anyone Mandaric appointed under him without consultation would have been cause for suspicion. In the end, Smith and Bond stayed as Redknapp and Mandaric patched up their differences, but the spat was to be the first of several in which chairman and manager would show themselves to have memories diametrically at odds with one another.

Portsmouth's good form continued into the new season with the team comfortably positioned in mid-table, but by early November 2004 the relationship between Mandaric and Redknapp was again at breaking point. This time the disagreement centred on Mandaric's decision to bring in the Croatian Velimir Zajec, from the Greek club Panathinaikos, to be director of football over Redknapp's head, and it was to prove fatal. Redknapp took this to be a direct challenge to his authority and wasn't shy about making his feelings known – an entirely predictable reaction that Mandaric, a man who is nobody's fool, must have seen coming. This suggests that he can only have intended to provoke the inevitable response from Redknapp. So why did he want to have a head-on confrontation with a popular manager who had lifted the club from one that bumped along the lower reaches of the First Division to one that looked entirely at home in the Premiership and who had just been voted Premiership manager of the month for October?

Some supporters reckoned it was little more than a clash of egos. Before Redknapp had come along, Mandaric picked up all the plaudits for having rescued the club from going under. Normally, the only time a chairman's name is sung on the terraces is when the fans want him out, but Mandaric had been used to hearing his chanted with something approaching devotion. But when Redknapp arrived and the team started playing well, it was the manager's name, not the chairman's, being heard at Fratton Park. That may have stung, but a businessman as shrewd as Mandaric wasn't in the habit of making important decisions based on a fit of pique, so there had to have been more to it than that. And that was the amount of money Redknapp's transfer activity was costing the club in fees, wages and – in particular – agents' fees. During Redknapp's two and a half years in charge, he had bought in thirty-eight players – either as transfers or loans – in deals that had cost the club £11.5 million, of which more than a third had been raked off by agents.

Zajec's arrival was a clear if clumsy signal to Redknapp that this level of expenditure was no longer going to be tolerated. It's less evident, though, why it was necessary. Redknapp's spend, spend, spend approach can't have come as a surprise to Mandaric – it's what he had done at both Bournemouth and West Ham – and the chairman and managing director, Peter Storrie, would have had the final say on every deal as they were the ones who legally signed them off. Redknapp could have wanted anything he liked, but Mandaric had the power to say no. Why couldn't Mandaric, then, have just told Redknapp enough was enough? Or had he said exactly that, and Redknapp hadn't take him seriously?

It's impossible to tell if Mandaric was using Zajec merely to limit Redknapp's powers or as a means of forcing him out. Redknapp, though, would have been alert to the latter possibility. He had been parachuted into Portsmouth above Graham Rix and had replaced him within a year, so there was a precedent. It was a modus operandi with which both Redknapp and Mandaric were familiar; added to this were Redknapp's own feelings that the position of director of football was a total waste of space. If Redknapp felt that way, then he probably reckoned others did, too, and therefore the only reason Zajec would have taken it was if he had had his eye on the bigger prize of the manager's job.

For a short while after Zajec's arrival, an uneasy truce was reached with the Croatian being appointed executive director, with responsibility for developing a youth academy and European scouting, rather than director of football – a semantic quickstep to try and save everyone's pride in front of the media. Portsmouth released a statement saying, 'Any issues that the manager had with a new appointment were pure speculation. Harry Redknapp remains manager of the club which was never in doubt. The board will continue the expansion of the club with the appointment of a new executive director who will be Velimir Zajec. Speculation that he was joining as a director of football was ill-founded and he will become a main board member.'

Redknapp responded rather more bullishly. 'I'm the manager and I'm in total control of the club,' he said. 'He [Zajec] has other specific duties and if he does those jobs it will be for the benefit of Portsmouth and that's what matters. I've spent two days chatting with the chairman and he's assured me that I'm completely in charge of my own job. No one will interfere and my responsibility will be exactly the same. It's fine by me.'

Not so fine, though, that Redknapp ever planned to talk to Zajec face to face. After losing to local rivals Southampton in mid-November, Redknapp was asked how he felt about the Croatian. 'I will never meet him,' he said. Hardly a peace offering and, within a week on 24 November 2004, Redknapp had resigned after Mandaric once more voiced his concerns about Redknapp's transfer dealings and the amount of money that was finding its way into agents' pockets, leading many to conclude that the chairman thought his manager was personally benefiting from these transactions. Redknapp's resignation announcement made no mention of this; rather, he asked everyone to believe that his departure was 'something I have been thinking about for a while. I made it without any pressure from the chairman or the board.'

Mandaric pushed the charade still further by declaring, 'Harry and I remain good friends. People will obviously make their own minds up and say Harry has stepped down for reasons that have been intensely speculated over in the media. That could not be further from the truth. The truth is Harry sees this as a perfect opportunity to bow out.'

The fans did make up their own minds and came to the same conclusion as everyone but Redknapp and Mandaric. Within minutes of Redknapp's resignation, the supporters' websites were condemning the chairman with messages such as 'Harry Redknapp has been a revelation at Pompey – regardless of the money MM has put in, without Redknapp's football wheeling and dealing nous, Pompey would still probably be a decent Championship team . . .' and 'I'm really at a loss to understand MM's motives. He says he wants to improve the football structure, but unsettling the one man who has proved to be so pivotal is a contradiction in terms.'

If Portsmouth hoped these statements would draw a line under the bad blood between its chairman and manager, it was mistaken. A week after Redknapp's departure, Mandaric issued another public statement – one that had all the hallmarks of having been forced upon him by Redknapp's lawyers – saying that when he had complained about Redknapp's transfer dealings and the large sums paid out to agents, he had never intended to imply that the manager had been involved in taking bungs. 'At no time did I imply there was any wrongdoing,' Mandaric said. 'I was simply saying that agents take too much money from the game. All transactions and fees have been registered with the Football Association.'

Mandaric also held out a further olive branch – the possibility of Redknapp reconsidering his decision to resign and returning to the club. Redknapp responded by accepting the chairman's public apology, saying, 'This needed to be done. I don't deserve the innuendoes and we needed to clear the air. Milan's done that. I've done nothing but good for the club.' He did, though, reject any return out of hand. 'There's a future for Milan [at Portsmouth],' he said, 'but not for me. I decided to quit because it was time to move on and it was one million per cent my decision.' Redknapp went on to say he was planning to take a break from football. 'Have I spoken to other clubs? None at all. I haven't gone down that road.'

Redknapp not having spoken to anyone was hard enough for

anyone to imagine. But it was to whom he was about to speak that would really get jaws dropping.

Just 27 miles of the M27 separates Portsmouth from Southampton, but culturally they couldn't be more divided. Portsmouth is a working-class town, dominated by the Navy and not much else; Southampton is more genteel and upwardly mobile, a port more used to ocean-going liners than destroyers. Their physical proximity and class differences have generated a fierce rivalry that has been played out between their football teams for more than a century. When Portsmouth fans travel to away derby games at St Mary's, they are often greeted by a banner hanging from one of the motorway bridges that says, 'Welcome to Civilization'; seldom has civilization been made to seem more threatening.

You can't work at either of the clubs without being aware there is no love lost between them, and Redknapp had given a public assurance that he understood this when he resigned from Portsmouth. 'I will not be going down the road. No chance,' he had promised.

Within two weeks he had been appointed manager of Southampton. This drew an immediate response from Portsmouth, accusing Southampton chairman, Rupert Lowe, of having made an illegal approach to Redknapp and agreeing the outline of a deal before Redknapp had resigned from Portsmouth. 'It would give the impression,' Peter Storrie told the BBC, 'that he has been in negotiations for some time and has used the appointment of Velimir Zajec as an excuse to leave the club.' Both Lowe and Redknapp denied these allegations but the sense of betrayal still cut deep throughout the city.

Teasing out exactly who did what and when in any football transaction is always difficult as selective memory is one of the key qualifications for any manager and chairman, but there is no evidence that the move was in any way pre-planned.

Southampton had been in freefall for some time. Gordon Strachan had resigned as manager in February 2004 amid rumours he was to be replaced by Glenn Hoddle. Hoddle never appeared and Strachan's assistant coach, Steve Wigley, was brought in as caretaker before Paul Sturrock was given the job. Sturrock lasted just four months, before being fired to make way for Wigley to take over full time in August. Wigley had been no more successful than Sturrock and the club had won just two games all season and were facing relegation. So another change had been on the cards for some time and Redknapp's sudden availability was Southampton's apparent good fortune.

Redknapp characteristically refused to see his move to Southampton as a betrayal. 'I don't owe anybody anything,' he said. 'It's my life and this is a great opportunity for me. I left Portsmouth halfway up the Premiership table and circumstances at the club had changed. It did not suit the way I wanted to work and I decided to move on. A new chap was director of football which wasn't a situation that suited me. I've sat at home for the last two weeks watching football on TV and didn't enjoy it. I got a phone call late on Monday from the chairman and it was too good a chance to refuse.'

Apart from being an outright contradiction – something Harrywatchers had grown used to even then – of his previous statements that the appointment of Zajec had played no part in his resignation from Portsmouth, it wasn't quite true that Redknapp had spent two weeks just sitting at home. He had gone out of his way to put himself in the frame for a possible move to Wolves and had gigs lined up as one of Sky Sports match pundits, so he wasn't short of options. And yet he took on the Southampton job, even though he must have known he didn't have the full backing of Southampton chairman Rupert Lowe. 'He wasn't really my choice,' Lowe told Les Roopanarine, 'but the board wouldn't support my wish to reappoint Glenn Hoddle. I probably should have resigned when the board wouldn't do what I wanted to do with Hoddle but, being a team player, I followed the board's wish and ended up working with Redknapp – much to my regret.'

Once Mandaric had pointedly given interviews after Redknapp's departure saying how good it was to be now working with a man, Zajec, whom he thought he could trust, Redknapp would have had to have had the self-denial of a Buddhist monk not to have wanted to stick two fingers up to his former club, and taking the Southampton job would have been the ultimate in the two-fingered salute. Or he might simply have had the lack of awareness of a complete fool. As we've seen, though, Redknapp is neither a saint nor a fool. But there were also other attractions to Southampton – not least its geography. The two towns weren't merely close to one another, they were also close to his home in Sandbanks. Taking the job would cause no major upheavals for him.

A further reason for the rivalry between the two clubs was that, for all the perceived class and cultural differences between them, they actually had a similar profile. They were both clubs – despite Southampton's FA Cup Final defeat to Arsenal the previous year – that had experienced little by way of success for some time, clubs that were visibly shrinking in front of their supporters' eyes, clubs of which little was expected. Much the same could also have been said of West Ham and Bournemouth when Redknapp joined them. So Southampton would have been a club at which he instinctively felt at home, one at which he understood he could be a big fish in a little pond, where his every move wouldn't be under the microscope and relatively small successes would bring him big headlines and the gratitude of the fans.

In his first game in charge, Southampton contrived to squander a two-goal lead and Redknapp was not slow to do what he usually did when he arrived at any new club – expressing grave reservations about the squad he had inherited. Lowering people's expectations is never a bad way forward, and proposing his familiar solution could do no harm. 'For us to stay up now would be a terrific achievement,' he said. 'It's the toughest job I've taken on. I will have to try to beg, steal and borrow a few players because this group would not even get us out of the Championship. Somehow, this club has accumulated a lot of players but we are short of quality. I can't make them better. I haven't got a magic wand. We need to get some players with a bit of character who might just turn us around.' And in a warning shot to his new chairman, he added that Lowe had to accept a bit of a blow to his wallet. 'He has got to know that it's no good saying we have got all these good players, because they're second from bottom. We need to strengthen somehow.'

If Redknapp had imagined Lowe would be an easy touch, a posh public schoolboy with more money than sense, then he had misjudged his target, as for the first time in his managerial career he came up against a chairman who didn't pull out his cheque book every time he said 'Open Sesame'. Lowe was a man who took the club's finances as seriously as its football and Redknapp was also expected to balance the books. Having declared he was desperate to retain striker James Beattie, Redknapp discovered he was obliged to sell him when Everton offered an irresistible £6 million and, for once, Redknapp's transfer radar was seriously off with the players he was allowed to bring into the club with some of the proceeds. Henri Camara and Nigel Quashie couldn't stop the rot, and buying his own son, Jamie, from Spurs was an unrewarded act of faith as his knees were almost completely knackered by that stage of his career.

But his worst signings were at the back. It had been Southampton's defence that had been mainly responsible for the position the club was in, and plugging the holes by bringing in Calum Davenport and Oliver Bernard looked inadequate even to the most optimistic Saints supporter.

There were a few wins – most notably an FA Cup win against Portsmouth in which Peter Crouch scored a last-minute winner from the penalty spot that prompted a 'I thought he was going to head it' Harryism in the post-match press conference. But in the league, Southampton were equally prone to conceding last-minute goals and were relegated on the last day of the season. There had been speculation that Redknapp would call it quits after Saints dropped into the Championship but, a week later, after talking to Lowe, he announced he would be staying on. 'We had a good meeting,' Redknapp, said. 'It was nice and positive. When I walked off the pitch on Sunday, the fans were fantastic and there was no doubt that I wanted to stay at the club.'

Some of the fans had misgivings, though. 'I'd been thrilled when Harry arrived at the club,' says Jason Rodrigues, a life-long Southampton supporter. 'Paul Sturrock and Steve Wigley had been a disaster and Harry had done well with Portsmouth. The fact that we had annoyed everyone in Portsmouth by taking their manager was just an added bonus. The line that Harry kept feeding us was that we would have stayed up if the chairman had allowed him to bring in more players. And there was some truth in that, but he totally ignored the fact that the squad of players we did have – among them Peter Crouch, Kevin Phillips, Graeme Le Saux, Antti Niemi and Anders Svensson – should have been good enough to stay up regardless.

'Harry came billed as a great motivator but he couldn't get the side to play for him and we never seemed able to hang on to winning positions. Nor did he seem to have the tactical nous to think round problems and change the shape of the team when the formation he was playing wasn't working and he never got to grips with the team's defensive frailties. It was fair enough for Harry's Plan A to be to buy new players but, when that wasn't on offer, he should have been able to adapt and come up with a Plan B. But he couldn't and he didn't. It wouldn't be fair to blame him entirely for us going down, but seeing as he would have been happy to take most of the credit if we had stayed up, he has to shoulder some of the responsibility.'

There was further trouble looming when Lowe appointed the English World Cup-winning rugby coach, Sir Clive Woodward, as the club's performance director. With no experience of professional football, Woodward was a strange choice – the notion that all performance skills were completely transferrable between rugby and football was completely untested – but Redknapp instinctively perceived him as a threat, in much the same way as he had Zajec at Portsmouth the previous year, though with far less reason. Lowe had been openly toying with the idea of bringing Woodward into the club long before Redknapp's arrival, so he couldn't have been taken by surprise and the demarcation lines should have been clear.

So his reflex response suggests there is something more to Redknapp's difficulties with working with people imposed on him than mere – sometimes justified – paranoia or a guilty conscience. It also indicates an inability to work with people who might disagree with him. When Redknapp had joined Southampton, he had brought with him Jim Smith and Kevin Bond, both solid journeymen who understood football but could be relied on not to question his judgement. In football, a manager surrounding himself with yes-men is often mistaken for a sign of strength, when it's actually a sign of weakness. One of the reasons Redknapp had no Plan B for the latter half of the season in which Southampton was relegated is because there was no one else at the club capable of working it out for themselves or who dared tell him what it was. A manager can't be expected to think of all the solutions, so he needs to have assistants who can see things he can't. Throughout his career, Redknapp has always been deeply suspicious of people with a different world view; more often than not, this insecurity has not cost his teams that much. At Southampton, it did.

By the end of September 2005, relations were so bad between Redknapp and Woodward that the club had to call a press conference to let everyone know how well they were getting on together. 'I have no problem with Clive . . . we get on fine,' said Redknapp. 'We want to clear the air once and for all. There's been so much written about how we don't get on. There has not been one problem. Clive does not come in and tell me, "You should do that . . . you should play him . . ." and everyone knows I wouldn't stand for that. Clive is here to help with the youngsters and does not interfere with me in any way. Clive is a high-profile person so we know you are always going to get these stories. He's given up rugby and wants to try his hand at football.'

No one was fooled. By saying that Woodward had 'given up' rugby and was 'trying his hand' at football, Redknapp could hardly have been more dismissive of Woodward and, from then on, everyone at Southampton was counting the days until he made his excuses and left. Even so, only Redknapp could have come up with a return to Portsmouth. And only Redknapp could have got away with it.

Having come unstuck with Alain Perrin, a Frenchman who had failed to live up to his billing as the new Arsène Wenger, Milan Mandaric was in the market for a new manager and appeared mysteriously to remember how much he missed Redknapp after bumping into his brother-in-law, Frank Lampard senior, in a restaurant. 'I can't encourage Harry on anything because I am not allowed to talk to him,' Mandaric said, having asked Southampton's permission to approach Redknapp and having been refused. 'I don't know how much Harry is enjoying it there. If he comes here, fine. If he doesn't come here, fine, we'll still be friends, no matter what. I don't think we fell out. I think it was created by the media. I have no problem with Harry whatsoever.'

It may not have been how everyone remembered the bitter feud between Mandaric and his ex-manager, but Redknapp was also apparently quite happy to slip into revisionist mode, promptly insisting he could no longer consider himself employed by Southampton once permission to talk to Portsmouth had been refused.

'On Thursday, December 1, I spoke to Harry,' said Lowe, 'who told me that he had been considering his future and that he believed Portsmouth to be his spiritual home.' The written request from Portsmouth to talk to Redknapp soon followed. 'I did not give that consent immediately,' continued Lowe, 'as I wanted to be sure that Harry meant what he had said, given some of the comments made by himself and Mandaric not much more than a year ago. I spoke to Harry again on Friday and he confirmed what he had said to me and that he wanted my consent to speak to Portsmouth.'

And that was that. Not for the first time – and not for the last – Redknapp's departure was messy, mysterious and undignified.

Within days of returning to Portsmouth, Redknapp set about mending the bridges he'd demolished a year earlier. 'When I went back, it felt like I had never been away,' he said. 'It's still the same people and they call everyone by their first names and not surnames. They're not addressed as "Redknapp" – the chairman calls everyone by their first names, Milan treats us as equals. It's nice to be treated like that by everybody, so it's good.'

Mandaric and Redknapp had always been a better double act than Lowe and Redknapp. Mandaric and Redknapp were both working-class, self-made men who – despite Mandaric's Serbian origins – spoke a noticeably similar language with one another than either did with Lowe . . . or most other people in football did with Lowe, for that matter. Yet for all they had in common, no one could quite work out just how or why there had been such a spectacular and unexpected rapprochement between Redknapp and Mandaric.

'There were all the usual rumours going round,' says Pete

Johnson. 'Deals here, counter-deals there, but I think it was just a simple matter of expedience. They both needed one another at the time. Harry was in a job that he hated, working for a chairman with whom he didn't get on, and Portsmouth had been going backwards since Harry had left, so Milan urgently needed a manager who could stop the club joining Southampton in the Championship. They also understood how each other operated and it was a case of "better the devil you know than the devil you don't".'

It's also possible that Mandaric knew he was on the way out and therefore reckoned he had less to lose. When Mandaric sold a fifty per cent share of the club to Alexandre Gaydamak in January 2006, the financial crisis was still a distant nightmare, and the arrival of the son of Russian oligarch, Arkady Gaydamak, was widely seen as the building block for a new Portsmouth empire. Roman Abramovic's bottomless money pit had bought Chelsea success; Gaydamak's would surely do the same for Pompey.

'I don't think Mandaric had any inside knowledge of Gaydamak's finances,' says Julian Guyer, 'and he must have believed the Russian would have been good for the money. But, admittedly with hindsight, I do think there was more to the timing of Mandaric's sale than was first thought. It had long been common knowledge that the only way the club could begin to pay its way as a Premiership club was to increase the ground capacity from 21,000 and, right from the time we won promotion, there had been various different redevelopment proposals on the table.

'But as time passed, more and more objections to all the proposals began to be raised. The Navy was unhappy about this and that, the old railway yard was also earmarked for a business park, and an out-of-town location was a possible Site of Special Scientific Interest. So Mandaric must have begun to suspect that redeveloping the ground would either be far more expensive than he thought or impossible; in both scenarios, the owner would have to bear the brunt of the ongoing salary and transfer bill.'

All of which would have made quitting while he was ahead quite attractive, because Mandaric could go out on a financial and football high. He knew the club needed fresh players to survive and he knew Redknapp was the man most likely to find them; he just didn't want to pay the exorbitant overheads Redknapp was likely to incur in the process. Under those circumstances, the timing of the Gaydamak deal was a win-win for Mandaric; he could do his best to ensure the club's future without having to take any of the risk. And he didn't have to take it personally any more when Redknapp inevitably started moaning about something.

With Gaydamak's money on the table in the January transfer window, Redknapp set about spending it with his usual panache. Redknapp is often described as a gambler, but his punting begins and ends at the bookies. In the transfer market he takes few chances, adopting the conservative approach of buying tried and tested talent, players who are in their prime or have been around the block and who he believes have a year or two of active service left in their legs. Only very rarely does he invest in young people with potential – that is something for managers with smaller wallets and more time on their hands. Bringing in Benjani for a club record £4.1 million, Pedro Mendes, Sean Davis and Noé Pamarot from Spurs for £7 million, along with Wayne Routledge and the Argentinian, Andres D'Alessandro, on loan deals was therefore par for the course.

Redknapp's approach paid off, but it was touch and go. For a long while, the new-look Portsmouth team was playing every bit as poorly as the old one had done under Perrin. At the end of February, Pompey were stranded at the bottom of the table eight points below the next club and, by the end of March, the team was still propping up the table. Only a late run of good results lifted the club to seventeenth, one place above the drop zone. If Redknapp knew why the team suddenly clicked so late in the season, he never said. Maybe it was a mixture of confidence and luck. Sometimes managers have to take whatever they can get.

In May 2006, Redknapp was feeling so comfortable that he told Sky Sports that Portsmouth would be his last job in football. 'I mean it this time,' he said. 'This is the end for me. This is my last job. I feel comfortable here – I'm in charge here. I love being here.' Portsmouth fans with longish memories might have started panicking at this point as, two years previously, he had told the *Sun*, 'I would not take another job if I left here. Too many things happen in football which do your head in. If anyone thinks I'm angling for another job, then they had better think again as this will be my last one.' He left for Southampton seven months later.

But most fans were in a forgiving mood, prepared to overlook the many inconsistencies and contradictions in their manager and remained open to the possibility that when he made both statements he actually meant them, because life at Portsmouth was good. And about to get a whole lot better.

During the summer of 2006, Gaydamak bought the other fifty per cent of Mandaric's holding in the club and, for Redknapp, it might as well have been Christmas. Finally, he appeared to have a benefactor who was prepared to put his money where Redknapp's mouth was and, having signed his own new three-year contract, Redknapp went on to reshape the squad entirely by buying Sol Campbell, David James, Niko Kranjcar, Glen Johnson, Nwankwo Kanu, Lauren, Andrew Cole and Djimi Traore, as well as replacing his ever-trusted lieutenant, Kevin Bond, who had followed him back to Portsmouth from Southampton, with Tony Adams.

Not all the signings immediately won over the fans, but Redknapp's radar for getting the best out of players who had been overlooked elsewhere was spot on this time and the club finished the season comfortably in ninth place – tantalizingly out of reach of a first-ever UEFA Cup place. Away from football, the troubles that were to hound Redknapp for the next five and a half years began to close in on him. Throughout his managerial career, there had been whispers about Redknapp's financial dealings and lifestyle, but no one had ever put their head over the parapet and accused him of wrongdoing in public. In September 2006, that changed when a BBC *Panorama* documentary accused him of making an illegal approach to (or 'tapping up') the Blackburn defender, Andy Todd.

Redknapp denied this, saying he was the victim of an attempted sting by the BBC. 'I was a complete innocent party,' he told the *Daily Telegraph*. 'The guy rings up, who I haven't seen for seven years. He's setting up a new company for £2 million for some guy and could he have five minutes with you, Harry? So the guy I haven't spoken to for six or seven years comes down, sits opposite me and starts filming me but I don't say nothing, not a word to him. I know what I've done and I've done nothing wrong. I sat down with this guy and he wasted his time with me, really.'

Redknapp then went on to ridicule the allegation that Kevin Bond had taken illegal payments – 'bungs' – while working as his assistant at Portsmouth. 'All this talk and all these idiots who keep on about bungs in football. It doesn't happen, it isn't happening, it can't happen. You tell me that you're going to be a manager and earning plenty of money, and you have to go to sleep at night knowing any idiot can pick up a phone and ring a newspaper and finish your career. You walk into a dressing room, every player, they've got agents who might say to them, "I've given your manager a few quid." You're going to get respect from those players? They can stand up and say, "I know all about you." It's bullshit.'

Despite Redknapp's protests, the BBC aired the programme. Redknapp didn't sue for libel; Bond threatened to, but dropped his claim shortly before it came to court in 2009. If the tactic was to make no fuss so that the problem would go away more quickly, then it didn't work. While concerns were raised about a racehorse that had been given to Redknapp by former Portsmouth player Amdy Faye's agent Willy McKay, Redknapp was cleared of taking illegal payments in the Rio Ferdinand transfer from West Ham to Leeds by the Stevens inquiry into football corruption in June 2007. Redknapp's house was raided at dawn by a combination of the police and a photographer from the *Sun*, and he, Mandaric, Peter Storrie and McKay were subsequently arrested on suspicion of conspiracy to defraud and false accounting in connection with the purchase of Faye.

These charges were subsequently dropped, although as a result of the investigation Mandaric and Redknapp would later wind up in court over the Peter Crouch sale. The police were later ordered to pay £1,000 and legal costs for the unacceptable manner in which his arrest had been made. But some of the mud stuck as Redknapp was thereafter branded in many people's minds as the human face of all that was dodgy in football.

Redknapp has always been outraged by this, blaming the media and the public both for making lazy and incorrect assumptions based on class prejudice, and ignorance of how football works and the volume of transfer transactions in which he was involved. He's probably spot on, but his innocence does raise other rather more philosophical questions: how is it possible that so many people were so insistent for so long that professional football was riven with players, agents and managers taking illegal payments from transfer deals and salary negotiations, and yet the police have been unable to acquire sufficient evidence to get a single successful prosecution?

These matters were the last thing on anyone's mind in Portsmouth during the 2007/08 season. Gaydamak's cheque book had paid for three more class players – Sulley Muntari, John Utaka and David Nugent – in the pre-season and Lassana Diarra and Jermain Defoe in the January window, and the team now began to look like a solid Premiership club, rather than a bunch of chancers and hopefuls whose sole aim was to avoid relegation. Portsmouth finished tenth in the league but the heroics came in the FA Cup, where, after a nail-biting and totally unexpected away win against a full-strength Manchester United – their first victory at Old Trafford for more than fifty years – in the quarter-finals, the team lifted the trophy in May.

For Julian Guyer and all Pompey fans, it was a dream come true. 'Some people sniped that Gaydamak's money had basically bought the cup and that we'd only had to beat West Brom in the semis and Cardiff in the final,' he says. 'But none of us cared. Every other team that was winning things had also essentially bought their silverware, so why shouldn't we be allowed to gate-crash the party? And I felt we'd earned those victories against West Brom and Cardiff for all the years I'd been travelling up to places like Carlisle and Oldham to watch us play crap football.

'I'd never thought I'd ever see my team win the FA Cup at Wembley and being there as we collected the trophy was one of the happiest and most emotional moments of my life. When I got home, I gave my grandfather a programme to put alongside his from our only previous FA Cup win in 1939; it was quite an emotional moment for both of us. Better still, we had qualified for Europe. It's hard to explain what that means to fans who take European football for granted. The closest any Pompey fans had previously got to Europe was the ferry port to Le Havre. Now we would be taking on top clubs, like AC Milan, on equal terms.'

Portsmouth's success during that season did not go unnoticed. David James and Sol Campbell were recalled to the England team and, for the first time, Redknapp's name came up as a possible contender for the England job in late 2007 when Steve McClaren was sacked in November after England failed to qualify for the finals of Euro 2008. The job was eventually given to Fabio Capello in early December and Redknapp felt that the police raid on his home a few months earlier had been largely responsible for the FA's decision to overlook him.

The investigation probably did influence the FA's thinking – no one knows for sure as the FA doesn't publish the minutes of its selection procedures – but equally, and perhaps counter-intuitively, it did help to create the groundswell of opinion for Redknapp to become the next England manager after Capello, one that would grow ever louder over the next four years. Capello was never popular with the media and his so-so results didn't buy him any breathing space and, within a year or so of his appointment, it seemed to have become a preordained truth that his successor would have to be English. Eriksson and Capello hadn't performed any great miracles because they were foreigners; they didn't understand the English game or English players. If England were ever to be successful again, then the team would need an English manager in charge.

Few came more English than Redknapp, and the police investigation in some ways enhanced his credentials. The police hadn't charged him and the public mood was that if Redknapp had done anything a bit dodgy it hadn't been *that* dodgy. More importantly, a large cross section of football fans didn't care if Redknapp had done anything wrong or not. He'd been picked on by the police just because he looked and behaved like the archetypal English football manager. He didn't dress in fancy Armani suits and talk corporate management bollocks. He wore – at least in the public's perception – a sheepskin coat and spoke the same language as the fans and the footballer, along with added gags. And if Redknapp had a wedge full of used £20 notes stuffed into his top pocket, so much the better. When he told the writer who ghosted his magazine column, 'A grand is peanuts . . . I can do that in an afternoon at the races,' everyone just laughed. It somehow made him even more English.

The more you looked, the more English he became. What could

be more English than an East End cockney? Especially one who had played and drunk alongside Bobby Moore, Geoff Hurst and Martin Peters; there was almost a strand of DNA linking him to the World Cup. Who needed all those poncy foreign tactics, when you had an English bloke who could do everything and more with a good half-time talk, a couple of wingers and a solid 4-4-2 formation? Why complicate things? Even Redknapp's canteen at the Portsmouth training ground was English through and through. Sod the nutritionists, lads, just tuck into egg and chips.

Strangely though, in all this glorification of all things English, there was little consideration of just how English was the main foundation of Redknapp's success. If being a constant presence in the transfer and loan market was an English virtue, then it was a comparatively recent one. And Redknapp was hyperactive again at the beginning of the 2008/09 season, buying Peter Crouch – yet again – for £11 million from Liverpool in preparation for his first European examination. Redknapp had proved he could mix it in the Premier League, but did he have the tactical nous to cut it against tricky European teams?

Before anyone had a real chance to find out, Redknapp was gone. Earlier in the year, he had turned down the Newcastle job after Sam Allardyce had been sacked – the daily commute from Sandbanks would have been a killer – but when Daniel Levy came looking for someone to halt Spurs' worst-ever start to a Premier League campaign, Redknapp couldn't resist. Peter Storrie tried to persuade him to stay, but Redknapp's keenness to go and the £5 million compensation on offer sealed the deal, and this second parting from Portsmouth was a great deal more amicable than the first. The timing might have been better, though. Two days after joining Spurs, Redknapp returned to Portsmouth for the day to be awarded the freedom of the city in recognition of his achievement in winning the FA Cup, and the reception he received from the crowd wasn't all he might have wanted.

Once the initial disappointment had passed, most fans were philosophical about Redknapp's departure; they hadn't expected him to stay for ever, he'd been offered a better job and they had no reason to think the good times wouldn't continue to roll under a different manager. Four years on, the feelings were more mixed; in another piece of Redknapp timing, the club went into administration during Redknapp's trial at Southwark Crown Court. The ten-point automatic deduction just about guaranteed that Portsmouth would be playing in the First Division – two leagues lower than the Premiership – at the start of the 2012/13 season. That's if the club existed at all.

'I feel ambivalent,' says Julian Guyer, 'because I wouldn't have missed the excitement for all the world. But in hindsight, it was like a mirror image of the banking crisis; we had had a manager who had maxed out all the credit cards at Harrods and it was only a matter of time before the bailiffs came in. Harry spent money the club just didn't have and, though the chairman was ultimately responsible for our financial situation, he was to some extent complicit. There were always doubts about Gaydamak's solvency and Harry should have been more careful about putting the club at risk.

'A manager has long-term as well as short-term responsibilities to the club. Harry might have long gone, but the fans and the club have to live with his legacy. And it's not just a question of being sore because we've gone down two divisions since he left; that sort of thing happens and you can accept it. But going into administration is not a victimless crime. There are many local firms that are reliant on the football club; some have gone out of business and others are still owed a lot of money by the club. These are the ones who have really suffered.'

Right next to Fratton Park there is a mobile kebab stall. Match days used to offer up the best pickings of the week, but now the owner, Andy Wells, says it's hardly worth opening on a Saturday afternoon. 'It's unbelievable, really,' he says. 'We do far better now on a midweek evening when there's no game. The business has been hit hard. I know it's partly the recession, but it's also down to the way the club has been run. Do I blame Harry? Yes, I do a bit. Though I blame the board for not reining him in more.'

That, though, is often easier said than done, as one former club chairman who worked with Redknapp in the past explained. 'It sounds perfectly straightforward,' he said. 'Harry tells you he wants to buy this player and pay him so much, and you go away and work out whether you can afford it. But it doesn't work like that. Harry has a way of talking to the media and getting them on his side. If you try to say no to him, he will go behind your back and get a story in the local paper about how the chairman has no ambition for the club.

'This is the story that the fans take on board. They don't care if you can afford it or not. To them, every football club chairman is a millionaire with bottomless pockets and if you don't keep signing blank cheques then you don't have the team's best interests at heart. Before you know it, the fans are chanting, "*Chairman Out!*" at every match. You try to ignore it, but you can't. It does hurt. So you give in a bit. You tell yourself you'll let Harry get away with it just this once and stand up to him the next time. Only you don't.

'Harry understands all this perfectly and has tried to play the system to great effect at every club he's been at. I lost millions and millions of pounds trying to keep the club afloat and it just about bankrupted me. The stupid thing is that I cared more about the club than he did, which is why I kept on handing over money I couldn't really afford. I just sort of closed my eyes and hoped we'd have a cup run or a promotion that would help pay for it. I'm not looking for sympathy here. Just a chance to put my point of view across. In my opinion, the judge of a good manager isn't only the results on the pitch; it's the state of the finances when he leaves.'

A bankrupt club and some bitter-sweet memories aren't Red-knapp's only legacy to the city. In 2007, through one of his companies, Redknapp bought Savoy Buildings, a row of shops and nightclubs along the seafront in Southsea, intending to redevelop the site as ninety-two luxury apartments. When the recession hit and the council insisted that more affordable housing be included in the planning, the development was put on hold indefinitely. In August 2011, the site burned down, forcing many nearby residents to be temporarily moved out of their homes. Three months later, the council had to order Redknapp to clean up the burnt-out buildings amid concerns that the site was an eyesore and potentially unsafe. The rubble has now been moved but the site is still empty. As a metaphor for the city's football club, it could hardly be bettered.

8

Coming Up Short

April 2012

A hard-won home victory against Swansea at the beginning of the month proved to be a false dawn. There was no glorious revival, the slick machine did not slip effortlessly back into gear; rather, it continued to misfire as Spurs laboured to a goalless draw against Sunderland at the Stadium of Light the following week. The point did take Tottenham temporarily back into third place in the table ahead of Arsenal, but the ten-point cushion had been well and truly blown and it was clear the team was a shadow of the one that had taken Newcastle apart only two months earlier.

The simplest explanation – and the one most analysts instinctively reached for – was that the delay over the appointment of the new England manager had affected Redknapp and that the uncertainty was transmitting itself to the team. There was a satisfyingly linear cause-and-effect logic to this, albeit one that Redknapp had little choice but to deny, as to have done anything else would only have made a bad situation worse. Yet the more Redknapp insisted that the England job was not distracting him, the less he was believed. It got to the point where Spurs banned any questions about his England future at Redknapp's weekly press conferences. Or, to be more accurate, the club said the manager would not be answering any more questions on the subject. The questions still came; the ensuing silences were uncomfortable for all concerned.

Yet there was a growing feeling among some keen-eyed Harry-watchers that there was more to the club's decline than just the ongoing England drama. The feeling was one of *déjà vu*; that they were watching a repeat of familiar failings, that the very qualities that Redknapp brought to the team and could help make it perform like possible champions were also those that could all too easily expose its limitations and cause it to implode. It was the fear that within Redknapp's unquestionable touches of football genius lay the seeds of his own and his team's self-destruction and that, with Redknapp, the line between triumph and tragedy was finer than most. It was just that in previous seasons the stakes hadn't been quite so high, nor his limitations quite so exposed. The speculation over the England job had merely created the perfect storm from which Redknapp had no hiding place.

The warning signs had been in place for a while, with Redknapp having given a press conference before the Bolton FA Cup tie in which he said, 'If we finish in the top four I think we over-punched our weight really, to be perfectly truthful with you.' This was a classic Redknapp diversionary tactic of getting his excuses in early, and one that had worked quite well for him in the past; tell everyone the team has exceeded all expectations and protect yourself from the fallout when things begin to unravel. Except this time it made him look a bit foolish and panicky. Spurs may have played better than anyone had predicted in the first half of the season but, having got themselves into a commanding position, there was no escaping the fact that the team was now crumbling. Rather than just acknowledging the situation and dealing with it, Redknapp appeared to be in denial about it. He seemed to be expecting everyone to respond with, 'You know what, Harry, you're absolutely right . . . We should never have let ourselves get into such a great position as it was bound to end in tears . . . We'd have been far better off if we had known our place and then we could have been happy with fourth . . .' But that was never going to happen.

Apart from anything else, the idea that Spurs had somehow overachieved just wasn't true. It would have been of many previous Spurs teams, but it wasn't of this one. The midfield of Bale, Modric, Parker and Lennon was the equal of any in the Premiership, and a combination of van der Vaart, Adebayor and Defoe up front was the envy of many. For overachievers in the division, you could point to Swansea, Norwich . . . and Manchester United. Almost everyone who claimed to be in the know had been arguing that this United side was the poorest for many seasons and yet it was still well ahead of every other team, except its local rival, Manchester City. And in so doing, that success exposed the difference in managerial styles between Sir Alex Ferguson, the United manager, and Redknapp. Whether by terrorizing his players or instilling a culture where failure was unacceptable, Ferguson had turned good – though not necessarily great – footballers into a team that could find ways to win the unwinnable games; Redknapp had assembled a team of mostly great players but was seemingly unable to make them play with any consistency.

To understand why this was so is to get to the heart of the Redknapp paradox. Throughout his career, Redknapp has acquired the reputation for having a talent for man-management, and it's not hard to rack up a list of players who have openly given him the credit for either reviving or prolonging their careers. What you don't hear so often are the stories of those who have fallen out with him. Players who moan about their manager quickly acquire the 'awkward customer' tag, and in a head-to-head popularity contest with Redknapp in the media, there is only ever going to be one winner. But Redknapp does have favourites. If you're in with him, he'll put his arm round you, tell you jokes and make you feel loved; if you're out, he can ignore you to death.

It's not that hard for an outsider to tell who is in favour and who is not with Redknapp's teams. The in-crowd are in the first team; the frozen-out are not. You can't blame a manager for preferring some players to others, it's only human; some people are naturally much more approachable and friendly, others have strops and sulks as their default setting. But a manager has to be professional enough to work with different personality types and tease out the best qualities in a group of often quite dysfunctional players; it's not exactly therapy, just a matter of getting everyone working well enough to put aside any differences and play as a team for ninety minutes. Part of that is making every player feel as if he has an equal chance of getting into the side and that if he is performing better in training than a first-team regular, it will not go unnoticed.

That level of fluidity and opportunity is not generally a feature of Redknapp's teams. Once Redknapp has decided a player is or isn't worth a first-team place, it takes a great deal for him to change his mind. This kind of loyalty to his players paid dividends in the first half of the season; the first team responded to the way Redknapp treated them by playing with freedom and confidence. They weren't scared that one off game or a couple of miss-hit passes would cost them their place in the starting eleven for the following match. The trouble came in the second half of the season.

Towards the end of March, Vedran Corluka, the Spurs right-back and very obviously not one of Redknapp's in-crowd, who had been loaned out to German club Bayer Leverkusen in January, gave an interview in which he argued that the reason the team's performances had fallen away was because the players were all tired due to Redknapp's reluctance to rotate the squad. His manager rejected this out of hand, implying Corluka was merely getting his own back for not being given the opportunities he thought he deserved. 'When you lose a few, everyone suddenly has something to say,' Redknapp observed. 'I didn't hear anyone complaining a month ago when we were beating everyone and flying. Most of the players have probably played thirty games. I didn't play any of them in the UEFA Cup or FA Cup, and no player has said to me, "Gaffer, I'm tired." Bobby Moore, Geoff Hurst or Martin Peters were never rotated, playing ankle-deep in mud every week. Frank Lampard plays how many games a season? Ashley Cole, Wayne Rooney and Patrice Evra are not rotated, so it's a load of nonsense. It's an excuse.'

As ever with Redknapp, there was more than a germ of truth in what he had said. Nobody had complained a month previously; though, equally, the levels of tiredness had yet to kick in. It's true, no player had complained of being tired, but there's no way of knowing whether that was because no one actually was tired or because the rules of the squad – you're either in or out – were implicitly understood by everyone and to have done so would have been tantamount to career suicide. It was also true that some players have remarkable levels of fitness and quick recovery times and don't need rotating. But some do, and one of those in the Spurs team who clearly did was Rafa van der Vaart. In the previous season, van der Vaart had played brilliantly before Christmas, creating havoc in opposition defences and seemingly scoring at will, but in February, March and April he had noticeably faded and had become far less effective. It's something all the fans had noticed, so it can't have escaped the eyes of Redknapp and his coaching team.

Exactly the same thing had happened to van der Vaart in this season, and yet, if Redknapp had noticed, he did nothing about it as the Dutchman was virtually ever-present in the first team. More than that, the whole team was set up for van der Vaart to play a roving role between the midfield and the lone striker, Adebayor, and when van der Vaart was unable to fulfil that role effectively the formation came unstuck. Just as Redknapp had one Team A, so he had no Plan B. It was as if he had a single, idealized view – a platonic form – of how he wanted the team to play and was unable to react pragmatically when circumstances prevented him. Just once did he alter the team's shape by leaving out van der Vaart and playing a standard 4-4-2 formation with Defoe and Saha up front, and that was for the home defeat against Norwich. After that game, Redknapp shrugged, seemingly implying the defeat was as much the fans' fault as anyone else's, because it was the fans who had been calling out for a switch to 4-4-2 to accommodate Defoe – he had merely given them what they had wanted.

For Redknapp, that one game was proof enough he had been right to maintain his original formation all along. And in a sense you couldn't argue with his logic. You could hardly expect the team to play at its best when the players knew they had been lined up in a formation that the manager thought was second best. But it was also asking a great deal of his two strikers, Defoe and Saha, to gel immediately when they had played so little together and they were so obviously not Redknapp's first choice.

This also rather raised the question of Saha – why had he been bought by the club in January if the manager had so little confidence in him? Saha had blown hot and cold – more often than not cold – for every other club he had played for, and no one should have been surprised when he began to look disinterested at Spurs, so it's unlikely that Redknapp was. So either he had been hoping to squeeze just a couple of match-winning performances out of Saha and had not got lucky, or the former Everton striker had always been the choice of Spurs chairman, Daniel Levy. Whatever the truth, the repercussions would be felt later.

There was also an old-school, wilful Englishness in Redknapp harking back to the days of Moore, Hurst and Peters ploughing through the mud. This always played well with a section of the media and fans prone to periodic bouts of nostalgia for the old days when there was less money in the game, everything seemed simpler and England won the World Cup. It may even have been a subconscious plea to the FA to hurry up and give him the England job. Sod the European softies, make me the manager and I will win you trophies with old-fashioned English virtues.

But however attractive – or even preferable – that sense of Englishness may have been, turning back the clock to Old Albion wasn't an option. The reason why Moore, Hurst and Peters happily ran through the mud week after week was because they had no choice. No teams rotated their squads so every side was able to slow down at the same rate. In the 2012 Premiership, the big teams with big budgets did rotate their squads and those teams that either couldn't or chose not to almost always struggled toward the end of the season.

Squad rotation has further knock-on benefits to resting tired bodies. It also keeps players on their toes. It had become part of the White Hart Lane experience for those who didn't watch Spurs regularly to marvel at the brilliance of the Croatian midfielder, Luka Modric, but for those who followed the club rather more closely, it was evident that – just like van der Vaart – his late season performances, while still having flashes of genius, had little of the intensity of the early season ones. The same trend had also been apparent the season before, although in Modric's case the reason was less likely to have been tiredness than dissatisfaction. In both seasons, he had been eyeing up a transfer to a bigger club with a guarantee of more money and regular Champions League football, and both times he frequently gave the impression he had already left. Under a manager who rotated his squad, there might have been more inducement for Modric to maintain his focus. As it was, Redknapp's dogged adherence to his pre-ordained first team would end up costing him rather more than Modric.

The biggest advantage to squad rotation, though, is the way it helps teams cope with injury – not just by preventing players succumbing to those caused by overuse and fatigue, but by enabling others to slot in more easily to the side when a key player was out of action. One of the foundations on which Spurs' early season dominance had been built was the speed of their two wingers, Gareth Bale and Aaron Lennon, and their ability to terrorize defenders on each flank. In March, Lennon had been badly injured and was sidelined for about a month, forcing Redknapp to rethink his approach. Except he never came up with a workable solution. The team had grown used to playing with Lennon and struggled to adapt to his absence. Redknapp tried playing various others – including Bale – out of position to compensate, but nothing worked effectively and no one really plugged the gap.

There were players who might have done. Two seasons previously, another Croatian midfielder, Niko Kranjcar, had been one of the first-team regulars who had helped the team reach the Champions League, but he had now fallen out of favour with Redknapp and barely made the subs' bench. It wasn't immediately clear to anyone just what he had done wrong, although it was also fair to say he hadn't done himself too many favours in the interim, for when he was required he looked both unfit and bored – neither quality was the most professional of responses, but any Premiership manager should have had sufficient experience to deal with them before they became an issue. For whatever reason, Redknapp's man-management skills fell well short of being able to re-motivate a player he had signed twice – once at Portsmouth and again at Spurs. The distance between the two men had been allowed to become too wide.

As it happened, there was a player who could have fitted in easily as a replacement for Lennon, without Redknapp needing to have tinkered with the balance of the side by playing Bale and Modric out of position. Unfortunately, Steven Pienaar had been sent out on loan to Everton in the January transfer window, having only been bought by Spurs from Everton the previous year. On his arrival, he had started a few games, made minimal impression and then been abruptly cast aside – yet another of the players whom Redknapp had decided early on that he didn't really rate and for whom there would be no second chances. If not as quick as Lennon, Pienaar had been a useful, competitive, right-sided midfielder at Everton before he had arrived at Spurs and had been looking even better than that since his return. David Moyes, the Everton manager, knew how to get the best out of Pienaar; Redknapp either didn't know that trick or didn't think it was worthwhile making the effort.

Player loyalty was also an issue among the defensive players. For some years, the club captain Ledley King had not only been a talismanic figure but a miracle. His knees were so ropey that he couldn't take part in midweek training sessions and he barely managed to play in half the team's fixtures. But when he did play, his timing and his talent invariably carried him through and the Spurs defence always looked more secure when he played than when he didn't. It was inevitable that something would eventually have to give and it had become painfully obvious since Christmas that King could no longer get by on a wing and a prayer. He had given away a silly last-minute penalty – a clumsy challenge the King of former seasons would never have made – to deny Spurs an away draw at Manchester City, been run ragged in the heavy away defeat at Arsenal and was cruelly exposed in the 5-1 FA Cup semi-final defeat against Chelsea in the middle of April.

There was at least a certain nobility and graciousness in Redknapp's loyalty to King. The Spurs defender had done the club proud on countless occasions in the past and he deserved the benefit of the doubt, a chance to prove that he could come good again after all. But Redknapp, a manager who can be utterly ruthless on occasions with some players, didn't have it in him to say enough is enough to his captain and allowed him to continue for several games too many. Perhaps he couldn't quite believe the evidence of his own eyes and accept that King was no longer the player he once was. It would have been a tough call for any manager to have made, but one can think of several cold-eyed Premiership managers who would have made it. There's a time and a place for sentiment in football, but a tight end-of-season run-in with a jittery team isn't it.

Redknapp could – and did – argue that he had little choice. The team had been badly hit by injuries and, in the manager's own words, was down to 'the bare bones' of the squad. 'We are not in a position where we can pull one or two out,' he said. 'Everyone says "look at the strong squad we have", but there's every chance David Bentley could be back on the bench. He's not had a game. I'm struggling to find seven substitutes.' To which one answer might well have been, 'Who's fault is that?'

A long second-half-of-the-season injury list had been a recurring feature of Redknapp's four campaigns at Spurs. That could be a coincidence but, then again, it might not be. 'If a team is consistently picking up more injuries than expected,' says sports psychologist Martin Perry, 'it could indicate there was something wrong with the training methods being employed. Perhaps some of the players weren't quite as fit as they should have been. It's certainly something a manager should consider seriously.'

Even if all the injuries had been unavoidable, the buck still stopped with Redknapp. Stephen Caulker and Kyle Naughton, both defenders who could have been trusted to do a decent job, had been sent out on season-long loans to Swansea and Norwich respectively and had been doing very well for their new clubs. Sebastien Bassong had been loaned out to Wolves and Redknapp appeared to have little faith in his replacement, Ryan Nelsen, the thirty-four-year-old defender who had been acquired from

Blackburn in the transfer window. So much for Redknapp's complaint that various members of his squad hadn't yet had a game.

Even Redknapp's lucky touch deserted him in the FA Cup semifinal. Spurs came out for the second half a goal down, having dominated much of the first, whereupon Chelsea were immediately awarded a second for a Juan Mata shot that didn't cross the line. Thereafter, Redknapp's Spurs never recovered their poise and were taken apart as they chased the game. Yet even a heavy semi-final defeat couldn't stop the 'Harry for England' bandwagon from continuing to roll. 'He looks like he is going to be the new England manager and I think he fully deserves the chance to lead his country,' said Roberto Di Matteo, the Chelsea interim first-team coach, after the game. 'A lot of [our England contingent] know him very well and I think that the general view is that the players all like him.'

Better still for Redknapp was that the May edition – which came out in mid-April – of the influential football magazine *Four Four Two* featured Redknapp wearing a crown on the front cover under the strapline 'All Hail King 'Arry', along with an inside feature in which former players such as Paolo Di Canio, Paul Merson and Shaka Hislop paid tribute to his managerial skills. No one lost any sleep working out the subtext of that article.

The final piece of the coronation jigsaw appeared to be complete when the Bolton Wanderers chairman and FA board member, Phil Gartside, declared in an interview with BBC World's *Extra Time* programme that Redknapp would be 'an outstanding England manager' and described him as 'a good motivator with a winning mentality'. Although Gartside wasn't one of the four FA members on the selection panel he was considered to be one of the most influential of the FA's committee members. This was the first time that anyone from the FA had spoken in public about the England job since Fabio Capello's resignation, so Gartside's remarks were reported by every newspaper as a rubber-stamp of approval – a way of calming speculation – ahead of the formal announcement.

For his part, Redknapp continued to insist he was hardly even aware there was a job vacancy. 'I never think about it . . . honestly,' he said. 'I swear. I never think about anything other than Tottenham, trying to finish this season so that we get where we have been all year – in that top four. Other than that there is nothing to occupy my mind at all.' If true, he had a funny way of showing it. Not normally a man to turn down easy money, Redknapp had rejected an offer from a confectionery company to appear in a TV commercial to coincide with the Euro 2012 finals – possibly because it wasn't the sort of deal the FA would take kindly to an England manager making.

He also hadn't endeared himself to Spurs by saying that he hoped Chelsea beat Barcelona in the second leg of their semi-final Champions League tie, even though he had gone on to qualify this by adding that he couldn't see Chelsea winning the final against Bayern Munich. Chelsea were not just rivals for a top-four place in the Premiership; if the club won the Champions League, then it would guarantee itself a place in the competition at the expense of whoever finished fourth. As there was a good chance it would be Tottenham in that fourth spot, everyone at the club was praying for Chelsea to get knocked out of the competition as soon as possible, so that avenue of anxiety and uncertainty would be eliminated. Well, everyone except Redknapp. It was impossible to imagine Alex Ferguson or Arsène Wenger saying anything like that in a similar position. They might not have gone public with an 'I hope Chelsea lose' statement, but they would certainly have kept a diplomatic silence. There was no need for Redknapp to say anything. Even a man prone to speak first and think later would have worked that one out. So saying what he did, when he did, was just another way of saying, 'I'm already half out the door at White Hart Lane and I'm trying to talk like an international manager.'

If Gartside's backing had been intended to reassure Redknapp that the job was his and allow him to refocus his concentration on Spurs' remaining five games, then it had no immediate effect as the team slumped to an away defeat at relegation-threatened Queens Park Rangers and down to sixth place in the league. After the game, Redknapp said that Spurs had dominated the game and had just been a bit unlucky in not scoring. That wasn't the way it had looked to anyone at the ground. For the most part, Spurs had looked hapless and aimless, barely managing one shot on target. Redknapp himself had looked much the same. In most games, he could be found pacing the technical area and shouting the odds; at QPR, he remained mostly rooted to the dugout, sucking in his cheeks and shaking his head. This was a pale imitation of the jocular, cajoling, dynamic Harry Redknapp the fans knew and loved.

There was some relief on the last weekend of the month as Spurs managed their first win in five games, a 2-0 victory against Blackburn, yet another side battling relegation. When Kyle Walker scored the second midway through the second half, from a thirty-five-yard free kick, no one assumed it was a victory planned out on the training ground. Least of all Redknapp, who after the game admitted he had said to Kevin Bond that he hoped Walker wasn't going to take the kick as it would end up in Row Z. If it had done, it would have been no more than anyone else at White Hart Lane expected, as that's precisely where every other free kick Spurs had taken throughout the season had gone. Whatever else Redknapp was doing with the first team on the training ground, it wasn't practising dead ball situations.

Had Spurs turned the corner? And had Redknapp finally learned to deal with the pressure of being the England manager-elect? That last question proved to be academic within hours of the final whistle of the Blackburn game, when the FA announced they had been given permission by West Bromwich Albion to talk to their manager, Roy Hodgson, and that they had no plans to talk to anyone else. After all that, the job of England manager had been offered, seemingly out of the blue, to Hodgson.

9

Winning His Spurs

October 2008

By late October in the 2008/09 season, Spurs – managed at the time by Juande Ramos – were four points adrift at the bottom of the Premier League, having managed just two draws in eight games, and had been well beaten by unfancied Italian side Udinese in the UEFA Cup. After that kind of start, any football manager would have been looking nervously over his shoulder but, even so, the sacking of Ramos was brutal. Most sackings are preceded by a series of leaks, private briefings and counter-briefings in which possible replacements are sounded out and excuses made. If Ramos had any idea the axe was about to fall he didn't let on, and the club's announcement that Redknapp was to take over as manager with immediate effect caught both the media and fans on the hop.

Spurs had approached Portsmouth on the Friday night and, within twenty-four hours, had made the club and Redknapp an offer neither could refuse. Portsmouth got £5 million and Redknapp got a basic salary of £3 million along with the chance to prove himself at one of the country's biggest clubs; given that Redknapp had been earning nearly that much at Portsmouth, the opportunity was probably a bigger attraction than the money. If he'd ever truly had the ambition to climb the management ladder, at nearly sixty-two years old he must have imagined his moment had passed.

'It's a big opportunity to manage a big club before I retire,' he said. 'The chairman knows the team needs strengthening in two or three positions still . . . we are short in one or two areas and that is something I will be looking at. However, first and foremost it will be about getting the best out of the players who are here. There are some good ones who have not done as well as they should have done. We have got to get them playing to their maximum and, if we do that, then we will be OK.'

Redknapp's arrival at Spurs was greeted with pragmatism rather than joy. The club was in a mess and Redknapp was the kind of manager who could sort it out. 'I wasn't a fan of Redknapp,' says Adam Powley, a football writer and author of several books about Spurs. 'He came with a lot of baggage (deserved or otherwise) and his record of one devalued FA Cup in thirty years of management seemed to tell its own story. It was more a case of grudgingly accepting that a problem of the club's own making required a pretty drastic remedy. Spurs seemed to be paying for the "bad karma" of the way Ramos had been appointed, and Redknapp was the appropriate antidote – a short-term fixer who knew his way round the Premier League and could rescue what was a pretty risible situation.

'That's not to say that I thought Redknapp was a wholly negative appointment. I liked the way his teams played. I'd reported on quite a few Portsmouth games in the past and he set his teams up to attack and play passing football. It was simply that the appointment of a sixty-one-year-old none of the "big clubs" appeared to want seemed a retrograde, reactive and short-term step.'

Reactive and short-term would almost certainly sum up Levy's own assessment of his approach to Redknapp. Levy had lost a great deal of the Spurs fans' goodwill the previous season by sacking Martin Jol – one of the most successful and popular club managers since Keith Burkinshaw – for no very good reason and appointing Juande Ramos, the Spanish manager of Sevilla, in his place on a reported £6 million per year. Despite engineering a Carling Cup victory over Chelsea, Spurs had suffered a dismal end to the 2007/08 Premier League season and an even worse start to the current season. Levy needed a quick fix, a manager who was going to be able to shore things up, ward off the threat of relegation and who was, above all, available. Redknapp ticked all those boxes. A long-term solution could be sought once the immediate danger had passed.

The terms of Redknapp's contract appeared to bear out Levy's thinking. In the four-year deal he agreed with Redknapp, there were no conditions included by which Redknapp would be able to renegotiate an improved deal for himself. This might suggest that both men thought there was little chance of Redknapp lasting much longer than a year – eighteen months at most – at Spurs. The longer Redknapp stayed at the club, the more resentful he became at not being able to negotiate a better deal; and thereby ultimately hastening his exit from it.

The surprise wasn't that Redknapp saved the club from relegation – the squad had always looked too strong for that – but that he got it to play, at times, the best football of any Spurs team since the 1960s, and it wasn't long before Redknapp began to win over those who had doubted his ability to do more than a rescue job.

'I was a little uneasy when he was appointed, if I'm honest, although as there really wasn't much choice, I just had to face the facts,' says Martin Cloake, another football writer and author of many books on Spurs. 'The unease was because of the feeling that Harry is always more interested in Harry than any team he manages, and because I wasn't sure just how good he was. That probably makes me sound like one of those fans who always goes on about "a name big enough for Spurs", but I've always rejected that attitude. A "big name" isn't always the right name; managers should make their reputations, not simply transfer them.

'Harry, like Terry Venables before him, gets a great press because he gives plenty of quotes. But Venables was a great coach as well as a motivator. I think Harry's skills are more motivational – although I don't think he is as tactically naïve as some of his more vociferous critics say. Or as he would sometimes like us to believe. What we needed when he came was a motivator and he motivated the players pretty quickly. He had pretty much the same squad as Martin Jol; the difference was that Redknapp got rather more backing. His self-interest worked well for us. So my unease was outweighed by the fact that we had a strong coach who insisted on his own space, dealt well with the players and had good ideas about playing attractive football . . . and the fact that he turned things around fairly quickly.'

Redknapp got off to the perfect start with a 2-0 victory against Bolton after which he made suitably purring noises about the team, saying, 'There is real quality in this group of players here. You look at the quality and they shouldn't be where they are, but two points in eight games is an amazingly bad start. We have to start working as hard as we did today for each other, picking up points, playing as we did – they passed the ball with real quality which I was really impressed with.'

But it was the next game – a 4-4 away draw against Arsenal, secured through two injury-time goals – that really got people's attention. Spurs just didn't carve out those kinds of results when they were all but buried against their arch-rivals. Who cared if Redknapp was mainly out for Redknapp? If he could carry on upsetting the odds, then everyone was going to get along just fine.

Redknapp and Levy are often characterized as the odd couple, the manager and chairman who rubbed each other up the wrong way and barely agreed on anything. But their relationship wasn't always like that, especially at the beginning, when they had a respect for one another that went beyond the grudging. They had their own separate spheres of influence and were happy to let each other concentrate on what they did best. Levy had recognized that Damien Comolli's appointment as director of football in control of identifying and buying players had not been a success. Two of his acquisitions, though, Luka Modric and Gareth Bale, would prove pivotal to Redknapp's Spurs, so Redknapp was left to work in the way he liked, free from excessive interference. For the man who had left Portsmouth when threatened by Zajec and had bristled at Woodward at Southampton, the news that Comolli would be leaving White Hart Lane at the same time as Ramos was welcome indeed.

And there certainly weren't any obvious sounds of discord over Redknapp's first signings in the January window, as Redknapp played it safe by re-signing three experienced former Spurs players; true to form, he raided his own former club, Portsmouth, to bring Jermain Defoe back to White Hart Lane and completed the trio by buying Robbie Keane from Liverpool and Pascal Chimbonda from Sunderland.

Defoe was an instant success on his return, adding some much-needed sharpness to the attack, but neither Keane nor Chimbonda could recapture the form that had previously made them local heroes at Tottenham.

That Redknapp's first sortie in the transfer market had been rather hit and miss was long forgotten by the end of the season. By steering Spurs to the Carling Cup final, which was lost to Manchester United on penalties, and finishing eighth in the Premier League, Redknapp had done everything that had been asked of him and more. He had shown himself to be a more astute tactician than he had been billed – his decision to play Modric in a more forward role had made the Croatian and the team far more effective – and he had given back the players their self-belief.

Well, most of them. At home to Portsmouth towards the end of the season, the scores were level at 1-1 with about ten minutes to go when Darren Bent headed wide with the goal open. It was a truly horrible miss, but Redknapp's reaction was worse. 'It was a great chance,' he said at a post-match press conference. 'You are not going to get a better one than that to win a game. It was game over and we were going home with three points, as simple as that. My missus could have scored that. David James had given up on it. He had turned his back and was getting ready to pick the ball out of the net. He did not just have a bit to aim at, he had the whole goal to aim at. What can you do?'

Not rubbishing one of your main strikers in public would have been a start. Telling the media Sandra would have scored got plenty of laughs, but it also got plenty of headlines, and Bent's confidence, fragile at the best of times, was destroyed. He barely scored another goal for Spurs and moved to Sunderland in the summer. Redknapp later defended his remarks by saying, 'It was only the truth, wasn't it?' but that rather missed the point. You wouldn't have caught any other Premiership manager humiliating a player in this way, whatever he may have thought in private. A manager's role is to build up a player, to make sure the next time he has an open goal he doesn't miss. It's called looking after your assets; a £16.5 million asset in Bent's case.

Part of Redknapp's charm had always lain in the fact that he was unlike other managers. He saw the game as a fan and sometimes called it as one; he wasn't one of the drones who could find ten different ways of saying nothing very interesting. When his teams were playing well and winning, he was let off the hook because he was 'a bit of a character'; and when they weren't, he just looked a bit unprofessional. But he had largely got away with it, because up until now he had managed smaller clubs where every indiscretion didn't automatically make a headline in the national press and feelings weren't so badly hurt. At a club like

Spurs, the prospects of causing more serious damage through unguarded comments was infinitely greater.

Redknapp may sometimes exaggerate his 'cheeky chappy' persona – if he sees a reporter with a microphone, it's rare for him not to wind down his car window and give good quote – but it's not an act. It is the way he is; even the exaggeration is part of the way he is. Under his tough-ish façade, Redknapp wants to be loved; he wants to be understood. Comedians don't tell jokes because they want to make people laugh; they tell them because they crave the feeling other people's laughter gives them. It makes them feel included, desired and good about themselves; it fulfils a need they can't meet themselves. Harry Redknapp is no different; keeping everyone laughing is one of the ways by which he can make himself feel valued.

This gets to the heart of understanding Redknapp. Fans and critics often suggest that 'Harry is only out for Harry' as if this is some kind of business strategy, like a banker manipulating the LIBOR rate for his own personal gain. It isn't; it's far less calculating and deliberate than that. If Redknapp does always look to gain an advantage in any situation, it's an unconscious, reflex response driven by his own personality. This doesn't excuse his behaviour, it merely explains it.

Redknapp – like many other extremely successful people – is self-absorbed; he sees other people largely as adjuncts to himself. If he weren't to exist, neither would they. This isn't to say that he isn't capable of empathizing with other people or is incapable of kindness or generosity. He clearly is, which is yet another of his attractions. Rather, it's that he can switch it on and off according to how he feels. If he feels generous and giving, he is; far more so than many. But when he doesn't, he's incapable of acting otherwise. So when people are caught in his warmth, he makes them feel like world-beaters; but when the light goes out, they feel hurt and a bit lost.

Seen like this, the highs and lows of Redknapp's career begin to fall into place. The great successes and the seemingly mindless acts of self-destruction are just two sides of the same coin, albeit a coin that had never been examined that closely as most of his career had taken place away somewhat from the main stage. There, his triumphs could be lauded as the work of the ordinary man taking on the football establishment and his failures could be brushed aside with a 'What else can you expect from a club with limited resources?' Even though Spurs had had little to show by way of trophies or league titles for many years, it saw itself with a big history and a great tradition. Success was expected and the lapses that Redknapp had got away with at his previous clubs would not so easily be forgiven at White Hart Lane.

Redknapp's greatest strengths can also, on a bad day, turn out to be his weaknesses. His directness, his need to be in charge and his ability to restore confidence to the players had been just what the club needed when he arrived. But on those days – or weeks sometimes – when his intensity and concentration were low, there was no one around to fill the vacuum his absence created. As so often before, Redknapp had brought his own coaching team with him to White Hart Lane, most notably his old sparring partner, Kevin Bond, who had been sacked as manager of Bournemouth a month or so earlier, as his assistant.

There was nothing inherently wrong with bringing in Bond, apart from the suspicion he had got the job more because he could be trusted to be loyal than on ability. It was a suspicion that Redknapp did little to dispel; Bond lived close to Redknapp in Poole and the two men used to travel up together to the Tottenham training ground every day and Redknapp regularly used to joke that Bond was his driver. It got a good laugh, but it didn't do much for Bond's reputation. On fans' message boards, Bond was known thereafter as 'the driver', and the lack of respect must have filtered down to the players. So when Redknapp was missing – either physically or emotionally – how could they take Bond seriously?

It's easy to be wise after the event, but Redknapp's 2012 trial did suggest one possible, hitherto unknown, consequence of this. Rob Beasley, the *News of the World* reporter, had phoned Redknapp with the tax-evasion allegations on the day before Spurs played Manchester United in the Carling Cup final. Much as he tried to keep himself focused, Redknapp could not have been anything but distracted by this, and, although the scores were level after extra time, Spurs played throughout with a noticeable lack of direction and ambition. Had Bond been a more powerful, respected figure in the dressing room, he could have compensated for Redknapp's absence and, even if the outcome had been the same, Spurs might well have played with more self-belief.

Redknapp's informal, jokey style could also rebound on himself. In December 2009, just after Spurs had lost unexpectedly at home to Wolves, it emerged that sixteen first-team players had each paid £2,000 towards a lavish booze-up in Dublin, despite Redknapp having banned his players from having a Christmas party. When the news broke, Redknapp was forced on to the defensive. 'Wednesday was their day off and Robbie [Keane] told me they were going to Ireland to play golf. I had no problem with that,' he said. 'However, it is widely known that I do not approve of Christmas parties and I've always made it clear players should only drink in moderation. Whatever happened in Ireland, I do not accept it had any effect on the result against Wolves. The squad trained brilliantly on Thursday and Friday and there were other reasons we lost that match.'

None of this said much for the players' sense of discipline or professionalism, but nor did it say much for the regard in which they held their manager. Few – if any – Premier League squads would have dared challenge their manager so directly over something that was almost bound to be discovered. And Redknapp was partly to blame for that; if you have a laugh at other people's expense, you can't complain too much when they have one at yours. Redknapp might well have believed he had only been guilty of being too trusting with his squad, of treating them like adults, but experience should have taught him that, with most footballers, you can never make the boundaries between what is – and what isn't – acceptable too plain.

Keane was disciplined, but the incident was forgotten when, after a brief and all-too-familiar mid-season stutter that culminated in a disappointing FA Cup semi-final defeat to Portsmouth, Spurs went on a remarkable late-season run that resulted in the team qualifying for the Champions League for the first time in the club's history. Not only did Spurs beat Arsenal, Chelsea and Manchester City in one epic four-week period – games previous Spurs sides could always have been counted on to surrender – they had beaten them in style. These weren't lucky, backs-to-the-walls, defend-in-depth-and-try-to-sneak-a-goal-on-the-break victories; they were ones in which the opposition were more or less swept off the pitch with virtuoso, fast, attacking football. The fans were ecstatic; finally, after years of hope more than expectation, they had been given back their long-held vision of the type of club Spurs was meant to be. And the credit was nearly all due to Redknapp.

Redknapp's success wasn't just in getting the big-name stars to play like stars – though that was something which had eluded many previous Tottenham managers – it was to turn hitherto unfancied footballers into stars. Gareth Bale had arrived from Southampton in 2007 heavily tipped as a name for the future, but had failed to deliver on that promise and, midway through the 2009/10 season, was on the verge of being loaned out to Nottingham Forest until left-back Benoit Assou-Ekotto got injured. Bale was brought in and looked a totally different player; his tentativeness had been replaced with confidence. The same could be said for Assou-Ekotto himself, who had morphed from liability to fans' favourite within the course of the season. Whatever Redknapp was doing with them was working.

'Harry worked wonders with Bale,' says John Williams. 'It wasn't so much about spotting his potential, as many others had already noticed it. Rather, it was about playing him in a more advanced position and getting him to believe in himself. Gareth may appear confident, but he hasn't always been that way. There was a time when he didn't feel he could play unless he was a hundred per cent fit. Harry managed to get through to him that there are times when everyone has to play with a slight niggle. If every footballer only played when he felt physically and mentally on top of his game, most would struggle to take the field.'

The most pertinent question at the beginning of the 2010/11 season was whether he could maintain it and, if so, for how long? Sports psychologist Martin Perry points out that there are various ways of motivating players. 'There's the straightforward putting your arm round players and rousing speeches telling everyone they are great and that they can go out and win,' he says. 'That's the standard fare of football management and can work well, especially with teams from the lower divisions. But it's less effective over time for the top players because they are looking for other more sophisticated forms of motivation. They need to feel the manager will help them improve their skills and develop their careers.'

In the past, this had never been Redknapp's strong suit. Players were expected to be experienced, not to be helped to acquire it. Those who didn't come up to the mark were either sold or loaned out. Having got his Spurs team to play at a high level, that philosophy was no longer going to be enough to ensure they maintained it consistently. The players wanted more from their manager, and the old 'Agincourt' Harry style of motivation that had worked initially was now only ever going to work intermittently – when Redknapp had the intensity and the players didn't find it stale.

* * *

Picking the single moment when the relationship between Redknapp and his chairman began to deteriorate is next to impossible, but Levy can't have been too thrilled when Redknapp was charged with two counts of cheating the public revenue in January 2010 as no football club wants the possible scandal or distraction of ongoing legal action against its manager. Having been named in the Tom Bower book and been investigated by the Stevens inquiry, Redknapp would have been asked by Levy for assurances that there were no hidden skeletons before he had been offered the job at Spurs. Likewise, when the *News of the World* story alleging Redknapp had made money illegally from the sale of Peter Crouch at Portsmouth had finally appeared in print in October 2009, Levy would have wanted again to be reassured that it had no substance.

So for Levy to discover that HMRC now thought it had enough evidence to take Redknapp to court must have raised doubts in his mind about his manager's judgement. He also could not have failed to take note of the coincidence that Peter Crouch – the player whose transfer sparked the police investigation – was now on the Spurs playing staff, having been bought from Portsmouth by Redknapp before the start of the 2009/10 season. The timing could not have been more unfortunate.

In public, Levy backed his manager but the dynamics between the two men began to alter, in financial matters at least, because from that point on Levy appeared to take a more hands-on role in regard to transfers. A note of caution: 'more hands on' as far as Levy is concerned is a relative concept. He is known to be a hard man to do business with, someone who likes to get involved in negotiations and keep the purse strings held tight, someone who wants to get value for money from his players. So Redknapp's track record of preferring older players on high salaries with little sell-on potential was always going to meet with some resistance.

Even so, in his first year at the club, Redknapp had been allowed a degree of independence in the transfer market. It might not have been the total freedom Redknapp had anticipated when he had first eyed up the size of Spurs' potential transfer budget, nor might he have been allowed to buy everyone on his shopping list, but the players who had been bought were very much his men – Defoe, Keane, Crouch and Kranjcar – whom he had identified as his kind of footballer around whom he could fashion a team that fitted the Redknapp blueprint.

Come the summer of 2010, there appeared to have been a defi-nite – if subtle – shift in power and it was Levy who seemed very much in charge of transfers. For Redknapp, who prided himself on his ability to judge a good footballer and had – apart from a year at Southampton – always had chairmen who were prepared to act on his say-so, it must have been a humbling experience. His frustration showed throughout the summer. Redknapp has never been shy of linking himself to any player, available or not, but for a few months he seemed out of control, declaring his interest in Joe Cole, Raúl, Cardozo; Forlán, Cahill, Falcao, Gallas, Hunt-elaar, Bellamy, Parker, Fabianao, Ashley Young and Ozil. Where Redknapp's gobbiness had once been endearing, he now began to look a bit silly – a manager desperate for attention – as not even the most optimistic Spurs fan thought there was any chance of the club acquiring more than a couple of the players on his wish list.

As it happened, Redknapp got just one. William Gallas was a typical Redknapp buy; he was an experienced player whom other clubs thought was past his sell-by date but whom Redknapp reck-oned had a good two or three seasons left in him. Redknapp's assessment of Gallas was spot on, but the pre-season landmark signing, Rafa van der Vaart, was almost entirely the work of Levy. 'My phone went at 4.00 p.m. on deadline day,' Redknapp told reporters, 'and the chairman said, "I've got a gift for you."

207

I thought it was going to be a new club car. He told me he had got me van der Vaart on loan, then it soon became apparent we could sign him permanently for £8 million. I had mentioned his name on a list of players but I can't pretend I was banging on the chairman's door saying we needed him desperately.'

Van der Vaart quickly became a pivotal player in the side, around whom Redknapp planned his playing formation, enabling Spurs to make a good start to the 2010/11 Premier League. But it was in the Champions League that the team really caught the eye, though their European campaign almost ended in disaster when Spurs found themselves 3-0 down after half an hour to Young Boys of Bern in the qualifying round. Young Boys were very much the underdogs and it looked for all the world as if Redknapp had been taken in as much as everyone else by the pre-match predictions that Spurs only had to turn up to win. It was no secret that the Swiss club played on an artificial pitch and yet the Spurs team appeared to be taken entirely by surprise. Intended passes were either flying straight into touch or bouncing well in front of the recipient before steepling over their head. Two completed passes was a rarity. It wasn't bad – it was awful – but Spurs somehow got out of jail with two undeserved goals before winning the home leg with some ease.

Things hadn't looked much more promising when Spurs went 4-0 down to Inter Milan at the San Siro, but Redknapp's team was a great deal more resilient than other Spurs sides had historically been and fought back to 4-3 through a Bale hat-trick that did more than just restore respectability. It also set up the second leg, the 3-1 win at White Hart Lane, which would turn out to be the defining game of Redknapp's time at Spurs, the one everyone associated with the club would remember for years. 'My dad reared me on stories about the Glory Nights games against Gornik and Benfica,' says football writer Adam Powley, 'but they might as well have been fairy tales, they seemed so distant. The

Inter match was *my* generation's Gornik. A packed and deafening White Hart Lane, under the lights, the all-white kit and Spurs tearing the champions apart with thrilling, scintillating football that all of Europe noticed. Without wishing to sound like Ingrid Bergman in *Casablanca*, whatever else happened with Redknapp we'll always have that magical night.'

Redknapp wasn't so tactically shabby in Europe, either. Many had predicted that Redknapp's inexperience of top-level European football would leave him being out-thought by the game's cannier strategists, but Redknapp had taken on all-comers playing attacking, stylish football and Spurs had finished top of their qualifying group. Come the knock-out stages, Redknapp showed he could mix it with the best of them by out-Italianing the Italians, defending in depth against AC Milan at the San Siro with a weakened team and sneaking a crucial late goal on the break to steal an away victory. Redknapp applied much the same tactics for the return home leg and held on for the 0-0 draw that took them through to the quarter-final. These weren't the results of a hopelessly tactically naïve manager.

Losing to Real Madrid in the quarter-final was no disgrace and Redknapp could rightly claim Spurs' first Champions League adventure had been a great success. The team hadn't been overawed, had competed with the best of the best and, if or when Spurs again qualified for the Champions League, no side would look forward to being drawn against them. The fly in the ointment was the 'if' part of re-qualification. As well as the team had performed in Europe, Spurs' form in the Premier League tailed off badly towards the end of the season. 'At times we had played some of the best football I have seen in my forty-six years of going to White Hart Lane,' says long-term supporter Pete Crawford, 'yet at others we had played like a Sunday morning pub team. We lost out on a Champions League place after only gaining fifteen points from our last twelve games, with only three wins in that period. We ended up in fifth place, six points adrift of fourth.'

Redknapp had never had the easiest of relationships with many Spurs supporters who objected to the way he always referred to them as 'you' or 'they' and never 'we'. In many ways, this was just a statement of fact. Redknapp wasn't a supporter, he was a manager. Football was his business and he could have – and had – been in charge of any number of different clubs. His job was to get that team playing the best football it could and, if he didn't, he would be out on his ear. There were no loyalty points on offer and none was expected.

Almost every other manager knew better than to point out the exact relationship between club, manager and supporters that starkly; etiquette demanded that a manager should always make the fans feel included and important – not least because having the fans on side could buy a little breathing space in a bad patch. Redknapp never bothered with this; not as an act of deliberate provocation, but because his egocentrism never allowed him to put himself in the fans' shoes. The relationship was what it was, and there was no need to call it any differently.

When the team was playing well this wasn't an issue, but when it wasn't there was conflict. Matters came to a head when Redknapp responded in public to supporters who had criticized him on a sports radio phone-in. 'The reaction doesn't hurt me,' he said. 'The reason I don't listen to phone-ins is because you're talking about idiots. Who rings up a radio station? They're idiots who don't even watch football. They say, "We were rubbish today." The guys on the radio ask them if they were at the game, and they say, "No, I heard it on the radio." When I start worrying about what they think, I'll be in trouble. Ninety-nine-point-nine per cent of people who go to Tottenham have loved everything they've seen. That's all that matters. Maybe expectations have been raised, but they don't have any brains, they don't understand. If they think we should have Champions League football every year, then what's been happening during all those years we didn't qualify? It's so hard to get into the top four now.'

This was yet another variation of the familiar 'You've never had it so good' Redknapp refrain – one that, as Adam Powley points out, was becoming increasingly ironic 'given that Redknapp had never had it so good to be managing Spurs at this stage in his career'. It was also one that he couldn't get away with any more without looking unnecessarily antagonistic to the fans and defensive about his managerial capabilities. His Spurs team had exceeded expectations but there had also been some very obvious and worrying self-destructive lapses, many of them Redknapp-related.

One of the reasons that Redknapp cited for the team's failure to sustain its challenge for Champions League qualification was injuries – in particular, one to Bale that had ruled him out for the previous five games. Yet, as was to be the case the following season, being down to the 'bare bones' was to a large extent self-inflicted as it was Redknapp's job to make sure there were players available to fill in when needed. The apparent lack of players whom Redknapp thought good enough raised questions both about his transfer targets and his decision to withdraw the reserve side from competitions two seasons previously.

Traditionally, the reserve team had acted as a stepping stone for emerging players to get a taste of competitive professional football and for first-team players to ease themselves back to match fitness after injury. Redknapp did away with a reserve team, arguing that the young players would be better served playing tailor-made fixtures. 'I just think it gives you the option of fixing up a game where and whenever you want rather than being tied to a fixture schedule which can sometimes prove difficult around first-team games,' Redknapp said. 'This way we can create our own schedule and play games when we want to. There are always clubs looking for games so I think this will suit us better. The youngsters need to go out on loan and get playing like they did last year. It was a great experience for those lads who went out, so we will be looking to do the same again this season.'

In theory, this might have seemed reasonable but, in practice, the policy hadn't worked. Youngsters who might have been ready to break through to the first team were nowhere near White Hart Lane, and keeping tracking of just how well each and every player who was out on loan was performing was a logistical nightmare. More importantly, though, it sent out the same message that Redknapp had given at his previous clubs; namely, that whatever he might say to the contrary, he wasn't terribly interested in bringing on youngsters himself. His focus was the first team and you were either in or out. When injuries did require Redknapp to pick his less fancied players, it was self-fulfilling that they looked out of their depth.

Most concerning of all, though, was that Redknapp didn't seem to be aware of a failing that had been blindingly obvious to everyone since long before Christmas. Spurs' problems weren't, for once, a leaky defence; it was a strike force that couldn't score enough goals. Redknapp didn't rate the Russian striker, Roman Pavlyuchenko, and insisted on playing Peter Crouch up front ahead of Jermain Defoe, despite Crouch being unable to buy a goal in the Premier League, where defenders didn't give him the same space as they did in European competitions. The consequences were felt throughout the season as – for the want of a striker – Spurs lost league games they should have drawn and drew games they should have won. It was baffling that Redknapp hadn't bought another striker in the January transfer window or had varied his tactics by rotating his squad and starting with Defoe more often. His public courting of an ageing David Beckham had brought most fans out in a cold sweat.

Crouch was shuffled off to Stoke at the end of the season, so

Redknapp can't have been unaware of his limitations, but his replacement – Emmanuel Adebayor, who was signed on loan from Manchester City shortly before the end of August – was again primarily a Daniel Levy deal. Scott Parker and forty-year-old goalkeeper Brad Friedel were Redknapp's. Parker was a no-brainer, a bargain at £5.5 million, while Friedel was another example of Redknapp's knack of spotting players whom others thought were past it.

As for handling the speculation over high-profile players potentially leaving the club, Redknapp's approach was erratic. The Modric 'Is he going to Chelsea or not?' saga is a case in point – it had been ongoing since the end of the previous season when the Croatian announced he wanted to leave Spurs. Redknapp would have been better advised to say nothing rather than offering frequent and not necessarily informed updates. But then Redknapp had never been one to keep quiet and, once Levy had outmuscled Modric and forced him to stay, his team began to play some of the best football in the Premier League and get the results to match.

The only blot on the horizon was Redknapp's trial, which had finally been scheduled for the following January, and the strain of that appeared to have told when he was admitted to hospital for a heart operation in early November. Typically, though, Redknapp tried to play it all down. 'I have a running machine at home and run or jog for around half an hour several times a week to help stay fit,' he told the *Sun* newspaper. 'But this time I went on and had been running for no more than about two minutes when I felt pains in my chest. I had hardly got going when it went tight and I was struggling to breathe. As soon as that happens you know the best thing to do is stop immediately, which I did. I wasn't that frightened if I'm honest, but it was clearly a warning sign from within. I just stopped running there and then and I went to see the club doctor at Spurs. He got me in to see a specialist on Saturday and by Monday I was in hospital. I've had narrow or blocked arteries for some time. I've been taking tablets for it just like a lot of people my age do. It's no big thing. They didn't even put me out. This isn't going to stop me doing the job I love. I love my football and won't be walking away any time soon. I can assure everyone I'm doing OK.'

And so he was. Within ten days he was back at White Hart Lane where his side were maintaining their early-season run of form and being talked about not just as certainties for Champions League qualification, but as possible Premier League title contenders. It was an incredible achievement for a club that was being run on a shoestring compared to the other contenders – Manchester City, Manchester United, Arsenal and Chelsea. Even his policy of not taking the Europa League seriously so he could concentrate on the Premiership – a decision that had annoyed many Spurs fans who reckoned the club was not yet so overloaded with success it could afford to be picky about which competitions it tried to win – seemed to be paying off. By and large, Redknapp had been forgiven. To top it all, Fabio Capello had announced he was planning to step down as England manager directly after Euro 2012 the following summer and no one was looking any further than Redknapp to replace him. At the age of sixty-four, Redknapp was within a now well-regulated heartbeat of achieving everything he had ever dreamed of in football . . . and a great deal more.

What could possibly go wrong?

10

Bouncebackability

May–December 2012

The fall from grace was spectacular. From being the clear favourite to replace Capello, the Football Association hadn't even bothered to interview Redknapp for the job. Whatever Redknapp might – or might not – have had to say about the England job and what he thought he could bring to it, the FA weren't interested in listening. Given the delay and speculation over the appointment – not to mention the very obvious effects they had had on both Redknapp and Tottenham – it was, at best, tactless not to go through the motions of talking to Redknapp even if the board had made a decision. It would have saved face for Redknapp. And them.

Redknapp responded magnanimously as required. 'I'm history with that job,' he said. 'Roy deserves it, he's got it and I just hope he makes a great job of it. I'm not disappointed at all. It's saved me a decision, if I'm honest, because I'm very happy at Tottenham. I'm lucky I'm managing a great club. I've come up the ladder from Bournemouth, I get very well paid and I have a fantastic job. I don't feel as though anyone owes me [an explanation]. Roy wouldn't have gone for the interview with the FA if they were going to be interviewing someone else, and neither would I. That wasn't going to work, going back to your club with your tail between your legs. They wanted Roy, and that's good enough.'

The generosity didn't make the statement any more believable. Redknapp was disappointed; the notion that being interviewed for a job you didn't get was somehow more humiliating than not being interviewed at all was laughable and he was most certainly owed an explanation. Hodgson wasn't a totally left-field appointment – he had had international experience, having managed the Finnish, Swiss and United Arab Emirates national teams at various stages in his career – but he hadn't been a front-runner, and his time in charge of Liverpool, his only really big job in England, had been a disaster. And yet the FA never said a word other than to express its support for its new manager.

Within days, rumours began to circulate that it had been Sir Trevor Brooking, the FA's director of development and one of the three-man selection panel, who had stuck the knife into Redknapp as a result of ongoing animosity between the two men, dating back to when Redknapp replaced Billy Bonds as West Ham manager. Brooking had been a close friend of Bonds and is believed by many to have regarded Redknapp taking his job as an act of disloyalty. Brooking dismissed this as mere gossip. 'I've heard the whispers and I've seen one or two things which have been written, and it's just outrageous,' he said. 'That business has got to be, what, nearly twenty years ago, hasn't it? Sure, I wasn't happy at the time, but I made my points then. To suggest I could be so petty is just absurd.

'I've met Harry many times since then and it doesn't even cross my mind. I never give it a thought. Listen, if you can bear a grudge for nearly twenty years, then it's time to take a look at yourself. There were a number of candidates discussed and I had no problems with any of them. It wasn't an issue.' He went on to say that, as the only ex-professional footballer on the selection panel, his role was bound to come under sharper scrutiny and that he didn't believe the timing of the appointment had been at all disruptive. 'It happens,' he said. 'You've just got to deal with it, because the general reaction to Roy has been really good. We knew his peers would be supportive, but the rest of the country seems to have reacted well. And Harry has conducted himself with a lot of dignity. By getting Roy in now, he's got a month with the squad to prepare. And a month is what an international manager only gets every two years.'

Brooking wouldn't have been the first person in football to hold a grudge for twenty years, and his idea of the timing not being disruptive was myopic to say the least. But even taking his explanations at face value, it was still difficult to explain why Redknapp had fallen so quickly out of favour. If he had never been in favour, the FA could have saved itself and everyone a great deal of trouble by ruling him out months ago. So what had gone wrong for Redknapp? Had Spurs' poor end to the season exposed previously hidden limitations in Redknapp's managerial skills? Hardly. The limitations had always been on show, as had his many capabilities. Had the FA begun to doubt his willingness to take an active interest in the England Under-21 side? If so, it was a bit late in the day to realize that youth-team football had limited appeal for him. Was the FA worried Redknapp might have other skeletons in the closet that would come back to bite him? Possibly. Redknapp had insisted he had had nothing to hide at the Stevens inquiry, but that hadn't stopped HMRC from later taking him to court, although as the police must have scoured every available document for evidence, the prospect of any future criminal proceedings would have been vanishingly slim.

Alternatively, had the FA fudged the issue and gone for the soft option? Hodgson was a safe pair of hands, a man who could be guaranteed not to rock the boat, a manager who could be relied on to do a good enough job. There was a precedent for this. After

Don Revie's controversial resignation from the England job to manage the UAE national side in 1977, the FA chose to replace him with Ron Greenwood, rather than the more charismatic – and successful – Brian Clough. Ever since then, Clough had been described as 'the best manager England never had'. Would Redknapp hereafter be known as 'the second-best manager England never had'?

Talksport presenter Sam Delaney thinks it possible. 'The very qualities that sometimes got in the way of Harry doing a good job at club level could have worked to his advantage at international level,' he says. 'The England manager has to play the cards he is dealt; he can't go dabbling in the transfer market. While Harry was quite good at wheeler-dealing, it could be very distracting. As England manager, his focus would have been maintained on his existing squad. In the same way, an international manager doesn't have to worry too much about building a squad and developing talent; his job is merely to pick the best players who are available to him. Nor does the team ever play so frequently that the squad needs to be rotated. Injuries permitting, Harry could have picked the team he wanted time and again with no adverse consequences.'

Steve Claridge also reckons England may have missed a trick. 'Harry has mellowed with age,' he says. 'He's less confrontational than he was. He's learnt to take a deep breath. He now understands there's a time to shout and a time to manage. He doesn't take the chances he once did; he plays safer, preferring to deal with quality rather than quantity of players. His main asset is he's good at getting those players he rates to be the best they can be and that's something from which England could have benefited.'

Redknapp may not have been the greatest tactician – Rafa van der Vaart once remarked that the tactics chalkboard in the Spurs dressing room was usually kept blank – but he was good enough.

And his motivational skills would have more than compensated, because at international level where a manager is mostly trying to achieve a short-term lift – for a single game or a four-week tournament at most – Redknapp's basic enthusiasm and down-to-earth common sense were precisely what was needed. Over the course of a full Premier League season, telling a striker – as Redknapp famously once did to Roman Pavlyuchenko – to 'fucking run around a bit' might end up doing more harm than good, but to get a result over ninety minutes it's very effective street football. He might also have been just the man to tackle the north-south tensions between some England players that many insiders believed had plagued the national squad for much of the past decade.

Redknapp did secure his seat at Euro 2012 a few days later when the BBC announced he would be joining their team as a pundit in Poland and Ukraine – no doubt hoping he might upset Hodgson in the same way he had Capello from the same vantage point over his deployment of Steven Gerrard at the World Cup in South Africa. But his immediate task was to ensure Spurs qualified for the Champions League. They were currently in fourth place in the Premier League, which would ordinarily have been good enough. Yet Redknapp had been granted his controversial wish and Chelsea had beaten Barcelona in the semi-final of the Champions League. If they were to go on to beat Bayern Munich and win the competition, then only third place would do.

Having previously always denied that the England saga had affected him in any way, Redknapp now admitted it had – up to a point. 'Some people will feel it has,' he said. 'People who work with me think it's definitely had an effect but I don't know really, I'm not sure. It's dragged on a bit, I suppose. That's the only thing. Other than that, I've got no problems. They choose whoever they want to choose. So I'm very lucky to be managing such a great club with great players. It's not something I thought about or I haven't spent the last six weeks thinking, "Oh my God, what's the squad I'm going to take . . . what am I going to do?" I've just been concentrating solely on Tottenham and that's not changed.'

He hadn't, of course, but he did have some fence-mending to do with Spurs now that he wasn't leaving for England. He wisely started with Daniel Levy, promising not to make a fuss about his contract. 'It's up to the chairman,' he said. 'I don't go running to him asking for a new contract. I'll see what happens in the next few weeks and what the chairman has to say. It's his club. He does what he wants. If he wants to talk to me about a contract, we will talk about it. If he doesn't, we'll take it from there.'

Redknapp also went some way to effecting a rapprochement with the fans when Spurs swept to a 4-1 victory away to Bolton – the first time Spurs had ever won at the Reebok stadium – playing the same fast, attacking football that had characterized the first half of their season. Even Modric looked up for the fight for the first time in months. Redknapp, too, was on his feet, out of the dugout, waving to the fans and clapping them – something he hadn't bothered to do in ages. This prompted a chorus of '*We want you to stay*' from the visiting fans, but it was almost an automatic response rather than a genuine plea; it certainly wasn't as heartfelt and genuine as when the chant had been sung at the Newcastle game immediately after his trial.

Something had changed in the Spurs fans' relationship with Redknapp. It was as if they recognized they had been manipulated somewhat and had come to realize their affection wasn't as long-lasting or genuine as it had once felt. During the hiatus following Capello's resignation, Redknapp had come to resemble the girlfriend who took you for granted while making eyes at the handsome bloke with the sports car. Only the handsome bloke with the sports car had run off with the dullest, plainest girl in the class instead, leaving your girlfriend no choice but to come running back and tell you she had only really loved you all along. At which point, many Spurs fans woke up and thought, 'Hang on a minute . . . I'm not quite sure how much I love you now.'

Four days later, what goodwill Redknapp had recovered was tested once again when Spurs played their penultimate game of the season away to Aston Villa. The previous day, Arsenal had unexpectedly thrown Spurs a lifeline by only drawing at home to Norwich; if Spurs won their last two games, they would be guaranteed third place and qualification for the Champions League. Having gone a goal down and had a man sent off, Spurs had equalized and were pressing hard for the winner when, with ten minutes left, Redknapp substituted the attack-minded van der Vaart with the defensive Scott Parker, while both Defoe and Saha were left sitting on the bench. With a win the priority, Redknapp's decision-making appeared incomprehensible. 'When you've gone down to ten men, you'd say it was a point gained but, on the balance of play, maybe it was two lost,' he said gnomically after the game.

There was a momentary sense of excitement the following week when it looked as if Roy Hodgson might finally do Redknapp an overdue favour when his West Bromwich Albion side went ahead against Arsenal, but once Spurs' north London rivals had got their noses in front, Tottenham's own 2-0 victory against Fulham felt entirely anti-climactic. 'It was no coincidence,' says Spurs fan Pete Crawford, 'that during that game there were more songs praising Martin Jol [Fulham's manager] for what he had done for us when he was manager than there were for Harry. The Spurs fans have retained a genuine affection for Jol, and it's something he gratefully acknowledges. Harry has always done what's best for Harry and stuff the consequences. I don't think he had a clue how badly the Spurs fans felt at seeing an almost guaranteed third place slip away.'

It was tough on Redknapp that fourth place should have

been regarded as a failure. Only two years earlier, after Spurs had beaten Manchester City to secure fourth place, the celebrations had been uncontained. But this season, fourth place was only good enough to put Spurs in limbo. The misery was complete a week later when Chelsea held off Bayern Munich to win the Champions League. It may have been bad luck for Spurs to become the first-ever English team to finish fourth and not qualify for the Champions League but, deep down, Redknapp and the players all knew they had no one to blame but themselves. Third place had been theirs for the taking and they had blown it.

There was a light comic interlude when the betting firm Betfair confirmed it had signed Redknapp as an analyst for the duration of the Euros; given Redknapp's luck on the horses, most punters would have been well advised to keep their money in their pockets. Just a few days later, the comedy turned to tragedy when Redknapp was sacked as manager of Spurs.

Having originally said that he was going to leave it up to Levy to decide whether his contract was extended or not, Redknapp announced in early June that he was bringing in Paul Stretford – the man who'd previously gone eyeball to eyeball with Alex Ferguson and secured a massive pay rise for Wayne Rooney – to negotiate on his behalf, and went on the offensive in an interview with Sky Sports.

'The simple situation is that I have a year left on my contract and it is up to Tottenham whether they want to extend that or not. Things couldn't have gone better since I've been there. We've finished fourth twice, fifth once, quarter-finals of the Champions League and played fantastic football,' he said, before going on to warn of the dangers of letting his contract reach its expiry date at the end of the following year. 'It's not a case of me looking for security. What it's about, really, is that when players know they have only a year left on their contract, it doesn't work. You don't let players run into the last year of their contract if you think they are any good, and you don't let managers run into the last year of their contract if you think they are any good. That is the situation, so it is up to the club.'

It was a huge misjudgement on Redknapp's part. He had had enough first-hand experience of doing business with Levy to know the chairman didn't react well to being threatened, and to do so when his own hand was so weak was a peculiar act of self-destruction. He should have known that Levy had not been impressed by Spurs' failure to qualify for the Champions League. He should also have known his suggestion that the players would be unsettled if he was not offered a longer deal, having previously claimed that the squad would not be affected by speculation linking him with the England position, was unlikely to have been well received. So why didn't he just keep his mouth shut and do things on Levy's terms?

It can't be ruled out that he might, subconsciously, have been trying to sabotage his career; he was no stranger to knee-jerk reactions, and the rejection by England must have played its part. If he couldn't have the best job, then he wasn't going to have any.

Steve Claridge reckons Redknapp just got fed up. 'He'd expected to get the England job and hadn't got it,' he says. 'Then he'd asked the Spurs chairman for a new deal and more money and was being stalled. Something snapped.'

If so, it was Redknapp's ego that let him down. He had managed to convince himself so well that he had done a brilliant job and was worth a great deal more money, that he wasn't able to see how his position might look to anyone else.

Levy didn't blink when challenged. As far as he was concerned, Redknapp had another year left on his contract and there was no need to do anything. If Spurs qualified for the Champions League the following season, then they could negotiate new terms; if not, then Redknapp had come to the end of the road at Spurs and they could part company with no hard feelings. And no hard cash. With his bluff called, Redknapp was left with nothing to negotiate but the compensation for terminating his contract a year early.

'I have thoroughly enjoyed my time at Spurs and am proud of my achievements,' Redknapp said immediately after his sacking had been confirmed. 'I have had a fantastic four years with the club . . . at times, the football has been breathtaking. I am sad to be leaving but wish to thank the players, staff and fans for their terrific support during my time there.'

His disappointment was more evident a day later in an interview with the *Sun*. 'If the club wants to go in a different direction, that's up to them,' he said. 'But even if I say so myself, I did a fantastic job there. I don't know what more I could have done there. No one was more loyal to Spurs than me. I wanted to stay, but that's life. I can't do anything about it.

'It's entirely up to the owner of the club. I was an employee and if they want to go down a different road, they own the club. I won't slit my throat over it. I want to get on with my life instead of moping about getting the sack. What have I got to have the hump about? It's football. I just want to move on with my life. My missus Sandra is going to be fed up with me for a little while because I'll be under her feet. But not for long. I want to manage a club again. I've not given any thought to where – but I will be back.'

Steve Claridge found the whole episode massively depressing. 'He got Spurs fourth place in the Premier League,' he said. 'No one could have asked for much more than that, especially as all the clubs who finished above him had far more money. He was just unlucky that Spurs didn't qualify for the Champions League.'

Many football writers, in particular those who had been close to Redknapp and had got good copy from him, were quick to condemn Levy for sacking him, arguing that Spurs had shown a lack of respect, tried to airbrush Redknapp out of its recent history and would inevitably pay for the blunder by going backwards the following season.

Martin Cloake gave a rather more considered verdict that spoke for the overwhelming majority of Spurs fans. 'I'm sad Harry Redknapp's gone from Spurs,' he said. 'We've seen some great football during his time at the club, and the record of fourth, fifth and fourth again speaks for itself. But I'm not going to join in with the kicking of the Spurs board for sacking Harry. I think a build-up of factors led to the decision to sack him, and I think Redknapp overplayed his hand when foolishly opting to negotiate through the press.

'Redknapp got a talented group of players to believe in themselves, set the team up in a straightforward manner, and encouraged it to play football the way we like to see it played. It didn't work every week, but things steadily improved during his time in charge. Any criticism of what he achieved seems to be based on a view about what the team could have achieved but didn't. It's a strange way of judging any manager's tenure, not least because it's only the success we had that meant we could seriously contemplate further success. When was the last time we were seriously talked of as title contenders? Or Champions League regulars?

'I still have a nagging doubt about whether we could have mounted a stronger title challenge in a couple of seasons when the so-called Big Four were stumbling or rebuilding and Spurs did not have the added pressure of the Champions League. One of my concerns about Redknapp never really went away, and that was that he was more focused on relative success than absolute. Harry never hesitated to point out how much Tottenham's rivals had going for them compared to us, always portraying himself as the underdog in order to play up any achievement and minimize the risk of blame for any failure. Under Harry, we were very successful – but it's not wrong to ask if we were as successful as we could or should have been.'

For all that Redknapp likes to portray himself – or is happy to be portrayed – as a straightforward, what-you-see-is-what-you-get bloke, he is anything but. If he is the quintessential English football manager, then the quintessential English football manager is a complex character. That his departure from Spurs aroused such conflicted feelings was entirely in keeping.

Under most normal circumstances, a manager who had achieved two fourth- and one fifth-place Premier League finishes, two FA Cup semi-finals, a Carling Cup final and a Champions League quarter-final within three and a half seasons would go down as a club legend at White Hart Lane. But, just as before at Bournemouth, West Ham, Southampton and Portsmouth, his legacy has been tarnished; the fans remember the good times – and there were a lot of them – but they can't somehow bring themselves to forget the bad.

It would be easy simply to explain this away as being typical of the lack of gratitude and general fickleness of the average football fan. Indeed, that can't be ignored, but to blame the fans for everything would be to miss a trick. Other managers have remained the fans' sweetheart for delivering far less, long after they've moved on. So there has to be something in Redknapp that contributes to the souring of the relationship.

In an interview with *The Times*, given before he was told he hadn't got the England job, he said, 'I get stressed out like I couldn't tell you. It's difficult to deal with on a Saturday night after a bad result. I often wonder what it must do to my health; I'd be lying if I said I didn't. It affects me so badly it stops me sleeping.'

Despite his public image as a man who wore his heart on his sleeve, he seldom showed it. Apart from the odd occasion when he lost it completely – such as when he was accused of being a wheeler-dealer by a TV reporter – he always came across as a genial bloke who didn't care as much about a defeat as the fans. There was no reason why he should, other than that it would have done him a favour. For a man who appeared so much to want to be loved and appreciated, Redknapp had a funny way of going about things. Then was Redknapp ever quite the man he seemed? Apart from with his family, was he really ever close to anyone? For many, it often seemed like the more they felt they were getting to know him, the more elusive he became.

Later in the same interview, Redknapp went on to say, 'If someone asks me to do something, I'll do it. If you stop me in the street, I'll talk to you, because if people have time for you then you should have time for them. Besides, I enjoy talking to people. It's in my nature.' That was true, most of the time. But, equally, it's hard not to forget the people he did know, with whom he didn't bother speaking as much as he should have done; the players to whom he gave the cold shoulder and whose respect he lost. Maybe if he'd spent more time developing better relationships with those to whom he was professionally close, rather than chatting so freely to strangers, he would have received the long-term affection he deserved.

Like Icarus, Redknapp got within a heartbeat of football immortality before his wings melted in the sun. And the fans got within a heartbeat of giving him their devotion, before that same sun exposed their love as something more transient, more ephemeral than they had ever expected. Under the glare of the light, the relationship was not quite as rose-tinted as either had imagined it.

After getting the sack from Spurs, Redknapp stood down as a pundit for the BBC at Euro 2012, so, for now at least, his feelings about the performance of the England team remain private. But while watching that tournament, he must have felt the slightest tinge of regret as Hodgson's side went out in the quarter-final after an uninspired, pragmatic, defensive display. Redknapp's team might have lost at the same stage, but it would probably have been a great deal more fun to watch.

Steve Claridge reckoned Redknapp might think enough was enough. 'There aren't any vacancies going at one of the top Premiership clubs,' he said, 'and even if there were, Harry probably doesn't have the kind of profile their chairmen would be looking for. So if I were him, I'd be inclined to chuck it in. Any new club would probably feel like a step down after Spurs, and how much longer does he want to traipse up and down the motorway twice a day?'

There again, Redknapp had always said that football was the only thing that interested him, so, even though he was now sixty-five, it felt unlikely he would be content to see out his life looking out to sea from his Sandbanks home, in between walking the dogs, playing the odd round of golf and doing the occasional stint as a TV pundit. But what managerial job could he do next?

It wasn't long before newspaper reports linked him with the job of managing the Qatar national side. It was a move that wasn't beyond the realms of possibility, as he could have done the job part-time. There had also been rumours he had been close to accepting a £6 million per year offer to manage Dubai side Al Ahli in 2010 – but the United Arab Emirates was still an awfully long way away from Poole.

Thereafter, the rumour mill went quiet for a couple of months. And yet . . . it didn't seem right that Redknapp could just fade away. He'd been a fixture of the football landscape for the best part of fifty years and a lot of the fun had always been wondering what he would do next. Whatever he said, the opposite was always just as likely. Redknapp may have been infuriating, difficult and contradictory but he was never boring. The speed and height of his fall might have had all the hallmarks of Greek tragedy, but it had cemented his reputation as a one-off English legend.

Football's need to resurrect Redknapp matched his own desire for a football afterlife. Both seemed diminished without the presence of the other. Without Redknapp on the back – and front – pages, the beginning of the 2012/13 football season felt just a little bit duller, a little bit more corporate. And without football, Redknapp had lost a dimension, a sense of purpose. He was marking time. So both Redknapp and football did what they had always done so well in the past: they worked hard together to find ways to contrive to keep each other in the news.

It is never entirely clear where any new Redknapp rumour starts – with him, his agent, a desperate football writer with space to fill or a bloke in the pub? Its genesis isn't really the point; what matters is that it exists as a background hum of football noise to keep everyone entertained, and that everyone does their bit to keep it alive for as long as possible. And they invariably do. Redknapp has long since perfected the art of denying a rumour in such a way as to leave open the possibility that it's true. Football writers never miss a chance to quote Redknapp denying a rumour that he could have started himself, and fans are happy to repeat any old nonsense they read in the papers or on Twitter. It's just another of Harry's games.

The first rumour to surface after Euro 2012 was that Redknapp had been included on the shortlist of candidates to take over as manager of the Russian national team from Dick Advocaat – an unlikely possibility given the commuting distance, even before Redknapp accumulated dozens of column inches with a denial. Thereafter, it was as if the floodgates had been opened as Redknapp was linked with virtually every managerial vacancy, real or imagined. Possible moves to Leicester City, Ipswich Town and Nottingham Forest came and went quite quickly; a move to Blackburn Rovers lingered rather longer, as the club dithered over announcing a replacement for Steve Kean, and Redknapp's responses to suggestions he might take the job were equivocal and enigmatic even by his own standards. A quick check of the distance between Blackburn and Bournemouth should have been all the information anyone really needed to work out the real probabilities. Still, it all kept Redknapp's profile high and everyone else amused until Blackburn appointed the Norwegian, Henning Berg, as manager at the end of October.

When not putting himself in the frame for another job, Redknapp found plenty of other ways to keep himself in the limelight. Initially, this was by giving his first in-depth newspaper interview since his trial, most of which was the standard fare of 'It's been very stressful . . . I wish Roy well . . . That's football.' But there was one revealing nugget and that came with a barely veiled attack on the management style of his replacement at Tottenham, André Villas-Boas.

'There are people out there who try to make the game sound too complicated for their own good,' he said. 'They are such geniuses, some of these boys. It's a simple game and it's about getting the best out of people. About managing them.

'If you've got a right-back who can't defend, you work with him. Make sure he's putting himself in the right positions. That's coaching. If Glen Johnson is getting caught with the ball behind him, you work with him on that.

'It's about moving Modric from left wing to central midfield. People said he was too small but I moved him into the middle. You don't need PowerPoint. You take him out on the pitch. It's simple and, if you can't see it, you shouldn't be in bloody football. Now you're getting seventy-page dossiers on this and that. Bullshit can baffle brains at times.'

On one level, this could be read as Redknapp being Redknapp, a simple reiteration of his management philosophy. But as ever, there was a subtext. Villas-Boas hadn't had the easiest of starts at Tottenham; the team had struggled to find fluency and form. So this was Redknapp laying down a marker, a reminder of the dangers of getting rid of him. But it wasn't necessarily a very well advised one, as it left Redknapp a hostage to fortune if Villas-Boas managed to reverse the early season decline. More seriously, it invited everyone to reconsider his own legacy.

For a while, it was true that some of the Spurs players had looked hesitant and inconsistent on the pitch, but the unarguable message coming from the training ground was that the players liked and respected the new manager. During Redknapp's regime at Tottenham, certain fringe players leaked sideways moans about Redknapp and his methods to the media; under Villas-Boas, every player went out of his way to back him. The jury may have been out on Villas-Boas's tactics, but the Portuguese was winning hands down on touchy-feely man-management.

Redknapp's next public outing was to reveal that he was now acting in an unpaid advisory capacity to his old club, Bournemouth. 'Just because it's League One doesn't mean you can't get it off the back four like Andrea Pirlo,' he said. 'They play proper football. I had a great day watching them against Yeovil last week. I was desperate for them to win. I just love the game. It's like Fergie. Get me and him together and we'll be talking about the good job Micky Mellon's doing at Fleetwood Town.'

On the face of it, this was nothing more than a heart-warming snapshot of a man who loved football so much he couldn't stay away and was happy to donate his expertise for nothing. True – but there may have been more to it. 'It wouldn't have been in Harry's interests to be paid,' says one ex-club chairman. 'For one thing, he wouldn't want to be too closely linked to a club that might struggle; it would devalue his own currency as a future manager elsewhere. I would also guess there were clauses in his severance deal from Tottenham that limited the amount of compensation he was due if he was offered another job. He'd have been a fool to jeopardize that for a part-time job at Bournemouth. And Harry isn't a fool.'

Redknapp's most bravura performance was reserved for his offer to act as a go-between in the ongoing dispute between Portsmouth FC and some of the playing staff over unpaid salaries that threatened the club with going into administration. He told the TV station ESPN that he was going to talk to two of the players, Nwankwo Kanu and Tal Ben Haim, whom he had himself signed, and ask them to reconsider their demands. 'If players have a contract and are owed money, you can see why they think they should get it,' he said. 'But if the club closes down, they won't get a penny. They need to think hard about that. Portsmouth has got to be saved. It's a great club with great traditions. It would be a disaster if this club went out of business.'

This took some nerve, considering there was a good argument for saying Redknapp's free-spending, hyper-inflationary wage deals during his time in charge had been a major contributor to Portsmouth's current predicament. The irony wasn't lost on one former football club chairman. 'For years and years, Harry had been persuading players to come to clubs he was managing by offering them huge salaries,' he said. 'And the Professional Footballers Association was complicit in this. Neither party paused for a moment to think about how much the club could actually afford to pay. So it's a bit rich for them both to start affecting concern that the club is in danger of going out of business.'

The main focus of Redknapp gossip, though, was in west London. Having struggled to stay up in their first season back in the Premiership the previous season, Queens Park Rangers had spent the best part of £25 million on strengthening the squad, only to find the team was continuing to struggle. By the beginning of November, with the team rooted to the bottom of the table without a single league win, it seemed a question of when, not if, manager Mark Hughes would be sacked. It also seemed to be a question of when, not if, Redknapp took over.

Queens Park Rangers and Redknapp were a match made in heaven; two more perfect partners you couldn't have found. QPR ticked all the Redknapp boxes; close enough to Bournemouth for him to commute daily; an underperforming, misfiring squad; and a rich owner in Tony Fernandes who had shown he was prepared to dig deep into his own pockets to ensure Premiership survival. Typically, Redknapp kept his cards close to his chest, insisting in one radio interview that he had received eight job offers in the previous week. At that rate, if he'd held on for another three months, he could have taken his pick of any of the ninety-two league clubs.

For seasoned Harry-watchers, the clearest sign that he fancied the QPR job came when he started talking about how tempted he was to be manager of the Ukraine national side. 'It's a fantastic job,' he told reporters. 'I found out about it a couple of weeks ago when they got in touch with my advisors. I am serious about it. They are an up-and-coming football country with some very good young players, some great teams like Shakhtar and some great stadiums. I will talk to them and see if we can sort something out. I'm definitely interested, without a doubt.'

The only person who could really see Redknapp going to Ukraine was . . . Redknapp. To everyone else, his Ukrainian courtship had all the hallmarks of a gentle reminder to Fernandes that he didn't want to hang around indefinitely and that he wasn't going to come cheap.

Planned or not, that's the way it panned out as Redknapp was offered the QPR job in the last week of November. All was now revealed. He wasn't going to be anybody's new Fergie, Wenger, Mourinho or Villas-Boas; nor even their temporary Di Matteo or Benitez. He wasn't ever going to be the kind of manager to whom chairmen of the big clubs looked to lead them to Premiership and European glory. That had been a beautiful, golden chimera that briefly seemed possible for two years at Spurs. Redknapp's number had been called. He was a scrapper, a typically English manager whose gift was to squeeze the best out of his players when the chips were down. A man to whom you would turn to get you out of trouble, but not to take you onwards and upwards once you were in the clear.

If Redknapp was disappointed in this judgement, he gave no sign of it. Within minutes of arriving at Loftus Road, Redknapp's stock phrases were wheeled out again, saying how pleased he was to have the job and how all his family were now QPR fans. It was also like *Groundhog Day* in most other respects, as he prepared the ground for possible failure by deflecting all the blame for the club's predicament on to the players, while talking up the insane idea of bringing David Beckham to play in the Premiership along with his desire to sign Darren Bent in the January transfer window, along with several members of his old Spurs squad. He could have been reading from one of his old scripts.

This time, though, there was no immediate Redknapp bounce. QPR were held to draws in his first three games against fellow strugglers Sunderland, Aston Villa and Wigan. A home win against Fulham hinted at a revival, but the year ended with three straight defeats, including a 3-0 home surrender to Liverpool. Redknapp's immediate response was to criticize several members of his squad in the press for not being worth the money they were paid – in particular, José Bosingwa, whom he had fined two weeks' wages for refusing to sit on the substitutes' bench for the game against West Bromwich Albion. His analysis was undoubtedly right; some of the QPR players were earning too much, although he could hardly blame them for taking the money that the club's owner and previous manager had offered. And what about humiliating his squad in public? It definitely didn't seem to be the best way to raise morale, even if it did echo the feelings of many QPR supporters.

Remarkably, though, the new year began with another of those totally unexpected results that have so often been a feature of his career and on which his reputation has largely been made – a 1-0 victory away at Stamford Bridge, thanks to some dogged defending against an under-strength Chelsea team, who had clearly thought they only had to turn up to claim the three points. It was, perhaps inevitably, eventually won via a late winner on the break. In just ninety minutes, the 'Harry Houdini' headlines were back on the sports pages.

Then came the game that somehow seemed more symbolic than most – the home fixture against Spurs. The old versus the new. A victory against the club that had sacked him would be worth more than three points won; it would be a sign that the revival had substance.

The media came rushing to Redknapp's door for pre-match quotes and he didn't disappoint, suggesting that 'you'd have to be a dope' to mess up managing Chelsea – an implied dig at Spurs manager, André Villas-Boas, who had been sacked by the west London club after just eight months in charge the previous season. Redknapp's timing was a little off, though, as the day before the game Villas-Boas was named Premiership manager of the month, and Redknapp quickly performed a volte-face, claiming his words had been taken out of context.

Both managers shook hands before the game and embraced for the cameras after it. In between, not a lot happened. There were no Harry chants from the away fans signifying any lasting devotion to their former manager. It was almost as though there had never been a bond between them and that the events of the previous three seasons had taken place in a forgotten universe.

On the field, Spurs were at their most anaemic, QPR defended in depth and the game petered out in a goalless stalemate. Both managers could leave with their pride intact, claiming it was a point earned rather than a couple dropped. But the truth was that a draw was of little value to either manager, and Redknapp in particular, as QPR ended the day still rooted to the bottom of the Premiership table with just fourteen points from twenty-two games, two points behind Reading in nineteenth place and six away from escaping the relegation zone. It was by no means all over for QPR and Redknapp but it was getting harder by the day and, if the club was to stay up, it would need grit and guts rather than fun and flair. Redknapp's own demeanour suggested he thought it unlikely his squad would be up to the challenge.

There again, game on. If he pulled off the miracle, his reputation would be enhanced and he would pick up a £1 million bonus. And if he didn't . . . well, he'd been through that situation before several times at other clubs, such as Bournemouth and Southampton. And perhaps the fact that he was still on the best part of £3 million per year at QPR would ease the pain a little.

It wasn't the worst situation to be in. And yes, he'd bought into bigger dreams and ambitions for a while, but they'd always really been other people's dreams and ambitions. All he'd ever wanted was to make a living out of football and he'd done far better for himself than he'd ever dared imagine in a virtually uninterrupted fifty-year career. Only fans and romantics think that football is all about the glory. It isn't – it is about survival. And Harry Redknapp will for ever be remembered as one of the greatest of all football's survivors.

Bibliography

Books

Anon, *I Am the Secret Footballer: Lifting the Lid on the Beautiful Game* (Guardian Books, 2012).

Steve Blowers, *Nearly Reached the Sky, West Ham United 1989–2005* (Football World, 2005).

Tom Bower, *Broken Dreams* (Pocket Books, 2007).

Steve Claridge with Ian Ridley, *Beyond the Boot Camps* (Orion, 2010).

Martin Cloake and Adam Powley, *The Glory, Glory Nights* (VSP, 2012).

David Conn, *Richer Than God, Manchester City, Modern Football and Growing Up* (Quercus, 2012).

Michael Lewis, *Moneyball: The Art of Winning an Unfair Game* (Norton, 2004).

Kevin Nash, *Cherries: First Hundred Years, AFC Bournemouth 1899–1999* (Red Post Books, 1999).

Harry Redknapp with Derek McGovern, *Harry Redknapp, My Autobiography* (Collins, 1998).

Les Roopanarine, *Harry Redknapp – The Biography* (John Blake, 2011).

Jim Smith with Bob Cass, *Jim Smith, The Autobiography: It's Only a Game* (Andre Deutsch, 2000).

Julie Welch, *The Biography of Tottenham Hotspur* (VSP, 2012).

Newspapers and Magazines
Guardian, The Times, Daily Telegraph, Independent, Daily Mail, Sun, Mirror, Four Four Two, When Saturday Comes.

Index

239

INDEX